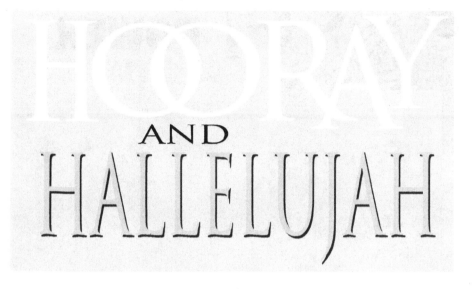

HOORAY

AND

HALLELUJAH

Escaping Tradition and Experiencing Power

70 Years of Christian Ministry

CHARLES CARRIN

FOREWORD BY JACK TAYLOR

What Others are Saying about *Hooray and Hallelujah!*

How invaluable it is to read and understand the generational background, upbringing, and life journey of someone who was destined to become a towering Christian leader and a champion of the full gospel of Christ. Charles Carrin is replete with relational treasures, both from his godly heritage and his early and later life experiences. He carries a great anointing that escorted diverse divine encounters over seventy years of ministry. So good Charles! So insightful, and so helpful. Thank you for writing Hooray and Hallelujah. I loved every minute of it!

—John Arnott,Catch the Fire, Toronto

For the past eighteen years, I, and the church I am privileged to serve, have received from the fruit of what is contained in this book. From our first meeting to this present day, Charles has been a man of humility, joy, and power, all as the result of the mighty work of God's Spirit in his life. I have met very few men who can say with integrity the things said in this book, but this man can! It is my prayer that all of us can walk such a journey where we live with "righteousness, peace, and joy in the Holy Spirit" while walking in the anointing of the Spirit. I believe this book will be a tool God uses to "spur us on" to such a life!

—David McQueen, Pastor, Beltway Park Church, Abilene, Texas

To read of Charles Carrin's experiences and conclusions regarding his more than 70-year ministry with the Holy Spirit reinforces the truth of the Book of Acts. Truly the Holy Spirit has directed Charles's ministry. To say "Jesus is alive!" becomes a vibrant and new reality in the pages of this book.

—Ralph Beisner, Supreme Court Justice, New York State, Retired

Charles Carrin occupies an exceptionally rare place in my life. He is a mentor, a father, and a friend. Every word Charles speaks or writes I take very seriously! I cannot remember a time of being in his presence that I did not come away with an increasing love for Jesus and a greater hunger for the things of the Spirit. Having read this book, I am enriched on so many levels. Simultaneously, I look back nostalgically with appreciation for what God has done, and I look forward expectantly to days of greater anointing. Thank you, Charles, for sharing a part of your life with us. We are better disciples because of you!

—Stephen Chitty, Pastor, Christian Life Church, Columbia, South Carolina

I have had the awesome privilege of traveling with Charles Carrin for over 20 years. His ministry is filled with some of the most amazing experiences I have ever heard. Some of them I have been a part of. May your journey with Charles be filled with laughter and revelation. Enjoy the history through time from a man celebrating 70 years of ministry! May you see the fruit of the Lord from a life sold out for God. Charles is a true treasure in my life, and after you read his journey, I believe he will be a treasure to you as well!

—David Rhea, Founder, The Father's Desire Ministries Inc., Boca Raton, Florida

What this book has imparted to me personally and will to our church-body will encourage our faith to believe God for greater things.

—Randy Turner, Executive Pastor, Beltway Park Church, Abilene, Texas

Cover art by Janet Unalp

www.BurkhartBooks.com
Bedford, Texas

DEDICATION

To
My wife Laurie,
Our Daughter and Son-in-law
Cecile and Neal McGuire

And to
Our Grandson, His Wife
and Children
Benjamin and Kendra McGuire
Evangeline Hope and Declan Charles

Thanks For The Memories!

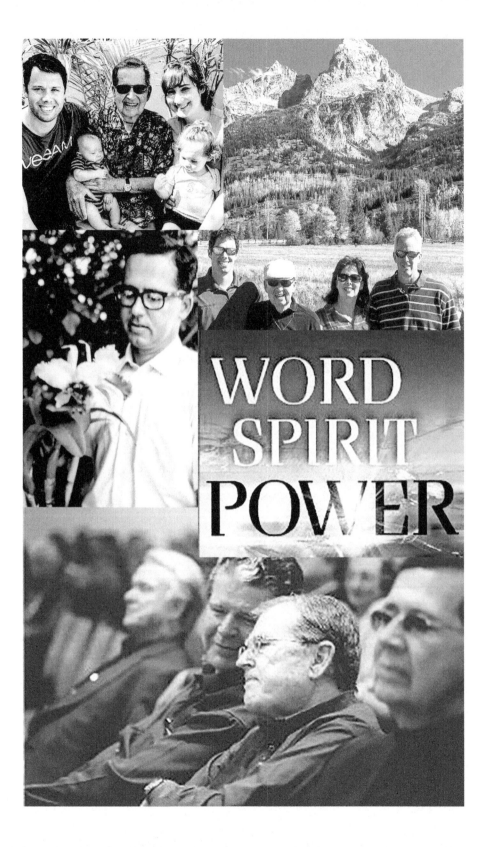

WORD
SPIRIT
POWER

ACKNOWLEDGMENTS

My heartfelt gratitude to my editors and proofreaders:

Cecile and Neal McGuire
Michael Peterson
Libby and Ray Simms

And to my
Financial Supporters

And to
My publisher, Tim Taylor
Burkhart Books

To God Be The Glory!

CONTENTS

Appendix

About the Author

FOREWORD

This is a rare and remarkable book from many standpoints. It goes beyond the norm in biographical significance because of the riches produced through this value-laden life. I use the word "beyond" in that it is far more than an interesting biography. Its intriguing narrative of events past is interlaced with little-known happenings and situations that give new meaning to well-known historical seasons.

Charles Carrin is one of the greatest thinkers among us and possesses a striking ability to put words together for the most exacting and precise conclusions imaginable. He is easy to read as well as stunningly interesting to hear.

In many cases, as he tells stories familiar to history, it is like discovering the "rest of the story." There is inestimable value to living long and Charles Carrin has carefully harvested the riches of his life and shared freely with us who read his words and hear his voice.

This is one of these literary productions that will bear reading again and again and will, I believe, prove valuable in making eternal sense of the strange issues that face us in Twenty-First Century life.

Thanks, Charles, for paying the price and taking the time to present us with this valuable volume which will surely serve to escort us to new levels of understanding as well as joy. We are happily in your debt!

Jack Taylor
Dimensions Ministries
Melbourne, Florida

INTRODUCTION

Labor Day, 1935, my brother and two cousins came running into our house in Miami, wide-eyed, soaked with rain, and screaming, "A hurricane is coming! A hurricane is coming!"

My parents stopped abruptly and stared at each other in panic. Mother rushed to the window and looked at the trees shaking in the wind. She and my dad had barely survived two previous hurricanes that killed thousands in South Florida. Like the one now approaching, those storms in 1926 and 1928 hit without warning and left a path of death and wreckage across the state.

Unknown to them, the wind now blowing was the beginning of a category five hurricane with gusts of 200 miles per hour. Weather instruments would blow away at that incredible speed, and eleven cars of an escape-train on Key Largo, crowded with World War One veterans, would be swept from the track and lie wrecked on its side. The lowest barometric pressure ever recorded in the Western Hemisphere lay in the storm's vortex. Whole towns would soon be washed away, and an unidentified number of men, women, and children would be swept to sea. One family would lose 50 members. We faced all this.

Our little house, still under construction, offered no protection from the wind. We were in the grip of America's "Great Depression," when there was no money to repair anything the hurricane might destroy. Worse still, my father had become seriously crippled and could be of little help. An injury from World War I had revived and left him in a near-immobile condition. Standing in the kitchen doorway that morning, seeing my parents' faces gripped with fear, a permanent mark was left in my memory.

Looking back, my life has covered an era of incredible change. For that reason, this book is not just about me. I am telling my story against the backdrop of World War I, the Great Depression, the Japanese attack on Pearl Harbor, World War II, and other events that are significant to American Christians. Everything has been told just as it happened: The good and the bad, the fun and the failures, the humorous and the humiliating.

Today, I am the only survivor of my family. My parents, brothers, and cousins are gone. In 2020 I will be 90 years old. Memories of my era are a treasure I do not want to be lost when I die.

More importantly, this book tells about my life in two spiritual experiences: God's calling me into ministry in 1948, and baptizing me in the Holy Spirit in 1977. Both were pivotal, life-shaking events. I am now celebrating 70 years of Christian ministry.

Following my Baptism in the Spirit, God increased the effectiveness of my ministry exponentially. Since that revolutionary day in 1977, I've seen thousands of people be visibly impacted by the power of God. Many have experienced deliverances from addiction, suicide, depression, and other crises. Many have been healed physically. It is my firm conviction that the Holy Spirit wants all believers—including you—to experience His fullness in every area of life. He will then empower you to minister miraculously to others.

This book is divided into three sections:

Section One contains my personal story with significant parallels in American and world history.

Section Two begins with how God led me to my "Ananias" at the Atlanta Federal Penitentiary, through whom I received the Baptism in the Holy Spirit. That encounter produced amazing changes in my ministry, and the Lord used it to set many other people free. Numerous testimonies of their experiences are included in this section.

The Appendix includes testimonial letters from people whose lives were changed by the Holy Spirit.

Hopefully, you will stay with me to the end of this exciting, 90+ year adventure!

Charles Carrin

Beginnings

Chapter 1

INFAMOUS 1935 "LABOR DAY" HURRICANE

Southam Florida, like other parts of the nation, has long been a target for hurricanes. My family, being pioneer residents, has experienced many of them. My cousins who rushed into our house with my brother that morning in 1935, screaming that a hurricane was coming, had barely survived the 1926 storm. That one was a category four hurricane with sustained winds of 150 mph. It blew the roof off their house, smashed the building and forced them to escape with their mother to an overturned railroad car.

In that storm, a wall of water 12-15 feet high plunged over the near-by town of Coconut Grove, and the surge on Miami's Biscayne Boulevard was 12 feet deep. More tragically, when the "eye" passed over the city, many assumed the winds were finished and rushed out to see the damage. Numerous cars were lining the Biscayne Bay causeway when the second half of the hurricane hit violently and swept them into the water. No one survived. All of Miami was damaged, and much of it was demolished. Statewide, 43,000 were left homeless (nearly a third of the county's population) and 372 were killed.

Two years later, the 1928 hurricane blew Lake Okeechobee's 730 square miles of water onto the south shore, drowning thousands of Everglades families and farm workers. There was no final count of those killed, but the number exceeded 4,000. Every Florida family was affected.

At that time, my father was an officer with the U.S. Immigration Service and was dispatched into the area to assist in burying the dead. Local police and National Guardsmen were also enlisted. So many corpses were found that they were piled in huge mounds, drenched with oil or gasoline and set ablaze. Columns of black smoke rose from burning funeral pyres south of the lake. Some corpses had to be cut from trees. People had tied themselves to trees with rope, wire—anything—to escape the rising water and keep from blowing away. Many of these victims drowned. Others perished from snakebites, and a few were killed by alligators.

My parents' memories of those horrific storms brought terror about the one now approaching. Mama did not wait for another second but darted about the house, stuffing food supplies and clothes into a box. She rushed from room to room, grabbing things we might need. Snooky, our Boston Terrier, chased after her, barking nervously. Our only place of refuge was my grandparents' house five miles away. Granddaddy had wisely secured his home by stretching steel cables across the roof and anchoring them into concrete columns in the yard. These were embedded into the coral rock below ground. He was a strong, spiritual man. Just being near him made us feel safer.

As Mama made preparations, a blast of wind suddenly hit the roof, howling and shaking it in a deafening roar. Stopping abruptly, she stared at my dad in terror. Our house was not strong enough to survive the wind, and with Dad's paralysis, all the responsibility for our safety fell on her. My cousins ran home, and their family left without offering us aid. Mama ran to the window and watched them drive away. Although our car was on the protected side of the house, getting to it was dangerous.

Daddy went first down the steps but did not go to the car. Instead, he braced his back against the wind, leaned on his cane, and tried to get to the mailbox across the road. His veteran's pension-check was due that day. As we leaped from the door to the car, Van and I were blown to the ground. Mud covered us, and we were soaked with rain. At the same time, the wind slammed the front door against my mother's arm, nearly breaking it, and leaving her with only one usable hand.

Her box of supplies went blowing across the yard. By this time Daddy was midway across the road, and Mama was screaming, "Come back! Come back!" Van and I were shrieking, watching our father blow away. Had he fallen, he could never have regained his footing. Beyond him, tall pines began snapping in the middle and crashing to the ground. Mama pushed us into the car, and through the window, we watched him slowly move back to our side of the road. Catching hold of a wire fence, he pulled himself into the yard and to the car.

We were wet and terrified, but the worst news was yet to come: When Mama turned the key in the ignition, the only sound was a grinding noise. The rain had blown under the hood, and the engine was drowned-out. She stared at my dad with an expression of fear I will never forget. More gusts slammed the car, but that is where we stayed—-shut up inside, bouncing back and forth. Snooky squeezed into the seat between Van and me, buried his face under the cushion, and whined with each jolt of the car. Mama shrieked; Daddy shouted his prayer. Within minutes, the storm's fury was upon us.

How long we sat there in our little 1932 Ford, screaming each time it pitched in the wind, I do not know. Hours passed and, miraculously, we never tipped over. What I remember most is that the wind abruptly stopped. The rain ceased, and everything became strangely still. We were gripped in a weird, death-like calm. No one moved. A few minutes later we looked up and saw my uncle's car racing toward us. Mom yelled that we were drowned-out.

Instead of jumping into his car and racing away, in the panic he started pushing our car, with Mama's foolishly trying to start the engine. A mile away she was still grinding the ignition. The road was littered with fallen trees and debris, and we had to detour around them. Time was running out, and we had no way of knowing how quickly the violence would return. Finally, with only seconds left, we arrived at my grandfather's house. Rushing inside, Grandma slammed the front door behind us, and the final and most severe part of the storm hit. Noise from the wind was deafening; water blew under the doors and around window sills, and all the adults were busy trying to keep out the torrential rain.

During the night the storm finally passed, leaving us crowded together awaiting the sunrise. When morning came, we cautiously went outside. All the fruit trees were uprooted, and the windmill was totally demolished. Its tall metal legs and blades were twisted like crumpled foil. Only the coconut palms were standing, with their fronds hanging limp and ragged. Thankfully, we were still alive. Returning home, we saw from a distance that another building had blown into our house, and one wall was completely crushed. The frame was twisted, and everything inside was soaked with rain. A lengthy piece of lumber stabbed through mama's dresser and into the wall behind it. I remember seeing her pull a three-foot-long dagger of window glass from her mattress. Then, leaning against the wall, she broke into sobs.

Strangely, we spent the night there, sleeping on the floor, and we did not go back to my grandparents' house. Daddy was more concerned about

700 World War I veterans that were camped on the Keys than he was about our house. We were safe, but these men were living in tents and shanties, with no protection from the storm. Some were his friends, who were helping build the overseas highway from the mainland to Key West. Unknown to us, in a last-minute effort to save them, an 11-car train was backed into Islamorada from Homestead. Hundreds of men scrambled on board. The train moved forward, but within minutes, a surge of sea-water eighteen feet deep swept across the island. Nine cars were knocked off the track. Chaos and screaming filled the train as the cars were thrown onto their side.

A few days after the storm, a mass funeral with military honors and flag-draped caskets was held in Miami's Woodlawn Cemetery for more than 100 veterans killed on the Keys. Other bodies were shipped to Washington for burial in the Arlington National Cemetery. In some places, corpses were decaying faster than they could be buried, and Florida's Governor David Sholtz ordered their coffins to be doused with gasoline and set afire. Some stacks were five caskets high with flames towering above them. For days after the storm, corpses were still found floating in Florida Bay.

In that day, there was no advance warning about such storms. Hurricanes were not named, but this one was remembered as the infamous "1935 Labor Day Hurricane." The winds and high tides destroyed most of the structures between Tavernier and Marathon Keys and totally devastated the town of Islamorada.

At that time, my uncle was a Station Agent for the Florida East Coast Railway. Two weeks before the storm, he was assigned to Key Largo. Not wanting to move his family off the mainland, he traded posts with another agent. This unsuspecting family transferred to Key Largo a few days before the storm and vanished without a trace.

My parents were committed Christians but had not been baptized or united with the family church, "Little Flock," in Coral Gables (Luke 12:32). Their deliverance from the storm awakened their gratitude to God; and on a beautiful Sunday morning two weeks after the storm, I stood with the congregation at the edge of Biscayne Bay and watched them wade into the water for Baptism. Ten others took part. The sky was blue; the bay was smooth as glass, and birds were singing in the coconut palms. As they stepped into the water, the congregation gathered on the bank and spontaneously began worshiping in beautiful, a capella harmony. The words of the hymn were far more prophetic than anyone realized; nor did I understand the impact they were making on my life:

> *On Jordan's stormy banks I stand*
> *And cast a wishful eye,*
> *To Canaan's fair and happy land*
> *Where my possessions lie.*
> *I am bound for the Promised Land,*
> *I am bound for the Promised Land,*
> *O who will come and go with me?*
> *I am bound for the Promised Land!*

Although I did not yet "know the Lord" (I Samuel 3:7), I stood there, hearing, seeing, and experiencing the Holy Spirit's awesome Presence. An impression was made on my five-year-old mind that time cannot erase. I will never forget the transforming impact of that song or the sacredness of the moment. Now, more than eighty years later, I can still close my eyes and re-live that beautiful morning on Biscayne Bay. Voices from the past seem to be speaking again:

> *No chilling wind nor poisonous breath*
> *Can reach that healthful shore.*
> *Sickness and sorrow, pain and death*
> *Are feared and felt no more.*
> *I am bound for the Promised Land,*
> *I am bound for the Promised Land,*
> *O, who will come and go with me?*
> *I am bound for the Promised Land!*

In that awesome moment, everyone felt as if he stood with Joshua on the banks of the Jordan River and saw the Land of Promise rising before him. My mother later said that her conviction was so great as she sank beneath the Baptismal waters, that she would have kept on sinking if the pastor had turned loose. Then, when she was raised, if he had not held her back, she would have risen out of sight! Such was the blessing of being "buried with Christ" in Baptism and being raised to "walk in newness of life" (Romans 6:4). That moment was preparing me to see future storms, not for their violence and harm, but as the darkness through which God's grace would reveal:

> *Sweet fields beyond the swelling flood,*
> *Stand dressed in living green.*
> *So, to the Jews, old Canaan stood,*
> *While Jordan rolled between.*

Chapter 2

1800s

MY FAMILY'S FLORIDA HISTORY

Both of my parents came from Florida pioneer Christian families. I am a fifth-generation Floridian on both sides. My great-great-grandfather, James Aaron Blanton, was a circuit-riding Primitive Baptist pastor. He came to the Florida wilderness soon after the Seminole War of 1835-1842. Traveling horseback, he preached the gospel and established churches in the northern part of the State.

During the Civil War, my mom's maternal great-grandparents James and Dorothy Dickinson, lived with their three sons near Madison, Florida. Refusing to defend the evil practice of slavery, they publicly renounced the Confederacy and declared their support for the Union. Immediately, Confederate vigilantes raided their farm and hanged my great-great-grandfather in his yard. They burned the house and stole their livestock. Dorothy escaped alone on foot to Georgia. Two days later, while crossing the Okapilco Creek, she learned her son George had also been caught and hanged. Hearing that, she disappeared into the swamps.

When the War ended, my great-grandfather Phabeon Dickinson returned home and found the house burned. The family had vanished, and his mother's status was unknown. He searched fruitlessly for her and finally got work in a sawmill in Quitman, Georgia. It was owned by my wife's great-grandfather John Hancock. Months later Mr. Hancock learned of two destitute women living alone in the woods, and he asked his crew if someone would take food to them. Phabeon volunteered.

After riding on horseback for an hour, Phabeon finally found the shack. A petite woman cautiously came outside and greeted him. When she realized Phabeon had food, she relaxed and went running back to the cabin, yelling, "We have food, Dorothy!"

Phabeon froze. It couldn't be! For a frantic second, he dared not hope. Then he bolted into the cabin and stood transfixed at what he saw. In the dim light of the room, his mother raised up in the bed before him.

"Mama! Mama!" he shouted, dropping the food to the floor. "I found you! I found you!"

"I knew you'd come, she cried, waving her arms toward him. "God told me you'd come! He told me!"

This amazing part of my family history is told in my book, *Island In The Sun*.

On my father's side, my great-great-grandmother Marie Catherine du Moline Carrin was a French Huguenot, who was born in Valenciennes, France, in 1798. She and her husband converted from Catholicism, but this caused tension within the family. To restore peace, she and her husband immigrated to the United States in the late 1850s with their teenage son Jean Baptiste. Her son was drafted to fight for the Union during the Civil War. He was wounded and contracted tuberculosis. Soon after that, Marie's husband died.

After the war, Marie realized her son needed to be in a warmer climate. She put her family, including Jean's pregnant wife, in an ox-cart and brought them to Florida. After traveling three months through the war-devastated South, they settled on the Suwannee River. Here they lived in peace. Marie later died and was buried at a site called "Old Wilmarth Cemetery." Florida became her Promised Land. After her death, the family moved farther south to the Esteinahatchee River, where my great-grandfather died and is buried.

My mother's Blanton family were enforcers of the law who came to America from England before the 1776 War for Independence. Their family contributed to the development of the young nation, producing Governors, Judges, Generals, and other public figures. Mom's grandfather was a member of the Florida Bar, an Attorney, a Representative in the State Legislature, Confederate veteran, and an Ordained Primitive Baptist preacher. It was his father who had been a circuit-riding preacher on the Florida frontier soon after the Seminole War.

My Blanton grandparents, including my father, mother, and others, moved to Miami in the 1920s. The road they traveled was a one-lane, shell-rock road that later became US Highway #1. The only other road giving access to the city was the highway that is known today as the Tamiami Trail. It crossed the Everglades from Miami to Naples on the Gulf coast and opened in 1915.

My grandfather Blanton's appearance in Miami did not go unnoticed. He was soon made Chairman of the Dade County School Board, a post which he held for many years of my childhood. Later, a Miami school was named in his honor, and my uncle was appointed Principal. My mother was a University-certified teacher, but she never sought a career in education.

Prohibition and The Great Depression

Wall Street was prosperous, and the nation was thriving. Suddenly, without warning, the Stock Market crashed on October 29, 1929. In a matter of hours, some thirty billion bank-dollars were lost. The U.S. and much of the industrialized world plunged into crushing bankruptcy. As the crisis went tidal-wave across the land, the effect was psychological as well as financial. Some investors leaped from office windows to their deaths. The day was quickly named "Black Tuesday," and that began America's ten-year era of the "Great Depression."

In Miami, unfinished high-rise buildings were abandoned to rust, while housing developments became overgrown with weeds and wild trees. Groves of Australian pines spread though partially-built neighborhoods and sprouted in uncompleted roadways. The Prinz Valdemar, a 241-foot steel-hulled schooner, sank in the mouth of the Miami harbor and blocked shipping-access to the city. A few miles away, a partially-built high-rise luxury hotel The Fritz was converted into a commercial chicken house. The "Great Depression" hit with an iron fist and my grandfather found himself owning acres of worthless land. My father recovered sufficiently from his war wounds and joined the U.S. Immigration's Border Patrol

During the depression, the national prohibition of the sale of alcohol provided criminals the opportunity to establish networks of illegal-liquor, prostitution, and other destructive activities across the nation. In effect, Prohibition gave birth to America's "Crime Syndicates." One of the most infamous names of that era was Al Capone. He lived in an elegant waterfront estate in Miami Beach. Florida appealed to him because of its beauty, warmth, and abundant smuggling opportunities. The Florida Keys, with thousands of unprotected islands, provided ideal sites to bring Cuban rum into the country. Homestead—the last town on the U.S. mainland—was an unavoidable entrance point for that alcohol into the U.S.

In 1929, the U.S. Immigration Department sent my father and other officers from the Miami Bureau to the Florida Keys to intercept the smuggling trade. Dad was a muscular man—six feet, three inches tall—who loved life and enjoyed his work with the Government. He, my mother, and my two-year-old brother, Van, moved from Miami to Homestead. It was here, in the most southern town in the continental US that I was born, although my birth almost failed to happen.

My dad captured a young crocodile to put in my grandmother's fish pool in Miami, but my mother was terrified and would not get in the car with it. Finally, with suitcases safely blocking it, mom got in the car, and they sped north. All went well, until she felt something claw her ankle. Looking down, she saw the crocodile's head between her feet. Screaming, she jumped onto the seat, knocking the steering wheel out of my dad's hand. The car plunged off the road, bouncing and swerving, and it finally stopped in a thicket of pines and palmettos. Fortunately, they hit no tree, and the car was undamaged; but both were terrified. Thankfully, on November 19, 1930, I arrived safely, with the crocodile living in my grandmother's pool.

Dad's Border Patrol squad seized and destroyed scores of illegal boats, dumped countless barrels of Cuban Rum into the bay, and arrested numerous aliens. There were wild boat chases across Florida Bay and automobile shoot-outs on U.S. #1. Dad and the other Immigration Officers became the target for mobster attack, and their lives were under constant threat.

My half-brother James was not with us in Homestead. His mother, my dad's first wife, died soon after his birth. Our grandmother kept him before my parents married. In effect, she became his mother and did not want to give him up after my parent's wedding. Although he lived part-time with her and with us, we felt no distinction in our family-bond. He was my full-brother in every way.

Chapter 3

The 1930s

SPIRITUAL WORLDS COLLIDE

1933

1933 was a significant year on both sides of the Atlantic. In Europe, only fifteen years after the end of World War I, a political newcomer was appointed Chancellor of Germany and began his rise to power. As head of the newly organized Nazi Party, he vowed to restore Germany to its lost prestige and supremacy. His name was Adolph Hitler. That same year in America, Franklin Delano Roosevelt was elected President and began what would prove to be the longest Presidency in the nation's history. Significantly, these two men—Roosevelt and Hitler—paralleled each other in the years of their rule, 1933-1945, and became parabolic symbols of life and death. They, more than many others, would leave lasting impacts on the psyche of mankind. One would create a worldwide wound; the other, a healing bandage. Dying only months apart, Hitler was 56; Roosevelt was 63.

President Roosevelt was elected during the Great Depression and immediately instituted his "New Deal" program that put millions of unemployed men back to work. This was implemented through the WPA—"Works Progress Administration" and the CCC or Civilian Conservation Corps. The five greatest achievements of these organizations were building the Lincoln Tunnel in New York, Florida's Overseas Highway to Key West, the Hoover Dam in Nevada, the Grand Coulee Dam in Washington State, and developing the Great Smokey Mountains National Park in Tennessee and North Carolina.

The same year Roosevelt became President, Prohibition ended, and public liquor sale was legal again. Rum-smuggling was no longer profitable, and my dad was ordered back to the main Immigration Office in Miami.

He and my mother found a comfortable house within walking distance of the downtown and quickly made the change. The structure had two stories, with a balcony on the second floor. As they were bringing furniture into the upstairs, a neighbor reluctantly approached my mother and introduced herself. She spoke admiringly of our family and said, "You have a lovely family! I know you want to stay here, but I urge you—beg you—please don't live in this house!" There was a fearful sound in her voice. Mom was startled at the strange request and asked, "Why?" "Because," she answered quickly, "Everyone who has lived here has had horrible tragedy! I realize the inconvenience this would cause you, but I beg you! Please don't stay! Go, find another place for your family. You will always regret having lived in this house!" A pleading, fearful tone shook her voice.

Mom looked at my dad. He said nothing but stared quizzically. My two uncles who were helping listened intently. They had already taken much of the furniture to the second floor, and my dad had to be in the office the next day. We had nowhere else to go. After a moment's hesitation, they thanked her for the warning but felt it necessary to stay. Staring fearfully at each of them again, she turned and walked away.

Soon after moving in, strange noises were heard throughout the house. My dad investigated from the attic to the garage but found nothing. Other times the sounds came simultaneously from underneath and overhead. One day when my uncle and aunt were visiting, the noise began in a disturbing way. This time it was louder, sounding like a heavy metal ball rolling between rafters above them. For a moment everyone listened intently, then the "ball"—whatever it was—suddenly raced across the attic and shot out of the house. With a loud bang, it hit my uncle's car, which was parked in the driveway below. Everyone raced outside, searching the yard and nearby areas for the object, but they found nothing; nor was there any dent in the car. Looking at each other with puzzled expressions, they went back inside.

A month after moving in, my mother lay down one afternoon to rest. She did not fall asleep but momentarily closed her eyes. Opening them, she looked to the right. Lying beside her was a phantom-like image of her dead grandmother. The form—whatever it was—looked astonishingly real and was wearing an identical shroud and cap in which her grandmother had been buried years before. Mother was terrified. For a moment she was too frightened to move. Then, slowly, she slid one leg off the bed and prepared to jump and run.

When she did, the image reached its arm across her body and stopped her, saying, "Don't worry! We are going to take care of you!" Even the voice sounded like her grandmother's voice. With that, mama leaped from the bed, looked back, and the form was gone. Rushing from the room, she ran downstairs, out the front door, and covering her face with her hands, fell against the wall weeping, shaking as in a chill.

She couldn't believe what had happened. Was it real? Was it God? If it were God, why was she so terrified?! She should feel joy at His presence, but she only felt fear. Both the message and the messenger were frightening. How could it be her grandmother? The Bible taught that the dead could not communicate with the living (Luke 16:26). What she had seen and heard violated every Scriptural truth she had ever learned, but it seemed so real! Worst of all, if the message were true, tragic events were awaiting our family but things about which she should not be worried. Someone—or something—would take care of us. Who would that be? Was it God? How serious was the problem we faced? What would It involve? There were too many unanswered questions, and she needed answers to all of them. Not realizing the connection between the neighbor's frightening warning and this demonic apparition, we continued living in the house.

Soon after that, as a three-year-old, I found matches, crawled under the bed in an upstairs bedroom and set fire to the bottom of the mattress. At that age, I was merely entertaining myself and unaware of the danger I caused. Later, mama was rushing us out of the house, taking Van and me on an errand, when she saw a wisp of smoke in the doorway. Going back inside, she checked the kitchen, other rooms, and found nothing. Still, in a hurry, she grabbed her purse from the bed where she had tossed it, and she felt heat touch her hand. Snatching back the cover, the bed burst into flames. There was no one to help and no time for delay. So, lifting the blazing mattress from the bed, she dragged it onto the balcony and tossed it to the ground. We were unharmed, and the house spared, but the neighbors warning of disaster had just begun.

A short time later, I was playing on the balcony, and I climbed too far forward and fell head-first to the ground. Striking my head on a heavy metal object, I suffered a severe concussion of the brain and cut a four-inch gash in my scalp. Blood spurted with every heartbeat, soaking the ground and covering my body. Mama found me and began screaming. Neighbors ran to her and raced us to the nearest doctor's office, arriving just minutes before I bled to death. The blood was stopped; the wound stitched, and I was sent home to recuperate. Nothing more could be done. Unknown to us, the worst effect from the injury was yet to come.

Mama awoke one morning to find Daddy still lying beside her in bed. He had not risen early and gone to work as he usually did. Pushing his shoulder to awaken him, he did not respond. Leaping onto her knees and jerking back the cover, she discovered he was unconscious, unable to move or speak, and totally paralyzed. Though alive, he had all the appearances of being dead. The sight was terrifying. Running to the phone, she called for an ambulance, which rushed him to the Veterans Hospital. For the next two weeks, he lay motionless, unable to move. He could not speak, blink an eye, or raise a finger. According to the doctors, the fifteen-year-old leg injury from the War had mysteriously revived and released a clot that struck his brain. His entire body was paralyzed; and, unknown to us, he would never walk normally again. That morning, his beloved work with the Immigration Department ended forever.

In the early 1930s, there was no penicillin to fight infection or clot-dissolving drugs to treat strokes. Nothing more could be done, and in a short time, the wound on Dad's leg became severely infected. Amputation was impossible, because of other complications. Weeks passed, and he was still unconscious. The hospital abandoned hope for his recovery and transferred him across Florida to the Veterans Hospital in St. Petersburg. In his absence, I went into shock and quit eating. No amount of coaxing could make me swallow food. I quickly lost weight, stopped talking or playing and became a shadow of my former self.

Mama, a young woman in her 20's, was in panic for all of us. Two weeks later she drove Van and me across Florida to see our father. The three of us were at his bedside staring. Mama was holding me, and Van was standing on his tiptoes. Daddy looked dead. He was motionless, pale, and his mouth hung open. No one was speaking, but while we stared, he moved one toe. That was all he did—moved one toe. I leaped in mama's arms—encouraged—and immediately revived. I began eating and was soon laughing and playing again. Daddy's recovery was slow, painful, and incomplete. Months passed before he was able to walk, and then he walked only with the help of a cane. Finally, the hospital released him to come home.

Not long after that, mother left Van and me in the care of her sister, while she took my dad to the doctor. I begged to go with them but was left at home. As soon as they drove away, I sneaked out of the house to follow them. I became lost and finally hid in an obscure place crying. Several hours passed before a stranger found me, and took me to a nearby grocery store, where they called the police. When the police arrived carrying guns and dressed similarly as my dad, I feared my running away would cause problems for him and told them my name was "Charlie Brown."(My aunt's last name was Brown). This added to the Police Department's complications in identifying me and delayed my return home. In the meantime, my parents arrived at the house, found me gone, and my auntie in hysteria. All of them were panic-stricken. Word quickly spread through the neighborhood that I had been kidnapped. A few years before, the infant son of Charles Lindberg, America's first aviator-hero to cross the Atlantic, had been kidnapped and killed.

Our neighbors were quick to believe the same had happened to me, and the evil reputation of our house became fortified with another horror story. Late that day, when I returned home sitting in the front seat of a patrol car between two policemen, the neighbors were crowded in our yard and onto the sidewalks. Seeing me, they started yelling, clapping, and thanking God for my safe return. Some were crying.

Finally, with my grandparent's financial help, we moved out of that horrible place into a newly-built house of our own. It was small and unfinished, but it was a welcome escape from the snake-pit where we lived. Neighbors who knew of our tragedy came to tell us goodbye as we pulled out of the driveway. Standing among them was the woman who appeared that frightening day and warned my parents about the crisis we faced. We had confirmed every fearful word she spoke. Would we always regret having lived in that house? Absolutely! Worst of all, when we moved out, all the demons were still there, awaiting their next victims. Years later we learned that someone set fire to the building one night and burned it to the ground. My reaction was, "Thank God! It is gone!"

Chapter 4

THE BIBLE'S REMEDY FOR DEMONS

The Bible is not silent about demonized places like our house. Thirty percent of Jesus's recorded ministry in the gospels was devoted to casting out demons. He explained, "If I cast out demons by the Spirit of God, surely the Kingdom of God has come upon you" (Matthew 12:28). In the Great Commission, He commanded the gospel to be taken into all the world and said, "These signs will follow those who believe: In My name, they will cast out demons" (Mark 16:17). Jesus never sent anyone to preach without specifically giving them that same responsibility and power. Exercising this authority should be a primary function of the church today (Matthew 10:8; Luke 10:19). Most of the American Church, however, refuses to fulfill its responsibility in "Deliverance Ministry," while significantly, some psychiatrists are doing it.

Dr. William P. Wilson, MD, Distinguished Professor Emeritus of Psychiatry at Duke University and Professor of Counseling at the Houston Graduate School of Theology (NC) wrote of "Demon Possession and Deliverance in Clinical Practice." As a medical doctor, he practices Deliverance Ministry and is a confirmed believer in demons and the Christians' power to exorcise them.

Dr. Richard Gallagher, a board-certified psychiatrist and clinical professor of psychiatry at New York Medical College, encountered demonic possession/oppression numerous times in his practice and wrote extensively about it. For more than two decades Dr. Gallagher was consulted on hundreds of such cases, some of which were medical conditions, while numerous others were the works of "evil spirits." Gallagher insisted that he had seen "the real thing." In some instances, the patients experienced "trances, enormous strength, levitation, and hidden knowledge." Dr. Gallagher declared, "I have seen more cases of possession than any other physician in the world."

Dr. M. Scott Peck (1936-2005), a Harvard-trained Psychiatrist, was a firm believer in unclean spirits and told about numerous demonic manifestations he witnessed in his practice. Of one such instance, he said, "An expression appeared on the patient's face that could be described only as satanic." Dr. Peck described how he later stood in front of a mirror trying to imitate the evil in the face he had seen. His effort failed. The doctor not only counseled those in psychiatric need and prescribed medication but routinely ministered deliverance to patients demonically affected. He described that part of his practice in his book The Road Less Traveled. Dr. Peck is joined by numerous others of his educational level who acknowledge the reality of unclean spirits. These men, like many other secular authorities, bemoan the church's refusal to exercise the power Jesus gave it. For the sake of clarity, from this point on, when I speak of the ministry of "Deliverance" from demons, I will capitalize the word. This will distinguish it from ordinary use.

Why did Jesus put so much emphasis on believers' having authority over demons? Why was it such a consuming part of His ministry? He did that because the need was real and protection from demons vital. The modern church, in contrast, not only ignores His teachings on that subject but often ridicules and defames those who obey Him.

At the time of my Ordination in 1949, I was taught nothing about demons or the believer's authority to expel them. It was not until my Baptism in the Spirit years later that my eyes were opened to the reality of this dark spiritual power. Now I realize our house in Miami was demonized and had been used for satanic worship, witchcraft sacrifices, séances, and other forms of devilish activity. The place was infested with unclean spirits. My parents' church, "Little Flock," was filled with beautiful, godly people, and our pastor was a dear man; but, as a hyper-Calvinist, he knew absolutely nothing about the Holy Spirit's gifts or the believer's authority over demons.

Defending us from the devil's attack was unknown to both him and the congregation (Luke 10:19). Instead of being established in the authority of Christ, the church taught that all of the Holy Spirit's miraculous gifts had been withdrawn. Specifically, "discerning of spirits," which we desperately needed, was no longer a viable spiritual gift (1 Corinthians 12:10). This New Testament provision, with all other "charismatic" benefits, had disappeared. Strangely, God took away the church's power but let the devil keep his. Where does the Bible make this claim? It doesn't. Search the Scriptures. It isn't there! When God said, "My people are destroyed for lack of knowledge," He was referring to circumstances exactly like this (Hosea 4:5). At the time Jesus said, "I give you power to tread on serpents and scorpions and over all the power of the enemy," He did not believe the Father would quickly revoke it (Luke 10:19).

The Apostle Paul never thought the Scripture would be changed when he wrote, "All Scripture is given by inspiration of God and is profitable ..." (II Timothy 3:16). The idea of Cessationism (God's removal of spiritual gifts and power) was invented by the church to justify its failure and unbelief. Consequently, my parents did not know their authority in Christ, and true to the neighbor's warning, I will go to my grave regretting that we lived in that horrible place. More so, I regret that we did not know to use the power God provided to exorcise the building. As New Testament believers, my parents could have cleansed the property themselves, lived there safely, and left it harmless for others to follow. We did not know that. Our church failed us.

I later found a Scriptural parallel between our circumstance and Simon the Sorcerer, a demonized man who bewitched the people of Samaria (Acts 8:5-26). As a false prophet, Simon made everyone believe he possessed the power of God, while the opposite was true. As an agent of Satan, he secretly plagued them with paralyzing forms of power. Identical to Simon's work, our family's crisis centered upon the paralytic symptom. This does not imply that all paralysis is demonic in origin. It is not. We are capable of self-injury. However, it seems that "spirits of infirmity" attack the body or mind in specific ways. For example, the maniac of Gadara was vexed by spirits that destroyed his mind but left his body with great strength (Mark 5:1-18). The opposite was true in the woman with the crooked back. (Luke 13:11). Though her problem appeared physical, in reality, it was spiritual. Jesus did not heal her, but He cast out the demon of infirmity that caused the problem. She was instantly normal. As then, so it is today. Medication is good, and we are grateful for it; however, it is of no value in treating demonically-based problems.

Psychics, clairvoyants, fortune tellers, and others like Simon, deceive the unwary with accurate predictions and powerful demonic demonstrations, while they cripple their victims with other crises. Be aware: such people are not foretelling future events. They are causing them! Someone argues, "No! That can't be!" Yes, it is. If we believe and submit to what they say, we agree for it to happen. We have the choice of believing we are helpless victims of the devil, or believing that Christ has given us "power to tread on serpents and scorpions and over all the power of the enemy" (Luke 10:19).

Jesus said, "The Scripture cannot be broken" (John 10:35). There is no way to deny the clarity and authority of this verse. "But!" Someone says, "It doesn't work. The Scripture no longer possess power!" In most cases that may seem true, but the failure is not in the Scripture. It is in the church's refusal to believe and teach it. Jesus said, "And these signs will follow those who believe: In My Name, they will cast out demons …" (Mark 16:17). Bible promises are valid only to the genuine believer. To the doubting Christian, they have no more power than a newspaper page. Tragically, the modern church is more confirmed in denial than in faith and needs to repent of its sin of unbelief and rejection of Scripture. Observe in the following two letters how the writers became demonic-victims by the verbal abuse of their parents. Both were delivered in public meetings. They wrote:

"Dear Charles, I'm free, I'm free, I'm free! Thank you for being my 'Ananias.' I have received my miracle! For 34 years I have been in bondage to a curse of homosexuality and rejection placed on me by my Dad. I had begun to contemplate suicide because I could not handle it any longer. I prayed one last time for God to send me the person that could help me get a 'breakthrough' —and the rest is history. No one could imagine the pain and suffering I've endured in my life but thank God it has been 'Swallowed up in Victory.' Charles, the church is so ignorant in this area. The homosexual behavior may be a choice but not the curse. I was five years old when my Dad threatened to castrate me and make me into a girl. I endured this abuse all during my childhood. I had forgiven my Dad years ago, but I never could break the curse until now. I not only experienced deliverance, but also inner healing. I now can begin the ministry God has intended for me. I could go on for days! To me, my miracle is as great as the lame man walking or the blind seeing … You are free to use my experience to help others …."

"Dear Brother Charles, I grew up in a home filled with alcohol, hatred, and abuse. I cannot remember ever feeling loved or wanted. I attempted suicide twice as a teenager. I have had two failed marriages and have lived forty-three years without one ounce of self-confidence or self-respect. My mother told me God didn't want someone like me. The night you said for those wanting deliverance to line up at the front. My feet got

up and took me. As I stood there, while you spoke, my insides began to tremble. But it was a very strange and different feeling. It was like it wasn't my insides that were trembling but something inside my insides that was trembling. The more you talked, the worse the thing in me shook ... it felt like a tornado ... very, very angry. I could barely hear you say, "In the Name of Jesus I command you to go!" That tornado ripped from my body with hatred, anger, and despite beyond belief. As it left, I passed out. Brother Charles, let me tell you, by the grace of God, I woke up as God's little girl who is loved! This thing is so overwhelming to me. Each day I love Jesus more than the day before ...."

These beautiful testimonies assure us that the gospel has not lost its original power. Instead, the church has denied it. It was not the will of God that these writers become victims of abuse; but, as children, they were cursed verbally and abused physically by angry parents. Demons took advantage of that damage. Thank God, the truth of Scripture rescued and set them free. Were these people "demon-possessed?" No. Not at all, and it is vital that we understand the difference between demonic "possession" and "oppression." Christians cannot be possessed by the devil. Possession implies ownership. Born-again people are owned by Jesus Christ. While our regenerate spirits are born-again and immune to demons, our bodies and brains have not yet been through the resurrection. Because of this, they can still be oppressed by unclean spirits. A demon can go anywhere sin and disease are present.

Paul explained why we are still vulnerable to their attack. He said, "Our mortal has not yet put on immortality, nor has our corruption put on incorruption" (1 Corinthians 15:53). Know this: The body will not become sinless until the Resurrection, and therefore, is still susceptible to demonic attack. Our regenerate spirit, however, is sin-free. It is immune to demons, and at death returns immediately to God. Paul tells about the body's future rescue:

So when this corruptible shall have put on incorruption, and this mortal shall have put on immortality, then shall be brought to pass the saying that is written, Death is swallowed up in victory. O death, where is thy sting? O grave, where is thy victory? ... Thanks be to God, who gives us the victory through our Lord Jesus Christ!

1 Corinthians 15:54-57

35

Charles Carrin

Be aware, as demons occupied my family's house, they can also occupy objects. Things like voodoo masks, Egyptian amulets, and Hindu images must be removed from our homes and destroyed. Demons regard these items as their "temples" and use them as a base of operation (Joshua 6:18). For example, Achan, an Israeli soldier, buried an "accursed thing" in the floor of his tent and caused Israel's defeat in their next battle (Joshua 6-8). His stolen items included a Babylonian garment and wedge of gold.

Once when I was preaching on a jungle-beach in Haiti, a number of people were saved. One of the women asked us to come to her house and burn her voodoo fetishes. We built a bonfire, and she brought out a basket of items and threw them into the flames. We all stood, staring at the blaze, and someone made a 35-millimeter photo of it. Later, when the picture was shown on the screen, a demonic face appeared in the lower right-hand corner of the blaze. The flames flickering upward, revealed the head, face, ears, and horns of an evil-looking being. Were demons actually present in the burning substances? Yes. Spirits inhabit a variety of material, including occult books. These must be destroyed.

We have a New Testament example of such a public fetish-destruction at Ephesus when occult writings valued at more than 50,000 pieces of silver were destroyed (Acts 19:19). If you have such objects or other talismans in your possession, you should destroy them. My purpose in telling this is not to incite fear or strengthen superstition, but to help believers realize the demonic-realm is very real and must be resisted. In my early years of ministry, I heard about a very naive, young American missionary who stood in a Hindu Temple in India and said to the idol, "If you're a god—strike me blind!" Instantly, she was blinded and never regained her sight.

Millions of Christians suffer needlessly today because the church refuses to teach the whole New Testament message. When Jesus delivered the Great Commission, instructing disciples to carry the gospel into "all the world," He included casting out demons. For the first 30 years of my ministry, I did not do that; and people in my congregation suffered from alcohol, drug addiction, emotional problems, promiscuity, habitual failure, and other crises. An example of that failure was an alcoholic-brother in my Florida congregation whom I was powerless to help. Their home was in chaos, the teenage daughter ran away to escape his drunken-tirades, and his wife was in a state of collapse.

On one occasion, I took him to a State-operated Rehabilitation Center that refused to accept him. Rather than take him back home, I drove away and left him on their steps. Later, I moved out of the state and knew nothing of him for many years. When I moved back to Florida, he and his wife came to a meeting where I preached. Both were radically changed and healthy; the addiction was obviously gone. When I asked him about his old problem, he replied, "Pastor, after you left, I went to a *real* church and got delivered!" As a result of his new freedom, he was in ministry sending hundreds of Derek Prince teaching tapes to pastors around the world.

Unlike churches today, Deliverance Ministry was a routine function in the early church. Literature of the second and third centuries gives us a good example of believers ministering exorcism in that day. Read carefully what these early Christians said:

"Numberless demoniacs throughout the whole world and in your city, many of our Christian men, exorcising them in the name of Jesus Christ … have healed and do heal, though they could not be cured by all other exorcists and those who use incantations and drugs."
—Justin Martyr: (110-165)

"Let a person be brought before your tribunals who is plainly under demonic possession. The wicked spirit, commanded to speak by a follower of Christ, will as readily make the truthful confession that he is a demon, as elsewhere he has falsely asserted that he is a god."
—Tertullian: (197)

"Sometimes they themselves (demons) disturb the habit of the body by a tempest of madness; but, being smitten by the Word of God, they depart in terror, and the sick man is healed."
—Tatian: (160)

More information on the subject of Deliverance is found in Section II, Chapter 23 of this book.

Chapter 5

THE SECRET CURSE DOMINATES OUR FAMILY

We had been in our new house only a short time when the 1935 hurricane hit. It demolished an exterior wall, twisted the frame, and smashed the windows. The beds, clothing, and everything inside were soaked. Mattresses, clothes, and linens had to be laid outside in the sunshine until they dried. Even in the hot Florida sun, it was days before the bedding could be used again. We were thankful to have our own home, even in its damaged condition. We had no indoor bathroom, and our outhouse had blown away.

One Sunday later that year, our Little Flock Church observed its annual "feet washing" service. This beautiful event was the highlight of the church year and was observed jointly with Communion. Members gathered at the front of the church, knelt before one another, and repented publicly, oftentimes weeping. They sought forgiveness, and, as Jesus taught, they washed each other's feet (John 13:5). For this event, everyone gathered at the front of the building. Mama knew the service would be lengthy and let Van and me go outside to play. We were soon bored with nothing to do. Sneaking through the front door, we crawled under the pews. Looking toward the front under the benches, we could see many bare feet, shoes, socks, and basins of water.

Van happened to have buckshot in his pocket, which he lined up in a crack between boards. Then he began thumping them at the feet. When he hit a foot and saw it jerk, we would giggle and shoot another BB. I probably hit no one but eagerly tried. Finally, the supply of buckshot was spent, and we left the building. Mama was unaware of our prank, but someone told her. Strangely, she said nothing until we got home. I remember undressing in my room and standing in my undershorts. She suddenly appeared and said, "Stay right there!" I thought she had new clothes for me to put on and gladly waited.

A moment later she burst into the room with a switch as long as her arm. I sprang onto the bed, but she grabbed my wrist with one hand. The switch became a blur in the other. Screaming, I leaped across the bed from one end to the other, but she held on and caught me in mid-air. My screeching and pleading did not stop her. Snooky, my dog, came racing to my rescue. Grabbing her skirt in his teeth, he began twisting it around her legs, snarling and tearing it. The scene was chaotic. Mama was yelling at me; I was wailing, and the dog was growling. Van ran to the yard, but mama saw him and hollered, "Don't run away! You're next!" When his time came, she locked Snooky in another room, more angered because of her ragged dress, and assailed Van.

The summer of 1936 passed uneventfully. Everyone assumed I had recovered from the fall; however, in autumn that year we visited relatives in High Springs, Florida, where I became violently ill. Before morning my face twisted, and my heart began beating irregularly. My leg stiffened, and my left arm locked rigidly against my side. Unknown to my parents, a clot from the old head injury struck my brain and paralyzed the left side of my body. That was a few months before my sixth birthday. Good medical care was nonexistent in the area, and the only doctor available misdiagnosed me as having polio. I was kept at home, given no medical treatment, and for weeks my consciousness came in fleeting moments. No one, not even the doctor, related the paralysis to the head-injury three years earlier. Worse still, it was a cold autumn, but I was too sick to return to Miami where warmth and better medical care might have helped. One of the few memories I have is sitting up and seeing my bed lined with the heads of people praying for me. My favorite auntie Nannie, a true believer and the most spiritual person I knew, had gathered her Nazarene Church prayer warriors to my bedside to pray.

Recovery was slow and incomplete, and I was sometimes tied in a chair with a broom against my chest to keep me from falling. I improved gradually, and as soon as I was able to travel, we returned to Miami. Even there, I had no further medical attention. Jimmy decided to stay with our grandmother at Monticello.

CHILDHOOD DISEASES

In 1937 there was no inoculation for childhood diseases, and my brothers and I experienced all of them. Measles, mumps, whooping cough, and chicken pox moved unchecked through school classrooms, sometimes sending every student home. Mumps was the worst. I caught it, my jaws swelled shut with pain, and any acidic-food brought spasms of agony. If I cried from pain and stretched my jaws, the anguish increased. Boys were carefully kept in bed, as the infection could move into the testes, causing greater suffering and damage. Foolishly, most children had their tonsils removed, and this was a terrorizing experience. I well remember the sickening smell of ether being forced against my nose until I was unconscious.

Poliomyelitis was the most feared of all childhood diseases, and every summer the population was hit with terrible outbreaks. Newspapers carried daily reports of epidemics. Large cities with dense populations were especially victimized. Public pools and playgrounds closed, and efforts were made to keep children apart. While youths were the usual target, polio could also attack adults with permanently crippling effects. President Franklin D. Roosevelt was thirty-nine years old when he contracted the disease and afterward spent much of his time in a wheelchair. In any large gathering of people, one would always see polio victims struggling with paralyzed limbs. It was not until my old-age that my paralysis was identified with my head injury and not polio.

In 1936, my parents bought a new home site three miles from downtown Miami. They had our little frame building put on a house-moving truck and carried to the new location. That was an exciting day. James, Van and I ran around our new yard, watching the activity and getting in the way. The house was set on a concrete foundation that had been prepared a week earlier. Wet cement was poured into coral-rock below ground to give us better anchorage during hurricanes. Mama climbed into the attic and examined every rafter to be certain that each was attached with metal-straps to the studs below.

My uncles built a tripod out of three young pine trees, and using a section of a heavy Australian-pine log, pounded a pipe fifty feet into the ground. Attaching a pump to the top, in a few minutes we had drinking water. That well remained our only supply for many years afterward, even though minerals turned it the color of tea when left overnight. Mama immediately began landscaping the yard. Coconuts palms were planted in front of the house, and brightly-colored crotons lined the sides. A mango, avocado, lime, and guava tree crowded the back. Huge Australian Pines bounded the road to the west of us. Across the street, a gravel-road was lined with tall Jamaican Coconuts, and within a year, our place was beautiful and homelike. A fish pool was later added to the front yard. I was excited about our new location as we were near Earlington Heights School and stores. We also had bus service to downtown Miami.

One of our biggest childhood hazards was going barefoot and stepping on rusty nails. This happened to me several times, but I never went to a doctor or had a tetanus shot. The home remedy of that day was to soak the foot in turpentine for half an hour. Visits to the doctor were non-existent. Dentists were my greatest fear, and my parents complained about the cost. A filling was $3.00, and an extraction was $5.00. A hospital room was also $5.00, unless you insisted on a private room, which cost $8.00. Our worst health-threat was snakes, which were abundant in South Florida. Twice I came within inches of stepping barefoot on a rattlesnake and a cottonmouth moccasin. Other times I had close encounters with coral snakes. Black widow spiders were abundant, as were scorpions, which lived inside the walls of our house and crawled across the ceiling at night. Once my Aunt Emma got trapped in the bathroom by a giant spider on the doorknob, and neighbors heard her screaming half a block away. The spider was in more danger than she was.

My favorite place to play was an abandoned rock pit not far from our house which contained a pool of clear green water, a jungle of plants, birds, and other wildlife. I would climb down the slope, explore the area and enjoy the solitude. There were lots of spring frogs, lizards, snakes, birds, and strange-looking insects. Once, returning home, my uncles were there, telling how they gigged frogs in the Everglades and cooked their legs. I listened carefully. They described how delicious they were. That gave me an idea: There were lots of frogs in the rock pit, and I would surprise mama with a big supply for supper. I told no one but got a quart-sized glass jar, took my bee-bee gun and headed to the pit. Two hours later I had filled the jar with small frogs. Putting a lid on it, I left it on a rock in the sun and played another hour. When the time came to go home, I did not notice that bubbles had formed in the jar and the color of the frogs had changed from green to brown. Their bellies had swelled to twice their original size.

Rushing in the back door at home I yelled, "Mama! Come here! I have a surprise for you!" She came to the kitchen. "Close your eyes!" I yelled excitedly. Then, pulling out a large metal pan, I said, "Look!" With that, I poured the jar of slimy, smelly frogs onto the tin. She shrieked and grabbed her face. For a moment she froze. "Get them out of here! Get them out of here!" She screamed and ran from the room. That night we enjoyed our usual meal of black-eyed peas and rice, and no frog legs were on the table.

My arm and leg slowly normalized, but the left side of my face did not. The greatest handicap was that I could not close the left eyelid, and it remained permanently open. The effect was horrific. I loved sports, but anytime I looked up to catch a baseball, I was blinded by the sunlight. Invariably, I missed the ball. My constant failure made other boys fight to keep me off their team. Many times I stood staring at the ground, while they argued with the teacher about letting me play. I dreaded getting up to bat and hearing the jeers that followed my strike-outs. Coaches did not understand my problem and ridiculed me in the presence of others. That powerfully re-enforced a spirit of rejection that dominated my life. Secretly, this sense of inferiority stayed with me into adulthood. I would pretend to be adequate, while inside I was more terrified. If another child rushed to me unexpectedly, I would throw up my arm in self-defense, but the greatest problem was my eye. Sunlight paralyzed me with inexpressible pain.

Two years after moving to our new location, my mom got her brothers to enlarge our house and build a cottage for winter rental. This would supplement our income. That fall, the first renter was a well-dressed northern family, the Nelsons. As they were moving into the cottage, I overheard my mother talk about the woman's expensive hat. It was black and white with a band of skunk fur around the rim. Immediately, I had a plan: A skunk had its nest in our pump house, and my mom would soon have skunk fur for her hat also.

I told no one my plan. One day when everyone left, and I was home alone, I sawed off the handle of the kitchen broom and drove a long nail into the end. Then I flattened the head with a hammer and filed it into a sharp gig. I knew mama would forgive my having ruined the broom because she would be so pleased with her own skunk-fur. Opening the pump-house door slowly and taking careful aim, I stabbed the skunk. But, I wasn't quick enough. In a second's time, he spun around and sprayed me with musk from my hair to my bare feet.

Stumbling away, gasping, with my eyes burning, I fell backward to the ground gagging and vomiting. The smell was nauseous, overwhelming, and I had gotten the full blast. At the same time, I heard my mother running through the house, yelling at the top of her lungs, "Charles!, Charles!"

Seeing me, she jumped back and slammed the door. Inside, she continued yelling, "Take off your clothes! Take off your clothes!" Cracking the door a few inches, she threw a bar of Lysol Soap at me. "Wash your hair! Everything!" she yelled, "You can't come in the house smelling like that!!"

But the odor would not wash off. I tried. Even with clean clothes, James and Van got sick when I came to dinner that night. The odor was overwhelming, and I was forced to eat my meal alone, sitting on the back steps. The next day I went to school, but my teacher would not let me in the classroom, and the Principal sent me home. It wasn't just I who stank. Skunk-smell covered the neighborhood. For blocks around, the whole area reeked with it. It even got into my bed sheets. The Nelsons threatened to move out. Worse still, the entire family began to stink, because it was in our hair and clothes. When my mother went to the local grocery, another customer stared angrily at her and moved away.

My reputation remained in the neighborhood long after the stench was gone. Years later whenever I passed a certain house, the woman would step onto the porch, pretend not to see me, sniff the air, cover her nose and go back inside. Fortunately, Mrs. Nelson never knew her hat was to blame for fouling the area. Later, when the family smell had lifted, my grandparents invited us back to their house for a dinner party.

The School Board had recently named a new Miami school in honor of my grandfather, Van E. Blanton School, and my uncle was made Principal. Some of the local teachers were at the dinner to congratulate him, as were politicians who sought his favor. Other guests came from Little Flock Church where Granddaddy was the church clerk. After the meal, he was seated with a group of men on the front porch when he suddenly called me to his chair, put his arm around my shoulders and in a loving, but loud voice, said, "Do you know what I think about you?" Instinctively, I knew it would be good, and answered "What?!" His reply shocked me. "You are either going to be a politician or a preacher!"

I was insulted. Jumping back a few feet, hands on my hips, I yelled, "I'll be a politician any day, but I'll never be a preacher!" Everyone laughed, and I stalked away, embarrassed that my grandfather thought so lowly of me. I was insulted, and it was apparent I did not hold preachers in high regard. Our Primitive Baptist Church, with long sermons and painful pews, was not on my list of priorities. Granddaddy felt differently. Before the Civil War, his father had been an ordained pastor, a State Legislator, Attorney, and member of the Florida Bar. His grandfather had heroically ridden the Florida frontier on horseback soon after the Seminole War, preaching the gospel and establishing out-post churches. Whether his forecast for my future was prophetic or a political guess, I do not know. I just know that when my "Call" to the ministry came, it was wholly God's idea and not mine, or my grandfather's.

Chapter 6

LIFE IN FLORIDA TOWNS IN THE 1930s

MIAMI

In spite of hurricanes, crises, or lack of money, Miami was a wonderful place for a child to grow up. The town was beautiful, friendly, and safe. Soon after our move closer to town, when I was eight years old, Van and I rode the city bus alone into town. We swam at a public pool, paid 10 cents to see a movie and 3 cents for a Coca Cola. The drink cost a nickel, but we got two cents back when we returned the bottle. Hot dogs were 10 cents, and coffee was five cents a cup, with all the free refills anyone wanted. Haircuts were a dime, as was a loaf of bread. Steak, which we rarely had, was twenty cents a pound. That was the same price as a gallon of gas. For a one-dollar bill, the attendant gave us five gallons of gas, washed the windshield, checked the air pressure in all the tires, and swept the front floorboard.

Miami had only six blocks of shops on Flagler Street, including Burdines Department Store, several 5 and 10 Cents Stores, the Olympia theatre, tourist boutiques, a few bar-restaurants, and several walk-up coffee counters. Two other streets, containing minor shops, paralleled Flagler Street. A few wood-frame houses from pioneer days still sat among the commercial buildings, and wild orchids hung from all the trees. Biscayne Boulevard had three major hotels, several Night Clubs, and the Miami Daily News Tower. The 27 story Dade County Court House, the tallest building in the State, towered impressively over the city.

My favorite spot was Bay Front Park between the bay and Biscayne Boulevard. It contained a tropical rock-garden, fish pools, and winding paths lined with exotic plants. To the south of the park, a grove of wild coconut palms crowded so thickly on the edge of the Miami River that it was impossible to squeeze through. Giant Manatees, some weighing 500 pounds, could be seen from the river banks. Homemade signs, nailed to the palms, warned about crocodiles. From the bank, we threw rocks at crocks on the opposite side. Our parents never worried about us. We were safe.

At 5:30 am, Van and I boarded a bus to go home. Mama always had dinner on the table exactly at 6:00 p.m., and we dared not be late, not even five minutes. Meals were simple. A ten-cent package of black-eyed peas and a cup of rice fed the entire family, and we ate dried peas, rice, and cornbread, at least five times a week. On Sundays, we sometimes feasted on one of our home-grown chickens, but I never had more than one leg. Other meals consisted wholly of collard-greens that Mama had grown by the back door. My grandfather raised pineapples, oranges, grapefruit, and kept us supplied with additional fruit. Grandma even had several coffee bushes in her yard.

Sometimes I would see big jugs of her homegrown pineapple fermenting in the kitchen. "I am making vinegar," she told me. Only as an adult did she admit that the result was brandy. My clothes were "hand-me-downs" that older cousins had out-grown, and my shoes had big holes in the bottom. Every morning I cut a piece of cardboard, put it in the shoe to keep my feet off the ground, but within a few steps, I could feel the dirt again. Since I could not remember any other kind of shoe, I thought the manufacturers made them that way.

Miami had no Spanish community in the 1930s and '40s, but a large Seminole village occupied the south side of the river. These beautiful people could always be seen on Flagler Street. Barefoot Indian women frequented the area wearing floor-length, brightly-colored patchwork dresses. Older ones combed their hair over frames above their faces and wore so many necklaces one could not see their necks. Seminole men were usually dressed in colorful long shirts that reached below their knees. Many wore no pants, no shoes, and spoke no English. Their dugout canoes could always be seen on the river bank, sometimes next to alligators and crocodiles. I loved being around them and was always grateful for the uniqueness they brought to the city.

Miles of open space surrounded Miami, and Seminole bands camped wherever they chose. A village which they occupied part-time was located between Allapattah and today's International Airport. It had open-sided cheekee huts with dirt floors, cooking-pits in the ground, and sleeping-shelves (unprotected from the weather), which fascinated me. Other times of the year a band of Seminoles camped across from our house to dig Coontee roots–a staple in their diet. I would venture close, hoping some of the boys would play with me, but a grunt from an older man with a gesture toward the hoe always sent them back to work. At the end of the day, they disappeared into the Everglades. These native Americans were a strong, noble group who were untouched by the "Great Depression" that gripped the rest of the nation. Seemingly, they lived unaffected by the White Man's crisis.

At that time Miami's airport, known as Wilcox Field, had one dirt-landing strip for private planes and no scheduled flights. Pan American Airlines landed pontoon planes on Biscayne Bay in Coconut Grove, and we sometimes went there, hoping to see a plane arrive. There was never more than one or two flights daily. They sometimes had to circle the area to warn fishermen they were approaching. When one landed on the Bay with a spray of water, people leaped to their feet, cheering, and clapping. After arriving at the port, swimmers would replace the pontoons with wheels, and a tractor pulled the planes ashore. This was an exciting time, and Mama usually packed a picnic basket for us to enjoy.

RURAL NORTH FLORIDA

My father's parents lived near Monticello, Florida, thirty miles east of Tallahassee and a few miles to the south. In the 1930's and '40's the area was unchanged since pioneer days. Rural houses had no electricity, telephones, refrigeration, or modern conveniences. All were unpainted and depended on a hand-dug well in the yard for water. A rope and bucket brought it to the top. I never liked the well, as it was dark and had lots of spider webs. Moss and ferns grew on the sidewalls, and bats sometimes slept in it during the daytime.

My grandfather Carrin died before my birth, and my grandma remarried. Their house burned, and she and her second husband, Grandpa Lacy, lived temporarily in their smokehouse. The tragedy of the fire was two-fold: Their home was destroyed. Secondly, my great-great-grandfather Jean-Baptiste Carrin was a jeweler and clock-maker by trade. He came to America from Valenciennes, France, with his wife and one son. Their only possessions were in a trunk they brought with them, which contained his father's original Army Bugle from his service in Napoleon's Army, as well as jewelers' tools, an antique wooden clock, a few gemstones, and other items. The day of the fire, my uncle (who was named for Napoleon) ran into the

49

building and lifted the trunk to the window. He was ready to shove it out when the roof collapsed. Diving out the window, he escaped; but the trunk and everything in it fell back and was destroyed.

When their new cabin was built, my grandmother cooked in a heavy iron pot that swung in and out of the fireplace. I will never forget waking in the morning to the fragrance of sausage cooking in my grandmother's cabin. That, with the scent of fresh biscuits, hot butter, and home-ground grits, will never fade from my mind.

There was no plumbing for kitchens or bathrooms, and many houses had no glass window panes. Wooden shutters kept out as much wind as possible, but cracks in the walls and floors allowed winter wind gusts to blow through the cabins. A common joke was about socks left by the bed at night being against the wall the next morning. I remember lying across the bed at my cousin's house and watching chickens underneath. Tragically, it was unheated houses like these that provided the 1918 flu-epidemic with all the components for thousands of deaths.

Water left inside the cabin sometimes froze overnight, and homemade quilts were piled on beds until their weight made it impossible to move. Most cabins had a quilting frame where women sewed every spare moment of the night or day. In the evenings, kerosene lamps provided light. Numbers of people went to bed with a "foot-warmer," a brick that been heated in the fireplace during the day. Beds were scarce, and children always slept together, and there was no privacy for anyone. Outside the back door, a water-shelf provided a bucket of water and work area for most tasks. Here, chickens were butchered, potatoes peeled, corn shucked, and all the routines of life carried on. Guinea hens, ducks, geese, ran free in the yard but often fell victim to fox and other predators at night. Those that roosted in trees were sometimes killed by owls.

Most families had their own outhouse, which was a safe distance away; but it was also a haunt for wasps, spiders, bats, and other varmints. Owls sometimes roosted there. Commercial toilet-paper had not yet reached the farm, and in its place was an old Sears Catalogue and a pile of corncobs. Kerosene lamps provided the only light for night-time walks to this important outpost, and the trip was terrifying to me as a child. I knew wild animals were nearby watching. Occasionally we could see their eyes in the dark. Night-prowlers were abundant, chiefly fox, raccoons, and possums, that scavenged around farms after dark. According to my cousins, they sometimes heard panthers scream in the swamps at night.

A few miles south of Monticello is one of the State's oldest Protestant Churches, Ebenezer Baptist, which was established before Florida's statehood and was my grandparents' place of worship. While I enjoyed visiting the farm, I was thankful I did not live there. Our lifestyle in Miami was very different.

While 1936 was a stressful year for me physically, spiritual events were taking place in South Africa that would someday affect other Christians worldwide. Unknown to us, Smith Wigglesworth, an English Evangelist, was in Cape Town, South Africa, preaching for David du Plessis. Early one morning Smith rushed into the church office, pushed David against the wall, and began prophesying. The message declared that God was going to bring renewal to mainline-denominational churches world-wide and David would be an instrument in that restoration. This was shocking news to both men. As Pentecostals, neither of them believed God had any further use for traditional Christianity. David had never been on a plane, but Wigglesworth explained he would be flying worldwide. Whether they understood it or not, God had spoken.

The South African Revival finally closed, and Wigglesworth returned to England; but instead of revival coming to the church, September 1, 1939, Hitler invaded Poland. That event plunged humanity into the Second World War. When it ended in 1945, there were 73,000,000 casualties worldwide. Wigglesworth died in 1947, never seeing the prophecy be fulfilled: "For the vision is yet for an appointed time, but at the end it shall speak, and not lie: though it tarry, wait for it; because it will surely come, it will not tarry" (Habakkuk 2:3).

Thirteen years after Wigglesworth's death, April 3, 1960, an Episcopal Priest, Fr. Dennis Bennett, pastor at St. Marks' Episcopal Church, Van Nuys, California, acknowledged to his congregation that he had experienced the Baptism in the Spirit and spoken in tongues. That announcement was the lightening-strike that declared the renewal had begun. When David du Plessis died in 1987, every word of Wigglesworth's message had been fulfilled: He had traveled worldwide, spoken to the highest church leaders globally—including the Pope.

In America, two years after the South African prophecy, 1938, my grandmother Carrin died, we went to her funeral, and I never returned to Monticello.

Chapter 7

WORLD WAR II: CRISIS FOR THE U.S.

In 1938 I was too young to be informed politically, but our family listened to the radio every night after dinner. My parent's favorite radio newscaster was a New York-based Russian Jew Walter Winchell who began every radio broadcast by saying, "Good Evening Mr. and Mrs. North and South America, and by shortwave to all the ships at sea, let's go to press!" Hearing his introduction always excited me. Winchell was well informed about Nazi hatred for Jews, and Hitler was taking command over vast areas of Europe that were home to millions of them.

Hitler's abhorrence seemed strange, as Jewish families had lived productively in every European country for centuries, some as far back as the Roman era. In many areas, they represented the intellectual, educational, and financial elite. Numerous doctors, bankers, scientists, and other professionals were Jewish and benefactors to the rest of their communities. In a sense, this professional lifestyle had been forced on them, because the Catholic Church had previously kept them in suppression for centuries. Jews had not been allowed to own land or be farmers, and this forced them into the business sector.

The week before my eighth birthday, Winchell's broadcast brought terrifying news: November 9, 1938, more than 2,000 Jewish Synagogues in Germany and its satellite nations were vandalized and destroyed. Thousands of Nazi Military Troops, armed police, and organized gangs made the attack. Hundreds of Jews were clubbed to death, while Jewish schools, institutions, and businesses were invaded and wrecked. Elderly patients in Jewish hospitals were dumped from their beds to the floor, kicked, killed, and another 30,000 Jewish men were forced into concentration camps. An uncounted number of Jewish women were jailed. Babies and children were ripped from their parents' arms, thrown onto trucks, hauled away, and were never seen again.

Our family grieved for them, but my father was especially astonished. Several of his fellow officers in the Immigration Department were Jewish. "They were some of the most brilliant men in our Office," he exclaimed to Mama. "I wanted them on my team!" Dr. Yosef Hartman, the M.D. who attended my birth at Homestead, was Jewish and was also one of my parents' closest friends.

Walter Winchell and other international observers kept exhorting America to realize Hitler was a madman whose warfare we could not avoid. My birthday that year, November 19, 1938, was overshadowed by the grief we felt for Jewish children trapped in Nazi territory.

Albert Einstein was also a Jew; however, he, fortunately, escaped to the U.S. He had won the Nobel Peace Prize in 1921 for his contribution to Theoretical Physics, and in the late 1930s taught at Universities in the U.S. Upon returning to Europe with his wife Elsa, they discovered their home in Belgium had been raided by the Nazi's. He then learned their names were on the Jewish assassination list. Fleeing first to England, they returned to the U.S., where his escape would prove to be one of mankind's great scientific blessings.

Tragically, our government felt powerless to defend the Jews, because it was not prepared for conflict with Hitler. That isolationist attitude was demonstrated again in May 1939, when the MS St. Louis, a passenger ship crowded with 937 German refugees, mostly Jewish parents and children escaping Hitler, came to the U.S. seeking asylum. They were denied entrance, as they had also been turned away earlier from Cuba. With America's refusal to help, the ship was forced back to Europe, where most of them perished in Nazi Concentrations Camps.

The era was tumultuous. Other frightening news came a year later on September 1, 1939. A radio news-flash interrupted the scheduled broadcast to announce that German troops had invaded Poland. Without warning, the German Luftwaffe bombed Polish airfields while Nazi U-boats and warships attacked Polish vessels in the Baltic Sea. The poorly-equipped Polish military quickly collapsed, and Nazi Germany took control. The Capital, Warsaw, was left defenseless.

At that time Poland had the largest Jewish population in the world, dating back more than 1,000 years, and it was the center of Jewish culture. Hitler's invasion meant the death-camp for millions of them. Two days later, Britain and France declared war on Germany, and Europe exploded into World War II. Again, that night, my parents sat by the radio and listened to Walter Winchell shout his warnings to America. My two brothers and I stood in the doorway listening. It was a frightening moment, but President

Roosevelt's grandfatherly voice and strong demeanor brought assurance to the nation. He reminded us that America had thousands of miles of ocean on the east and the west that separated us from the rest of the world. Temporarily, the U.S. remained neutral as situations in Europe grew incredibly worse.

I had no training in classical music but will never forget the first time I heard the Warsaw Concerto, a symphony written by an Englishman, Richard Addinsell, to depict the Polish resistance against the invading Nazis. Listening intently to the piano, I could almost hear the bombing of Warsaw, machine gun fire, fighter planes, and other sounds of war, which the concerto simulated.

Pearl Harbor

In February 1941, James, Van, and I awoke one February morning to hear a baby crying and learned that our youngest brother, Ellis, had arrived during the night. That completed our family of four boys, scattered seventeen years apart. My oldest brother James was seven years older than me. Ellis, the newest, was ten years my junior. In spite of our age differences, I cannot remember our ever having an argument. By adulthood, all four of us had become committed Christians.

Each of our parents filled a need the other could not achieve, and it was their mutual love for God and His Kingdom that dominated our lives. Mama was pretty, petite, and light-hearted but was also hot-tempered and loud. Even so, during the poverty years of the Great Depression, she kept us fed when other families were hungry. She clothed us when others were not, and because of her, we owned our own house and car. We were debt free and secure. Her strong will and determination was our salvation from famine. She would have fought bears to protect us—and would have won!

One time during a hurricane, the wind was howling, and coconuts were hitting the roof. The noise was deafening, and she yelled to Daddy— "Get to the back door!" Being crippled, he moved slowly. The next second, she shrieked louder, "Did you hear me?" He still did not hurry but replied calmly, "Yes, of course, I heard you! The Thompsons heard you!" This family lived a block away. I froze, fearing her response. Mama started to yell again but stopped—her mouth still open. For the first time, she saw herself as we saw her.

Daddy never raised his voice or lowered his standard. He was our spiritual rock and stabilizer. On Sundays, if we made too much noise playing in the yard, he would come to the window and calmly say, "Boys, drop your voices. Remember, this is the Lord's day." Had it been Mama correcting us, she would have been heard a block away. Daddy never spanked me in my entire life. My punishment came in knowing I had grieved him. Again, mama was different. She kept a "switch plant" growing by the back door and would burn our legs with it any time correction was needed.

Later that summer I went to downtown Miami to an "Electronics Exhibit" in which futuristic ideas were on display. Television was one of them. TV had not yet been invented, but scientists were working on the project. I was thrilled! When I got home, I rushed into the kitchen and excitedly began telling mama about Television. To me, it was top-news. "It won't be like radio!" I said, "We will be able to see the people at the same time they talk!" She laughed, momentarily stopping her cooking and said, "Your grandchildren may see television, but you never will!"

Significantly, the first television I saw about seven years later, was one my brother James built. Miami had its own television station! Jimmy had no college training but possessed a gifted mind. With parts ordered from various catalogs, he successfully built his own TV. I wasn't happy, because I had to hold the flashlight while he soldered the wires, installed bulbs, and fitted parts into place. The finished cabinet was about four feet square. The screen was seven inches wide, and the black and white picture had more snow than a Canadian winter. Even so, we stared at it spell-bound. As I had told mama years before, we were now seeing the people as they talked.

While our parents worshiped at Little Flock Church, Van and I began attending Sunday School at a church nearer our house, but I was never happy there. The services were more emotional than I liked, and in their urgency to pray for everyone, some of the older members would take people by the arm and force them to the altar for prayer. This happened once during the Sunday School Assembly, and I was escorted to the front. While I genuinely wanted to be saved, I wanted the choice to be mine, not their's. Reluctantly, I went, and in the next instant, I was surrounded by adults shouting their prayers for me.

One of the ladies pulled my face against hers and said, "When you get saved you'll see this Glorious Light! After your sins are gone, you will suddenly feel as if you are flying! You may see Heaven! Angels will surround you! You will hear God welcoming you into His family! Now, pray through to

Glory! Pray!" Suddenly, she started shouting. A few minutes later another woman interrupted my praying to ask me, "Are you saved yet?" "No," I answered honestly, realizing nothing had happened. "Keep praying!" she yelled, "You gotta pray through to Glory!" Nothing but Glory!"

Several more times they asked if I were saved. When I answered "No," I could sense they were troubled about me. Half an hour passed, and when I was aware that nothing was going to happen, I assured them I was saved and went back to my seat. But inside, I had a new problem: I had lied. There had been no bright lights, no glory, no angels, and I felt I had sinned more grievously by claiming to be saved when I was not. I continued going to Sunday School but felt like I didn't belong there. As far as I knew, I was the only one God did not want to save.

In December, 1941, I was alone in the yard on Sunday afternoon, when everyone in the house suddenly began yelling, running wild, and making noise. I had never heard my parents act that way before. Rushing to the window, I called, "What wrong?! What's happening?!" My dad shouted back. "The Japanese have bombed Pearl Harbor! We're at War! We're at war!!" I stood motionless on the spot. While I was only 11 years old, I knew this was a fearful moment. The sound of their yelling struck me with fear. I rushed into the house, dropped by the radio, and listened with the others to every frightening word. The announcer, in panic, shouted the message, "Pearl Harbor is blazing! Our entire Pacific Fleet has been destroyed! We're at war! We're at war!" Even in the newsroom near-hysteria reigned. There were shouts, interruptions, and confusion, as more frightening reports came in.

By attacking on Sunday morning, the Japanese caught many servicemen in their bunks and unable to reach their posts. In that defenseless state, Japanese bombers obliterated one hundred-sixty warships, battleships, submarines, PT boats, as well as supply ships. Workshop vessels, tenders, and various support craft burned helplessly. Huge oil-storage drums blazed like volcanoes, and gasoline tanks exploded as if they were bombs. Except for our Aircraft Carriers, which were at sea, the bulk of America's Pacific Fleet was destroyed. Some 3,700 U.S. servicemen lay dead or wounded. More than 1,000 were trapped in the Arizona alone. As Hawaii's sky blackened with smoke, our military defense lay mortally wounded.

That day, our lives changed forever. Cars were stopping in the street, and neighbors were rushing house to house. Strangers were yelling to each other, and panic quickly spread everywhere. Many were crying. All military leaves were canceled, and service personnel were ordered back to duty immediately. There were no exceptions. The next day President Roosevelt addressed Congress and the nation. Describing December 7th as a "Day of Infamy," he announced America's Declaration of War against Germany and Japan. When the Miami Herald arrived that day, its huge headline was blazing "Japanese Planes Bomb Hawaii!!" I saved it, with all other major-event newspapers during the War, and I still have them stored safely today.

One of our neighbor's sons was aboard the USS Arizona and killed. Thousands of identical stories were heard across the land, and many families suffered tragic loss. Young couples who were planning church weddings found themselves in railroad stations telling each other goodbye. For many, the weddings never took place, and their farewells were forever. I remember the anxiety at the wedding of my cousin, Dorothy, and her wonderful young husband who was immediately shipped to Europe and killed. His body remained there. She had been one of the cousins who rushed into our house that September morning in 1935, yelling that a hurricane was bearing down on us. Now, at age nineteen, she was a widow.

Immediately, German submarines began torpedoing American ships along our Florida coast, and the explosions could sometimes be heard for miles inland. None of this ship-sinking was reported in the press or on the air, although in 1942 alone, 56 Allied ships were torpedoed in the Gulf of Mexico. Only one German submarine was destroyed. The horrific damage Nazi U-Boats achieved in the Gulf and on our east coast was purposely withheld from the American public. In the first six months of 1942, more than 400 ships carrying an excess of three million tons of war materials were sunk in the Gulf and on the Atlantic seaboard. This loss of needed military supplies by submarines was greater than what the Japanese destroyed at Pearl Harbor. Such facts were kept from us. Had we known, we would have panicked.

The Gulf Stream comes nearer the U.S. mainland between Boca Raton and Boynton Beach, Florida than anywhere else on the U. S. coastline. These few miles saw more close-up ship-traffic and more torpedo activity than other place in America. Many nights, watchmen sitting in the tower of the Seacrest Hotel in Delray Beach and the Boca Raton Club, heard German U-Boats offshore charging their batteries. I personally knew some of those people and heard their frightening stories. Each time a ship was torpedoed on the Delray Beach coast, the Fire Department sounded its alarm. People in the area jumped from their beds at night and took their fishing boats into the darkness to rescue survivors. These were brought to the American Legion Post on U.S. Highway 1, which served as an emergency hospital. Here, they were loved and comforted but provided with no real medical help. During that time, a local fisherman caught a tiger shark that had part of a man's hand in its mouth. The thumb was fingerprinted and identified as a young American sailor.

After the war, it was believed that a beach front house in Delray Beach was used to send secret messages to the Germans regarding American vessels. In the few months following our Declaration of War, thirteen Liberty Ships were torpedoed off this beach, and one ammunition vessel exploded like a bomb in the night. People for miles inland were jarred from their beds by the blast. Another vessel near Delray Beach floated for days with its bow protruding from the water and smoke billowing into the air. In May 1942, in bright moonlight, a tanker off Jupiter Inlet was hit by two torpedoes that ripped a sixty-foot long hole in its side, exploding the ship and bursting it into flames. The crew, which was offered "rescue" by the Germans who sank their ship, refused, and local fishermen helped them to shore. This part of Florida was sparsely populated at that time.

Every night there were "Black Outs," and windows had to be covered, so no light was visible to the outside. American ships could be silhouetted against shore-lights and become easier targets for torpedoes. Block Wardens patrolled the neighborhoods to be certain everyone complied, and many nights we sat in the dark so we could have fresh air. Night driving was restricted, and all automobile headlights had to be partially darkened. Many areas were off-limits.

All of Miami Beach's hotels were confiscated by the Government and used as military barracks. My brother James enlisted and was stationed there. The Coral Gables Biltmore Hotel became the Veterans Hospital. Many food items were rationed, such as meat and sugar, as well as soap, gas and other items.

By 1942, many American newspapers gave frightening reports about the Jewish Holocaust underway in Europe, but a Gallup poll revealed that more than half of Americans did not believe the information was true. The facts were too horrific to accept as real. Even the U. S. Government denied they were authentic.

The following two years, battles raged worldwide in terrifying ways. Then, on June 6, 1944, our radio broadcasts were interrupted with the news that thousands of American troops, plus those of our allies, were invading the beaches of Normandy on the French coast. This began the land assault on territory controlled by the Nazis. Hitler's counter-attack was horrific. By that time three of my uncles were in the Pacific fighting Japanese, while other family members were scattered worldwide. My brother, Van, joined the Merchant Marines as soon as he graduated from High School.

During their absence, my beloved grandfather was critically injured in an automobile wreck and never recovered. Although he survived a few more years, it ended his long career as Chairman of the Dade County School Board. Miamians grieved for his absence. More than being an educator, he carried a godly "presence" that others trusted. His sons were in the Pacific Campaign where thousands of American lives were lost in the attempt to capture tiny islands. Some of these bits of land were only a few miles square but essential for U.S. airbases to be in striking distance of Japan. Americans at home were on their faces in desperate prayer during the battles of Guadalcanal, Iwo Jima, Midway, Okinawa, and others like them. While German troops quickly surrendered, Japanese fighters refused to submit, even when they were hopelessly defeated. The fighting in Europe covered vast amounts of land, while fighting in the Pacific involved thousands of miles of open sea.

During the war, I became the bicycle delivery boy and stockroom worker for our neighborhood grocery store, Ingram's Market. The hours were long, and my pay was $3.25 a week. Mrs. Ingram greedily watched every penny and lost no opportunity of benefiting herself. She lived in an expensive home on Biscayne Bay but was more grasping than a pauper. Customers quickly learned they had to watch her closely or be cheated. Sometimes she stood a broom beside the checkout-counter and charged for it. Once when my mother bought a five-cent jar of mustard, Mrs. Ingram charged her ten, which Mama swiftly corrected. This was a scene where two equally-strong women met face to face. Five cents was important, and Mama would not let her steal it.

My worst dread at the grocery store was when the cabbage became too old to sell. Mrs. Ingram would take it home to make sauerkraut. She canned it in glass jars and promoted it as "homemade." The problem was that she was not a good cook, and her canning was worse. Occasionally a jar would spoil and explode like a bomb in the stockroom, splattering rotted sauerkraut everywhere. The stench was horrific. I had to scoop it from the floor, the shelves, and off the ceiling. There was no ventilation, and I gagged with every step. The only thing worse than that was when a rat died in the attic, which we could not remove. That happened several times.

Soap was rationed during the war and became a very scarce item. Mrs. Ingram then remembered she had discarded a bag of soap powders years before and had it dragged under the building. I was told to pull it out. The crawl-space between the ground and building was very narrow, filled with scorpions and spider webs. I wedged in between the flooring and the dirt, only to discover the bag had rotted and could not be removed. Mrs. Ingram then ordered me to crawl back with paper bags and fill them. Some of the soap had hardened like rocks, other scoops had dirt in it, but I obeyed. These were placed on the shelf and sold as new soap.

German Prisoners of War, or "POWs," as we called them, became a common sight, and I frequently stood in our front yard and watched truck-loads of them pass our house. At one time, Florida housed more than 10,000 German POWs. We did not know where their camps were located, and we feared the men would escape and attack us. Rumors were terrifying. One rumor we heard repeatedly was that captured German submarines had American milk bottles on board. That meant the enemy was secretly coming ashore and returning to their U-boats undetected, or Americans on land where successfully smuggling supplies to them.

During that time a hurricane hit Miami. It did little damage except to trees and small structures, but there were huge piles of limbs and debris at intersections awaiting removal. Truckloads of German prisoners with huge POW signs on their uniforms, with armed soldiers guarding them, were used to clear the trash. Standing in the doorway of Ingram's Market, I watched a gang of them at work. What I saw, beyond their laboring, was men working with happiness and laughter. They tossed the trash with a spring in their step and cheerfulness in their mouths. Obviously, they were glad they had been captured and brought to America. Their life in Florida was far better than Europe's bombs and gunfire.

American radio stations occasionally broadcast Adolph Hitler's screaming tirades, and I sat motionless, listening to what I knew was the voice of Satan. We also heard Joseph Stalin and England's Prime Minister, Sir Winston Churchill, whose British accent was a delightful escape from our American drawl. "Tokyo Rose," the legendary but hated female Japanese disk-jockey who spoke perfect English, was occasionally rebroadcast in the U.S. Playing popular American music and telling "news from home," she taunted our troops in the Pacific with information about their wives, children, and families. She got this personal information from U.S. mail captured by the Japanese.

Though a number of women were involved in the Broadcasts, the primary one was an American-born Japanese, Iva Toguri D'Aquino. She returned to the United States after the war, thinking she would not be discovered. During her absence from the U.S., she had married a non-Japanese and assumed her name change would prevent her from being detected. Not so. She was recognized, arrested, convicted of treason, and sent to prison for a long term. American servicemen were glad to have her back in America—behind bars.

Chapter 8

TERROR OF WORLD WAR II

During the early years of the War, Van and I took the train to North Florida to spend time with our cousins, Donny, and Larry Odom, at Lake City. Hundreds of soldiers were crowded into the rail cars, and seats were hard to find. Many of the men were deeply wearied, fatigued, and slept in tumbled positions. They were going to Camp Blanding at Stark, Florida, not far from our destination at Lake City. I stopped in the aisle, staring at them. There were men of all ages, including many young fathers, who were forced to leave their children at home, perhaps never to see them again. Others appeared to be too young to be away from school. Van had already found a seat, while I continued to stare at these lonely-looking men.

My Aunt Emma's house had electricity but few modern conveniences like we had in Miami. She cooked on an old-fashioned 1728 wood-burning Jamb Stove. It was made of cast iron and contained a firebox to burn wood, along with space on top for five pots. Each of the "eyes" had a removable lid. A round, metal stack for smoke went through the roof, and a pile of hickory wood lay on the floor behind it. Kerosene or some other liquid fuel was used to start the fire. For maintaining the fire, my auntie relied on a hand-pumped can of fly spray. The spray used to kill mosquitoes and other bugs was made from petroleum and was highly combustible. If used cautiously, the pump could inject fuel safely into the fire-box of the stove. I was fascinated by watching my cousins use it and wanted the opportunity for myself.

Finally, my chance came. My cousins were gone, and Aunt Emma and I were alone in the house. She was ironing clothes, and she asked me to examine the fire. Her iron was also cast-iron and heated on top of the stove. I hurried to the kitchen and was disappointed that the stove needed no fuel. The fire was burning nicely. I stopped, realizing this was my only opportunity. So I went back, took the spray gun and shot the fire with a burst of fuel but it was more than I intended. The stove exploded like a bomb! Fire shot into the kitchen with a boom; lids lifted off the top, and biscuits blasted out of the oven. A big pot of collard greens splashed water onto the stove, while ashes filled the air, covering the floor and furniture.

Aunt Emma screamed, came running, and I fell back against the table. I was terrified but unharmed. She stopped in the doorway, hands against her face, and stood staring. Slowly, she came into the kitchen, replacing the lids. I got a bucket of water. She put the biscuits back in the oven, and together we mopped the floor. All the while, no one spoke. At the dinner table that night there was no conversation, only a painful silence in which my presence was ignored. I could feel Van's anger, as he made stabbing glances at me. The collards were good, but the biscuits were oddly shaped and tasted like smoke.

During that trip, I attended a Christian "Camp Meeting" on the Suwannee River that held preaching services under a large, tin-roofed Tabernacle. There were small cabins, encircling the area, where we slept. The sermons were very different from those I heard at Little Flock Church in Miami. Here, the evangelists told frightening stories of tornadoes, automobile wrecks, people killing others, and events that were terrifying. When one of the speakers graphically described a father killing his infant son, I began trembling and broke into tears. I had no conviction for my sin, only pain for the terrible crime the man committed. Immediately, others around me interpreted my emotion to mean I was unsaved and needed to go to the altar for prayer. I resisted until the preacher left the pulpit, came to where I sat and took me forward.

With his pulling on my arm, I went to the altar again, began praying earnestly, asking God to save me. I suddenly had flashbacks to the church in Miami when nothing happened. Again, I faced a silent Heaven and was seized with the replay of what had happened previously. My mind shouted at me, "You have not seen the Glory! There is no Light, no Salvation for you! It will never happen! God doesn't want you! You asked Him once before, but He said 'No!'" Instantly, I sprang to my feet, shoved everyone aside, and ran down the center aisle of the Tabernacle toward the front door. People I passed saw fear and panic in my face.

As I darted outside the building, I collided into the arms of my auntie who grabbed me and said, "What's wrong?!" I shouted loud enough for everyone in the building to hear me: "I am not saved, and I never will be!" With that, I disappeared into the dark. From that moment on, I accepted damnation as being my fate, and after returning to Miami, I quit attending Sunday School. It was apparent: God did not want me.

Two years later, the War was still underway. Germany was slowly crumbling, when Van and I returned to Lake City on the train. The next day, our Uncle John transported a prized stallion by truck to his pasture while Donnie, Larry, Van, and I rode beside him. We held onto the truck's side and stroked the animal to keep him calm. A rope tied the horse's neck to the cab. All went well until we rode into the yard and approached the corral gate that had a large wooden bar overhead. As the truck went under the bar, the horse suddenly panicked and reared into the air. Striking his head, he fell backward, and the rope broke his neck. As we watched in terror, the animal died, writhing and kicking in front of us.

Uncle John slammed on the brakes and jumped out of the truck. He leaped onto the rails, and, seeing the animal still squirming, he blamed us for its death. Angry, he drove to the barn, grabbed several shovels, and continued to the back pasture. There he dumped the animal, and, half-throwing the shovels at us, he yelled, "Bury it!" With that, he drove away. We stared at the animal and each other in terror. The day was hot, and the sun was bright. We began digging a pit beside the horse, but a huge problem was developing rapidly: The corpse was swelling faster than we could dig. Its belly began to bloat, and its legs and neck stiffened. No matter how furiously we worked, the animal continued to swell bigger than the pit.

Finally, we managed to dig the hole deep enough to contain the horse. The four of us rolled the horse into the grave, watching in terror, as sand broke loose and filled the area under its body. The horse was in the hole, but his legs were not. Like flagpoles, they stuck into the air. We were frantic. Moving him was impossible. We argued about digging the grave wider and turning the horse on its side. Suddenly, Donnie jumped up and started running to the barn.

A few minutes later he returned, with a saw in his hand. "There's only one thing to do," he said. "The horse has four legs, and there's four of us. We each gotta saw off a leg!" Our jaws dropped. I stared at Van in unbelief. No one moved. I must have looked more frightened than the others, for he shoved the saw my way, and said, "Charles! You start!" I gawked, unable to speak. The only place to stand was on the horse's belly. By this time it was distended like a huge balloon. I knew it would wobble if I stood on it. He glared at me, but I didn't move—-I couldn't. "Do it!," He ordered, and kicking his foot against one of the animal's legs, yelled again, "Do it!"

Finally, I picked up the saw and tried to balance myself on the horse's belly. I panicked when the gut wobbled under me. Instantly, I was sick, and my head began spinning. I grabbed the leg to steady myself. At that moment we heard a rumble in the distance. Looking up, we saw Uncle John's truck coming toward us. My memory goes blank at that point. I don't remember leaping off the horse's belly or throwing down the saw, but I do remember running toward the woods. That is where I stayed for the rest of the day. I never knew who buried the horse.

The War Ends

During the final year of the War, my dad received a surprising invitation to a Garden Party at the White House. He was greeted by President and Mrs. Roosevelt, and they thanked him for his contribution to the country, both in the Military and Immigration Service. Reasons for the invitation were never explained. Perhaps he couldn't tell. After his return from Washington, Daddy spoke of the President with a special reverence and awe. He and President Roosevelt were both crippled, the President from polio he contracted when he was 39 years old, and my dad from the First World War, when he was 24 years old. I still have a pressed-flower Daddy picked in the White House Rose Garden that evening.

April 12, 1945, radio broadcasts were suddenly interrupted. With very somber voices, announcers asked for attention before sharing the news: President Roosevelt was dead. The message was unreal, bewildering. Somehow, we believed he would live forever. FDR was only 63 years old, but his body had been severely weakened by disease. Though he died young, he was the longest-serving president in American history. Elected in 1933, he continued until 1945. As President, he led the United States through two of its greatest crises in history: The Great Depression and World War II.

Dying at Warm Springs, Georgia, in a polio-therapy center, his body was returned to Washington by train. After the casket's solemn procession through the Capital, he was buried in the Roosevelt family plot in Hyde Park, New York. His death felt very personal to us as if our grandfather had died. A sense of mourning lay not only on us personally but on the land. Everyone was grieving. Vice President Harry Truman was immediately sworn-in as President and, placing his hand on the Bible, he took the Oath of Office. I saved the newspaper with pictures of President Roosevelt's death and funeral.

During the days of national mourning, the radio played Christian hymns and patriotic songs. On a bigger scale, it was songs, both sacred and secular, that kept America alive during the War. Our radio stations frequently provided hymns and popular music interchangeably. Selections would sometimes vary from American tunes to British. One English song I came to love brought promise and hope to both sides of the Atlantic. The lyrics, speaking of the famous chalk-cliffs on the English Channel, were these:

> *"There'll be bluebirds over the white cliffs of Dover,*
> *Tomorrow, just you wait and see;*
> *There'll be love and laughter and peace ever after,*
> *Tomorrow, when the world is free.*
> *The shepherd will tend his sheep,*
> *The valley will bloom again,*
> *And Jimmy will go to sleep*
> *In his own little room again.*
> *There'll be bluebirds over*
> *The white cliffs of Dover—*
> *Tomorrow, just you wait and see ...."*

I had seen photos of those famous cliffs and pictured them in my mind as I joined in the song. The bluebirds I imagined were beautiful! Best of all, I believed the song's promise to be true. I hoped that English boys my same age were experiencing the same thing when they sang the words. It was like being in church and listening to hymns that spoke of Heaven. Our hope for a war-free future was beautiful!

May 7, 1945, I was in high-school when the announcement came over the PA system that Germany had surrendered. Students throughout the building leaped to their feet, threw books into the air and started yelling. Many were jumping up and down, and clapping their hands. The place became chaotic. Many had fathers on the front-lines who would now be coming home. I remember a girl near me burying her face in her book and sobbing out loud. Others faced the wall trying to hide their tears. It was too good to be true, but it was true! The War was over!! It was over!! We had won!! Families would be restored. Torpedoes and ship-sinking were no longer a threat. We could turn on the lights again. Blackouts were ended! Hitler is dead! Nazism was defeated!

There was a special meaning to the "Blackouts." At the beginning of the First World War, Sir Edward Grey, a British statesman, warned, "The lamps are going out all over Europe. We shall not see them lit again in our lifetime." My generation had also lived in that dreadful darkness of which Sir Edward warned. In 1942, a wonderful new song went to the top of the Saturday Night Hit Parade, entitled, "When The Lights Go On Again All Over The World." That wonderful day had finally come! We had sung the words in faith, and now we could experience them in reality:

> *"When the lights go on again all over the world,*
> *And the boys are home again all over the world,*
> *And rain or snow is all that falls from the skies above,*
> *A kiss won't mean "goodbye" but "hello to love,"*
> *When the lights go on again all over the world!*
> *And the ships will sail again all over the world,*
> *Then we'll have time for things like wedding rings*
> *and free hearts will sing,*
> *When the lights go on again all over the world ...."*

Everywhere, Americans were ready to celebrate. That night I went to downtown Miami where it was mobbed with thousands of happy people. The intersection of Biscayne Boulevard and Flagler Street was cordoned-off, and for blocks around, people danced, wept, prayed, sang hymns, and even kissed strangers. It was a melee of emotions. The Salvation Army Band played hymns on the sidewalk, and their choir repeated the line, "Onward Christian soldiers, ... onto 'Victory!'" At the same time, drunks stumbled out of bars holding beer-steins and yelling at the top of their lungs. Above the noise, everyone was shouting, "The War is over! The War is over!" Many were crying simply because they could finally say those wonderful words, "The war is over!"

Hitler was dead! Mussolini was dead! Berlin and Tokyo were in ruins, and tragically, President Roosevelt was also dead. So were thousands of young American soldiers and six million Jews. Britain was wounded to its soul but still free! France, Holland, Poland, and the rest of Europe could come back to life again. We had cause to celebrate! The plague of Nazism had been destroyed. "The lights would go on again all over the world!"

That awesome day our celebration ignored the Japanese who continued to fight. Though defeated, in their hypnotic-blindness they discounted Germany's collapse and America's offer of a beneficial surrender. Fanatically, they carried on the battle. In consequence, on March 10, 1945, the most destructive bombing raid in human history fell on Japan, and 16 square miles of central Tokyo were annihilated. More than 1,000,000 homes were destroyed and 100,000 civilians killed by incendiary bombs. The Japanese called it the night of the "Black Snow," but their leaders blindly refused to surrender. Seemingly, they had no concern for their people or their troops.

A final offer of surrender was made by the US, but the Japanese Prime Minister Kantaro Suzuki responded with an emphatic "No!" This forced a horrific decision on our military leaders. Except for a secret weapon, an American invasion of the Japanese homeland was the only option left. Such action would be ten times more costly in the deaths of U.S. soldiers than had been the invasion of Normandy, an event that destroyed nearly 30,000 American lives. President Harry Truman refused that possibility. Instead, he ordered the use of the Atom Bomb, a tragedy Japan brought upon itself.

On Monday, August 6, 1945, an American Boeing B-29 Super Fortress, dropped the first Atom Bomb on Japan. The city of Hiroshima became the target, and nearly 80,000 people were killed in a single blast. Another 100,000 were gravely injured. Three days later, August 9, a second bomb was dropped on Nagasaki, killing an additional 40,000 people. The effect was paralyzing to the Japanese, who, to that point, regarded themselves as invincible. Their national ego and pride were now burning as in a blast furnace. What they had foolishly begun at Pearl Harbor four years earlier had brought incredible devastation to their own homeland. At the same time, North America lay untouched. An enemy bomb had never fallen on the Continental U.S.

Within hours of the second atomic blast, Emperor Hirohito announced Japan's surrender, doing this without consent of his Cabinet. He feared a third bomb would bring incredibly worse devastation. Many Japanese leaders committed hari-kari, a ritual suicide in which they sliced their bellies open with a sword. Hirohito (1901-1989) survived and was allowed to live, only as powerless figure-head.

Albert Einstein, who fled Europe in a last-minute escape from the Nazis, was the super-mathematical brain who contributed most to the development of the Atom Bomb. He had done so reluctantly, as he knew the devastation it could cause in the wrong hands. He also knew the tyranny of the Germans and Japanese had to be stopped.

The day after Hiroshima's bombing, I sat next to my family with the Miami Herald spread in our laps, reading about this strange new Atom Bomb. We were celebrating the War's end, but at the same time, we were grieving for the Japanese people who had to pay for the sins of their leaders. One month later, September 2, 1945, Japan's High-Ranking Officials came aboard the USS Missouri in Tokyo Bay and signed the Unconditional Surrender before U.S. General, Douglas MacArthur. What the Japanese began in their treacherous attack on Pearl Harbor brought a thousand-fold disaster to them. Now, their own homeland was vastly more damaged than Hawaii. Again, I saved the paper with photos of the event aboard the USS Missouri.

Worldwide, the War was over, but it left more than 60,000,000 people dead and millions more permanently wounded. Hitler, who envisioned himself a hero, instead, would be remembered by mankind as a crazed-fiend and history's greatest madman. He committed suicide in the closing hours of the War and was never brought to trial. Heinrich Himmler, Wilhelm Bergdorf, Hans Krebs, and Joseph Goebbels—Nazi madmen—also killed themselves in the spring of 1945 without being captured.

When U.S. General Dwight D. Eisenhower explored the death-camps where millions of victims had starved, frozen, or been gassed to death, he ordered thousands of photographs to be made. His prediction was that someday, someone would claim it never happened. For that reason, he wanted an abundance of photographic proof. At the height of the war, there had been 23 main Concentration Camps, plus 20,000 lesser camps for forced labor and temporary detainment. The Burkina killing-center systematically murdered 6,000 Jews daily. By the war's end 6 million Jews had been slaughtered, plus 3 million Polish Catholics, 3 million Soviet prisoners of war, 700,000 Serbians, 250,000 Gypsies, and numerous smaller groups. While America had been thriving under President Roosevelt, Europe had been gutted alive by the madness of Adolph Hitler. I remember sitting in my chair, staring into space, wondering how such a man could endure himself.

President Roosevelt was gone, but in the mid-1950s, at the Miami Airport, I saw Eleanor Roosevelt being escorted to her plane. We were only a few feet apart when I recognized her. She was regal, wearing a huge orchid corsage, and walking with the confidence of a much younger woman. Eleanor had never been famous for beauty, but as we passed, I sensed an aura of nobility and greatness about her. Her personality was as strong as the President's, and she had successfully campaigned for him during his elections. We were only inches apart when I remembered that she created a national fire-storm in 1939 by resigning from the Daughters of the American Revolution (DAR). A racist-issue forced Eleanor's actions. They barred the famous Black singer, Marian Anderson from performing at Constitution Hall in Washington. Eleanor was furious. Later, Anderson sang to hundreds of thousands in the Washington Mall from the steps of the Lincoln Memorial. Eleanor outlived the President almost 20 years, dying in 1962 at age 78.

Almost twenty years after the War ended, 1964, I witnessed Hitler's anti-Jewish insanity in such a horrific way that I was physically sickened. I was in Hebron, Israel, in the Cave of Michaela, standing at Abraham's tomb. The site, according to Scriptural history, is also the tomb of Sarah, Isaac, Rebecca, Jacob, and Leah (Genesis 23). These were the Patriarchs and Matriarchs of the Jewish people. The present building was constructed by Herod the Great 2,000 years ago and is the world's oldest standing house of prayer. Today, it is a Mosque. My point is this: I noticed some strange, waxy-looking bars beside the cenotaphs of Abraham and the others.

When I asked the guide what they were, he was reluctant to respond. Then, dropping his gaze, said, "Those are bars of soap made from the body-fat of Jews killed in Nazi Germany." I drew back, stunned, unable to comprehend what he said. Seeing my reaction, he repeated it, "Those are bars of soap made from the body-fat of Jews killed in Nazi Germany." I was physically sickened and covered my face. What I was staring at had once been laughing, loving, people, killed for one reason: They were Jews. Their bodies had been butchered like animals and reduced to soap. This was the work of demonized insanity. The guide saw my sickening-grief and continued, "They were brought here to be interred by the grave of Abraham ...."

As a teenager, I despised Hitler's voice on the radio, but I did not know about the monster-demon that possessed him. There in the Cave of Machpelah, the depth of his madness was on full display. Years after that incident at Abraham's grave, I can still close my eyes and see those gruesome objects. But why such violent-hatred against Jews? More than

71

any other group, Jewish scientists, doctors, musicians, philanthropists, etc., have benefited humanity. The explanation for their national favor is found in the "Blessing of Abraham," which bestows the benefit of God on Jews ancestrally. It is available to all others who receive it by faith (Genesis 12:2,3; 28:3-4.Galatians 3:13-14).

As an ethnic group, the "Blessing" is still on Israel, and demons hate them because of it. Be aware: the Jewish population worldwide is about 14,000,000 or .02 of the world population. Even so, they have contributed 127 winners of the Nobel Peace Prize. Islam, by contrast, has 1.8 billion followers or 24 percent of the world population but has contributed only seven winners. Only God knows the number of great Jewish benefactors who perished in Nazi gas chambers.

With the War's end, my dad's gratitude for our being spared was expressed in his worship. He never quit singing, and it was his songs that influenced my young mind more than anything else. From childhood to teenage years, I learned more Bible facts from his hymnbook than I did from the pulpit. Sermons bored me, but I loved the hymns and heard them constantly. Both he and my mother sang throughout the day. Even while working with her flowers in the yard Mama sang. Thankfully, the neighbors heard her tender side when she was not yelling and being bossy. Mom was beautiful both in body and spirit but had come into the world with an extra amount of adrenalin.

Our favorite radio-preacher was Dr. Charles Fuller who broadcast his Old-Fashioned Revival Hour every Sunday morning from the Municipal Auditorium in Long Beach, California. His sermons were scriptural and encouraging; the music was wonderful, and he always had his wife read a testimony-letter from someone in the radio audience. These always blessed me.

Chapter 9

1945

WE CELEBRATE THE WAR'S END

Following the War's end in 1945, our attention was focused on the Nuremberg Trials of Nazi War Criminals in Germany, the rebuilding of Europe by America's Marshall Plan, and the Occupation of Japan. The "Plan" was history's greatest display of humanitarian and Christian charity. I call it "Christian" for a legitimate reason: In the past, nations who lost in war were frequently forced into bondage, starved, and their land confiscated. America did not respond that way either to the Germans or Japanese. Instead, our national attitude was "Love your enemies, bless them that curse you, do good to them that hate you, and pray for them which spitefully use you, and persecute you" (Matthew 5:44). Beginning in 1948 and lasting until 1951, the Marshall Plan, begun by U.S. Secretary of State, George Marshall, provided more than $13 billion to finance the economic recovery of Europe. America voluntarily rebuilt Japanese and European roads, public buildings, facilities, and met other humanitarian needs for those who tried to kill us.

It was at Nuremberg, Germany, where prosecutions were held for Nazi Party officials, high-ranking military officers, and others. In America, newspapers, and magazines routinely published pictures of Nazi executions in progress. Men, blindfolded and hands tied behind their backs, were dropped from gallows, while others fell before firing squads. Gruesome as the scenes were, they could not approach the gruesomeness of earlier pictures we saw of concentration camps, gas chambers, and crematories. The site of Nuremberg was chosen for several reasons. As far back as 1356, Nuremberg had been the ruling site of German Kings, and it was here in 1935 that Hitler stripped Jews of their citizenship and denied them other humanitarian rights. His massacre of six million of them, plus other atrocities, dictated that Nuremberg be the location for the greatest trial in German history.

To appreciate the billions of dollars spent in the "Marshall Plan" and the rebuilding of Japan, here are a few comparisons: At that time in

America we paid 8 cents for a loaf of bread, 21 cents for a gallon of milk or gas, 3 cents for a postage stamp, and 1 cent for a stamped postcard. Haircuts were 20 cents. When you divided the "Plan's" billions of dollars by nickels and dimes you get a better understanding of America's charity. We were Americans! We saluted the flag! We began the school day with everyone saying the Lord's Prayer and singing the National Anthem! Any student refusing to do so would have been mobbed by other children on the playground.

While the world was focused on Europe and Japan's recovery, my dad found a small news item in the Miami Herald that was important to him: Al Capone, king-pin of America's gangster world and nemesis to my dad's Border Patrol, died January 25, 1947. He was only 48 years old. Syphilis had destroyed his mind and wrecked his body.

High School Debate Team

World War II left huge financial and mental scars on every American heart but pushed the Great Depression into the past. Slowly, we came back to normalcy and life. The War also magnified the importance of every political topic, and two years after the Japanese surrender I joined the Debate Team at Miami Jackson High School to discuss international themes. The National Topic in my first year of competition was "One World Government," a concept I opposed then and do now. One of my arguments was simple: "America cannot help other nations achieve our level of economic success if we reduce ourselves to their level of political incompetence." Judges and audiences responded favorably to this presentation, which I supported by many historical facts, including the Marshall Plan, then in operation.

My girl-partner and I worked well together and soon defeated every Miami team we debated. After winning locally in South Florida, we went to the State Championship Tournament at the University of Florida. Here we rose through the ranks and soon became Florida's Champion Negative Team. This put us in the final debate against a team we had defeated several times in the past. If we won, we would represent Florida in the National Tournament.

In that crucial, concluding debate, we lost the State Championship. That was a devastating blow to us, one that momentarily paralyzed me in my chair. I was certain we had defeated this team again. Not so. Equal to that tragedy, however, was my discovery months later that I had won an all-expense-paid summer Workshop Scholarship to Northwestern University in Chicago. Tragically, I was never told about it, and I missed the opportunity. My team-mate was a girl, and our female debate-coach did not want mixed partners going off together. Instead, she sent another girl in my place, who was not even a successful debater. Of the three, I was the only one whose life-work would have benefited by the Northwestern University training. Even so, I did have the consolation prize of studying at the University of Miami Speech Department under an excellent professor. My grandfather who had spoken at many public events in Miami thanked me for the success I achieved in debate.

Soon after the State Debate Tournament, my partner and I were asked to address the High School Assembly and share highlights of the event. Several other students also spoke. We were seated on the stage, where heavy drapes partially shielded me from the audience. Since I was the final speaker and realized I had adequate time to visit the restroom, I slipped to the one back-stage. Quickly combing my hair and tucking my shirt, I was closing my pants' zipper when suddenly it came apart at the bottom. I panicked, frantically trying to get the zipper into place. It refused. Nothing worked. My hands began trembling, making it harder to told the fabric. I tried to tighten my belt and tuck the fly under it; but when I moved, the gap stood wide-open revealing my white underwear.

In desperation, I finally took off my pants, so I could better see the problem but without success. All the while, I could hear the final speaker ending his topic as I stood there with my pants in my hand. No one on stage knew where I was. Frantically, I began praying, urgently asking God to help me. The speaker concluded, and the students were clapping, when the zipper slipped into place. Frantically, I leaped into the pants, closed the zipper, tightened my belt, and heard the teacher introducing me as the next speaker. With only seconds left, I walked straight from the restroom to the microphone; and, except for the sweat on my face, I gave my message as though nothing had happened.

Soon after the Florida Championship Debate, I was invited to Cuba in an Exchange-Student program with other young Americans. My conversational Spanish was the best in the class, although I flunked all the written exams. I could not read the textbook, sentence structures, or explain verb conjugations. The same reading problem that harassed all my other studies plagued me in Spanish. My eye would jump from one line to the next and bounce backward. At the blackboard, math numbers seemed to move around, and the problem appeared in every subject. Strangely, if I stared at words without moving my eyes, my memory was almost photographic. I also gained much by listening.

Had I known of Rudolph Berlin's discovery of dyslexia a century before, it would have helped me. Berlin, a German ophthalmologist, realized that the problem some of his patients experienced was not bad vision but the brain's failure to properly control what it saw. He called it dyslexia, i.e., "difficulty." Reading problems or not, while flying from Miami to Havana and looking down on the dark blue of the Florida Straits, I had an "inside" feeling that my future would send me on many trips out of the U.S. This was thrilling, because I fully believed that someday I would live in the tropics as a botanist and explore the jungle. Now, on my first flight, I strangely thought of Orville Wright, one of the inventors of the airplane, who was still alive. He died the following year in 1948. In a short time, we were over the Cuban countryside and viewing its jungle and forests of Royal Palms from the air. More than anything else, I wanted to live in a place like that.

Our plane landed on a dirt strip at the Aeros Boyeros Airport, where we were officially greeted by a delegation and taken to the Hotel National in downtown Havana. On the way, we passed villages with thatched huts, dirt floors, and naked children. I was surprised that others still lived primitively this close to the luxury of Florida. At the hotel, we were welcomed by a group of Spanish High School students, Cuban Senators, and we feasted at a delightful Banquet. Afterward, we toured the Capitol Building, Morro Castle on the harbor, explored the Malecon Boulevard at night, and were entertained at Havana's famous Tropicana Nightclub. Daytimes were spent with young people our age. It was an exciting, whirlwind tour. On our final day, we were the honored guests at another High School banquet near Havana. The island was beautiful, and the plant life was rich—luxuriant. This was the tropical experience I envisioned for myself!

My greatest impact from the trip came inside Morro Castle, an ominous old harbor-fortress, built by slave labor in the 1600s. I was enjoying the tour until we passed through a series of dark chambers and came to a room shielded by a heavy drape. Before opening it, the guide explained, "This is the execution chamber where non-Catholics, Jews, Protestants, and other criminals were put to death during the Inquisition." With that, he jerked back the veil. Before us, was a life-like execution in process. I jumped back. Everyone gasped. Wax-images looked so real that we expected to hear the victim scream. A middle-aged man was strapped in a huge chair with an iron bar in front of his neck and another behind it. At his back stood the executioner—a large, muscular brute, turning a wheel that slowly brought the bars together and pushed off the victim's head.

The sight was incredibly gruesome, with the victim's eyes and tongue bulging out of his head and blood running down his neck. A black-robed priest stood by, holding a prayer-book and pad to record the victim's confession. Some of us were gripping our faces in unbelief. The "sin" that demanded his two-hour-long execution the guide explained was his having owned and believed the Bible. I spun away and closed my eyes in shock. That was the first time I had been confronted with religious evil. The attendant then pointed to what he called the "Iron Maiden," a heavy metal closet standing against the wall. Victims were stood erect in the chamber. The door, containing long metal spikes, was slowly closed until the victim's body was punctured and died.

There were other torture machines in the room equally as horrific, but the guide pointed to a stone table with a small hole opening into the sea. "This table," he explained, "was used to chop bodies small enough to push through the opening and feed the sharks." I closed my eyes, realizing the room where I stood had once heard the screams of dying Christians. At that time, I had not experienced my personal salvation, but the reality of this horrible place forced two questions into my mind: Why did some people love the Bible so much they would endure such horrific deaths for it? Why did others hate the Bible so much they would torture others in this inhumane, demonic way? What empowered the Bible's love and hatred that it had this effect on people? The question deeply troubled me.

It wasn't until years later that I found the answer. It was, in part, in Jesus's statement, "The words that I speak unto you are Spirit, and they are life" (John 6:63). Even when they are printed on a page, the words of Jesus are spiritual, not sensory. They are still alive, speaking in power today to those who hear them. It was this fact of "spirit and life" that enabled victims to endure such horrific persecution and martyrdom. Those devoted to powers of darkness were also enabled by that evil to carry out Satan's will against believers. Each response was personal to the individual.

Charles Carrin

Today, as a charismatic/evangelical, I have many friends who are Catholic, including priests, whom I love and do not hold responsible for the sins of their fathers, However, knowing the brutal history of the Catholic Church, I do not trust its religious-hierarchy. Thankfully, none of us are saved by our denominational affiliation. We are saved by personal belief and relationship to Jesus Christ.

After returning from Cuba, our group was interviewed by a local newspaper. We were photographed and asked for comments about the trip. I was not shy but gladly greeted the press. Like my grandfather, I excelled in public speaking, but unlike him, I failed in many other important ways. The only area in which I excelled was botanical science, and by the time I was sixteen years old, I could identify most of Florida's native orchids by their scientific names. Recognizing a *Cyrtopodiun Punctatum, Epidendrum Nocturnum,* or *Oncidium Luridium Guttatum* took no effort at all. Staring at the name briefly, I could easily remember the spelling and pronounce the genus and species. Dyslexia did not interfere.

Every free moment was spent in Florida's cypress swamps. The snakes, alligators, and insects did not bother me. Botany was the only subject in which I excelled, and I desperately wanted it as a life career. That motivated my love for the jungle. I was the youngest member of the South Florida Orchid Society and the youngest reporter to the American Orchid Society Bulletin.

During this time, two orchid experts, George and Cecile Wagner, adopted me as their student in orchid culture. They then moved to Ecuador and sent me orchid plants. I named my daughter after Mrs. Wagner.

Another friend secretly gave me the pollen of a rare Phalaenopsis-orchid, which I hybridized with a plant of my own. It was my golden opportunity to raise and sell quality plants. Orchid seeds are fine as dust, and sometimes one pod contains half a million seed. Planting them is a laboratory-process, much like raising medical-cultures. Months later when the pod ripened, I took it to another orchid grower in Miami who planted them for me. After a long wait, he called me, apologizing that the effort had failed, and he gave me a few flasks of worthless material. It was not until years later I learned from a reliable source that the planting had been very successful, and he had sold all of my seedlings. It took real effort to forgive his betrayal. Even so, my greenhouse was full of orchid species friends sent me from South America. Once when I received a shipment of Cattleya Maxima from Ecuador, they were blooming in the box.

78

One night I went camping alone at the southern tip of Florida, where crocodiles kept me awake until dawn. Their bellowing and fighting nearby were so noisy I could not sleep. Even so, it was music to my ears. I imagined I was in the jungles of Costa Rica, where I found Cattleya Dowianaaurea growing in its wild state. Dr. Charles Lancaster, Latin America's leading botanical scientist with whom I corresponded, had encouraged me to visit him in Costa Rica. He, more than anyone else, understood my botanical-mania. His orchid collection of 25,000 plants and 3,000 varieties was probably the largest in the world; and when he died, its 26 acres became the National Garden of Costa Rica. He was my ideal.

Although I was excelling in botanical science, my grades became so bad in algebra that I had to repeat the course in summer school. At the end of the term, the Dean called me in his office and sat me in a chair facing him knee to knee. Then he said threateningly, "Charles, you realize you flunked this math course!" I sat frozen, agreed nervously, and kept staring. "But!" He went on, "I am going to pass you under one condition!" I was frightened by his demeanor but thrilled to know that he might let me pass. I would eagerly say "Yes!" Still ogling me, he blared out, "You promise me you will never take math in this High School again!" My answer (with great relief) was "Yes Sir!! I promise!! I promise!!" He dismissed me, and I danced all the way back to my classroom. I was too happy to think about the monster of college-math that awaited my future.

Emotionally, I had several mental-escapes from my school-crisis: My backyard greenhouse was the most accessible. When I got home from a harrowing day at school, I could step into its moist shade, smell the fragrance of the plant-world, and feel my worries slide to the ground. The effect was almost narcotic. Another escape was Biscayne Key, an uninhabited island a mile offshore that was so overgrown with coconut palms. It looked like a South Pacific atoll. Numerous movies were filmed there, and I loved it. An unmanned lighthouse, built before the Seminole War in the 1830s, was the only structure on the island. No one lived there.

In the early 1940s, my dad had a small business selling coconut palms from Biscayne Key, and a friend brought them to the mainland on his boat. I was well acquainted with the island. In 1947, a causeway connected it to the mainland, and Biscayne Key became my most-frequent hide-out. I could walk long distances on the beach and see no one. The water around the island was incredibly clear and warm. Every shell was visible on the bottom, and the blue sky overhead made the scene idyllic. I ignored the threat of crocodiles. My favorite spot was a secluded area on the south end of the island, where I would sometimes drop my clothes on the sand and dive in. Seagulls and pelicans were the only eyes who saw me. There, quoting one of my father's favorite hymns:

"I bathed my weary soul in seas of heavenly rest,
And not a wave of trouble rolled across my peaceful breast."

While I treasure the memories of those idyllic times in Biscayne Bay, I also remember other times my cousins Donnie, Larry, Van, and I swam in dark, coffee-colored lakes in North Florida's woods that were infested with alligators. After one swim, we explored the edge of the lake and found a dozen giant 'gators someone had killed and left on the beach. We stood there, jaws dropped, silently staring at them, and we never went back in that lake.

Chapter 10

1948

MY UNEXPECTED CALL TO MINISTRY

Though the dead-horse crisis was a painful memory, there was also a good aspect of my visits to Lake City: My aunties were committed Christians. While Van and I were there, they made us promise to continue our church attendance every Sunday when we got home. Making that promise was a struggle for me, as I did not like Sunday School. I preferred Little Flock Church that had no Sunday School and held services twice a month. The one they wanted us to attend had a bus ministry that picked us up at home every Sunday. Tragically, for me, it also brought a number of mean-spirited street kids that I feared. Even the teacher could not control them. Van was more tolerant and had always been more spiritually-minded than I. When we were younger, he paid me ten cents to read my Bible. I accepted the dime but would turn two pages at once. He never understood the problem I had with dyslexia. Worse still, I had no motivation to read the Bible.

Like our aunties, Van joined the Church of the Nazarene and remained faithfully committed to it until the day he died. The rest of the family started attending the Miami Primitive Baptist Church, but there was never any tension over our church relationships. One Sunday morning in 1947, Van went with me to church. The building was crowded, and overflow-chairs were in the aisles. Our pastor, J. Fred Hartley preached. At the end of the service, the congregation stood, singing the invitational hymn. Van and I were in the last pew, nearest the door. I had not listened to the sermon, nor was I participating in the song. Instead, I was eager for the service to end. Suddenly, without explanation, something seized me internally, and I began to shake. My whole body started jerking visibly. Scared, I grabbed the pew in front of me and held on tightly. Van and others were staring at me, realizing something unusual was taking place. I was alarmed and very confused. Never had I known of anything like this in church.

Finally, pushing Van aside, I forced my way into the aisle and ran to the parking lot. My fright slowly gave way to a deep, inner conviction that I must repent, be baptized, and publicly confess Jesus Christ. The instruction was not a request but a command. I also realized it was the Holy Spirit who was shaking me, and He would not stop until I promised to obey. Finally, when I made the commitment, the quaking ended; and I felt normal again. Though I did not understand what had happened, internally, I knew I would never be the same.

I said nothing to my parents. We went home and had our Sunday dinner. It was not until late in the day that I tried to describe the encounter, but explaining it was impossible. Only years later I came to believe that during that strange shaking moment I was born-again. Like Saul of Tarsus, I had a "Damascus Road" encounter with Jesus and was saved. The experience was also prophetic: Like Saul, I would someday have a "Damascus Room" encounter with "Ananias" and be filled with the Holy Spirit (Acts 9:3-17). The afternoon passed slowly, and when we returned to the church that evening, I made a public commitment to the Lord and was baptized. At my request, the congregation sang the hymn I heard years before at my parents' baptism in Biscayne Bay:

"… Who will come and go with me,
I am bound for the Promised Land …."

Unknown to me, I was bound for the Promised Land, not as a layman but as one of its gospel messengers. In June school closed, and I got a summer job working as an elevator operator at the thirteen-storied Huntington Building in downtown Miami. Elevators were not automatic in those days, and each required a personal attendant who activated it. In total, I opened and closed two metal doors by hand about 800 times a day. I would then go home exhausted, fall asleep and immediately dream I was opening elevator doors. Sometimes the dream tormented me until daybreak.

Huntington was a Medical Arts building constructed in 1925. It had no central air conditioning, and the windows were open to the wonderful breeze from Biscayne Bay. The only problem was that seagulls, pigeons, and sparrows sometimes flew into the offices and were difficult to chase out. My break-time was spent on the thirteenth floor, where I had an unobstructed view of the Miami River, Brickell Avenue, the Bay, and several islands. This was a spot I loved and could look down on a grove of wild coconut palms that crowded the river's bank. My favorite scene was Biscayne Key in the distance, my hideout island. From that height, Brickell Avenue looked like a jungle of Poinciana Trees and Royal Palms

Doctors primarily occupied the Huntington Building, and some worked with psychiatric and mentally-disturbed patients. One day a man got on my elevator in the lobby, got off at the sixth floor, and on the next trip up, got on again at the sixth floor and got off at the ninth. He then walked into one of the offices, saw an open window and dived through it to the street below. When I returned to the lobby, not knowing what had happened, a police officer came running to me. "Get a sheet! Get a sheet!" He ordered, "A man jumped! We have to cover his body!" Trembling, I hurried to a doctor's office, got a sheet but refused to go outside to the scene. People who witnessed his plunge to the sidewalk quickly gathered in the lobby, where the druggist and several doctors assisted them. I did not know until later that the man's mother was waiting for him in a nearby car and witnessed the police covering his body.

A black delivery boy Gerald who was my same age and with whom I had become friends, worked for the drug store in the Lobby. He had been standing in the doorway a few months before, when another suicide-body landed in front of him. The experience was so traumatic that he refused to go near the door again. Instead, he used a side entrance only. The Pharmacist became concerned, cautioning him that he had to overcome his fear about the place. For the first time, he was standing in the doorway that morning when this second body landed in front of him. This time he was incredibly shaken. One of the doctors calmed him with a pill. I took him to my "secret place" on the top floor where he tried to compose himself, but the view of the river and bay had no effect. When we came back to the Lobby, my hands still trembling from fright, one of the doctors said to me, "You need a cup of coffee!" I immediately went to the food counter in the lobby and for the first time discovered the wonderful benefits of coffee. The doctor even paid the five cents for me. From then on, coffee was part of my daily routine.

Gerald was a gracious young man. Although I was white, and he was black; racism had never been a topic in our home. I grew up unaware that Miami was racially segregated. The day I realized that Seminoles were welcomed in downtown Miami, but Blacks were not, I became very angry. It wasn't fair, and my parents agreed. Significantly, Miami was never a southern city. The population was much more northern based. Interestingly, July 26, 1948, one month after my meeting Gerald at the Huntington Building, President Harry Truman issued a historic Executive Order: Number 9981, which ended racial segregation in the Armed Services.

In spite of the boredom of opening elevator doors, I was grateful for my job and the $13.50 it paid weekly, all of which was spent on my greenhouse and orchid collection.

In the late 1940's, during my High School years, I started writing poems, but I never wanted to be known as a poet; and I usually discarded what I composed. Even so, rhymes continued popping into my mind. Some were profound, others humorous and light-hearted. Later, a question about poetry challenged me: I puzzled over the fact that after a church service a poetic-hymn would be pulsing in my mind long after the sermon was forgotten. Then I discovered this: The rhythm of music embellishes the learning process; it excites the mind and facilitates progress. Some Christian schools now employ this musical tactic in teaching and students are learning the facts of history, science, language, etc., much faster by singing them.

Why is this so? In part, what we call "rhythm," or vibration, is fundamental to Creation. We are surrounded by sound waves, light waves, electric waves, microwaves, and others yet to be discovered. In fact, this principle explains in part the importance of poetic singing. Musical worship not only invites the Holy Spirit to come upon us, but its emotional structure connects us to other fundamentals of the Universe. Poetry contains a lyrical word-structure that is missing in other forms of speech. With the Holy Spirit's anointing, the combination of the two is awesome. It is this union of physical/spiritual harmony we experience in worship. Man's total body, soul, and spirit become affected. Today there is a field of science known as "Vibration Physics," which is the study of molecular shaking and attempts to explain the vibratory rates of everything—solid or fluid.

Jesus touched on this principle when He told the Pharisees that if His disciples were to restrain their praise, the rocks would immediately "cry out." (Luke 19:40) Apparently, every rock, grain of sand, piece of salt, water molecule, etc., contains a note of musical vibration. Paul further expounded this truth when he said that the earth is in a state of "groaning"–that is, making a deep humming sound while it waits for the revealing of the sons of God. (Romans 8:19-22) If that vibrating-groan were to reach high enough intensity, it would literally shake the planet. Significantly, there are numerous places around the world today where unidentifiable groaning sounds are coming from the earth. Science has no explanation for the phenomenon.

So also, the rhythmical effect we experience in poetry is more than mere words. I can best illustrate this vibration-fact with tuning forks. If two forks of similar structure are held aloft and one of them is struck, it will begin making a humming sound. The other tuning fork–without being struck–will intercept and duplicate the same sound as the first. Invisible airwaves from the first caused the reaction in the second. That vibration which affects the metal goes unrecognized in us.

True worship, instrumental or vocal, when accompanied by the Holy Spirit, brings us into harmony both with God and creation. Discordant music disrupts that perception. When the Father spoke in the beginning, saying, "Let there be light," the Holy Spirit was "hovering over the face of the waters." (Genesis 1:1,2) The word, hovering, *rachaph*, in Hebrew, means to flutter, move, shake. At that point, the Holy Spirit was awaiting His signal to energize the Universe with its myriad of natural laws

Poetry appeals to us for the same reason. It stimulates—and simulates—one of the most basic realities of the universe: Rhythm. This is a rhythm to which we unconsciously respond. Some fields of medical science employ vibration treatment in therapy. Even our hearts and brains create electrical waves that function effectively and free of conflict with the other. Many physicists now believe that if we could reduce the atom to its absolute "bottom"–to the point where there is no further reduction–the only thing left would be sound. What is sound? It is vibration. Poetry, in its own way, is merely thoughts and words moving in pulsation.

Charles Carrin

WORLDS WITHIN OUR WORLD
Charles Carrin

Ah, fools! Had we eyes to see
Into the realm of microscopic things,
To crawl inside the spider's egg
With its own suns and galaxies,
Here we'd behold Creation's full display
And the flawless pearl of system find
That touches every insect, leaf, or stone
With the same brush-stroke of design.
Astonishment would seize our breath
And silence us as quiet as death
Seeing creation's chartless realm
Compressed inside the tiniest cell.
But more than that—to understand—
God's whole design of nature
Engraved in every cell of man.

The Vision, 1948

After my return to the U.S. from Cuba, I concentrated more on my future in botanical science and was certain it would comprise my life's work. It never occurred to me that God had other plans; but, that change happened suddenly and radically. Early one morning in October 1948, I was walking to the bus stop on my way to school. I was at the intersection of NW. 54 Street and 19 Avenue, when I looked up and—in the air above me—I saw a "Vision" of myself preaching. Only a split-second long, it flashed as suddenly as a gunshot. I froze in my tracks, panic-stricken, and I knew what it meant. God was calling me to the ministry! It was not a request. It was a command! He was not asking me to preach. He was announcing that I would. In that blinding moment, all my dreams for the jungle lay dead at my feet.

I stopped, frozen on the spot and could not move. "No! No!" I half-yelled to the Lord, "Please! Please spare me!" He did not respond. "Please!" I begged, terror-stricken. My body began shaking in panic. Traffic was speeding past me, but I did not look up. If a car had hit me, I would have cared less. What had happened was the most devastating moment of my life. The impact of the vision was more tragic and more absolute than anything I had ever experienced. Inside I felt ripped apart. "Please, God!'" I begged, "Please!" The only response was an enlarging knowledge that my ministry would be divided into two parts: The first would be in familiar surroundings, traditional, and predictable. In the second, I would travel and minister in a style entirely different from the first. Beyond that, I knew nothing; but, none of that future distinction mattered anyway. It was now—today—that was in crisis, and I kept saying, "No! No! No!"

Finally composing myself, I continued to school. I told no one what had happened, but neither could I erase it from my mind. After the "Call" I wept for two weeks, begging God, and pleading with Him to realize that I was not a good choice. My brother, Van, should be the one who preached. He had always been more spiritually-minded than I was. My efforts were futile. God was unrelenting and remained unmoved by my tears. I told no one about my crisis and bore the agony alone, although my opposition continued.

Suddenly, one morning the "Call" was gone. I could not find it, feel it, or even imagine it. My joy was inexpressible. I was a free man again! God had canceled His plan. The future beckoned me more wonderfully than before, and the jungle had never been more inviting. I returned to church the following Sunday, eager to worship and thank God for sparing me, but something was terribly wrong. Spiritually, I felt dead inside, abandoned. My prayers, worship, and singing were hollow and meaningless. Everyone around me was rejoicing and experiencing the presence of God, while I felt nothing. Inside, I was disconnected from everything around me. Even in the church I loved, I felt like a trespasser, completely out of place.

The following week the effect was worse. When I went to a Wednesday prayer-meeting, I might as well have been in a department store. Slowly, the frightening truth struck me: In asking the Lord to remove the "Call," He had removed His total presence. Everything spiritual in me was dead. Even my greenhouse offered nothing. Its mystic-fragrance was gone. Thoughts of the jungle were blank, meaningless. I had become a young man without God, without grace, without purpose. A sense of panic took over, and I became more desperate than before.

In that abandoned condition even the jungle would be no joy. As much as I disdained giving my life to ministry, the danger of total-barrenness was more frightening. Another week passed without change. Suddenly one morning, when I could endure the deadness no longer, almost in a state of collapse, I begged God to return and said a desperate "Yes" to the "Call." Immediately the Call returned. With it, the "Presence" was restored. I still told no one what was happening in my life.

Without effort on my part, the Ministry began happening. I was only a spectator to God's work in my life. In the early spring of 1949, the Holy Spirit moved again, and a frightening "word of knowledge" (I Corinthians 12:8) informed me that I would preach my first sermon a month away on Easter Sunday, April 17th. That was terrifying because I had no preparation and had not been asked to preach. It was illogical, because Easter was the most important day in the Christian year, and no one wanted to hear a teenager attempt his first sermon on that special day. I knew the word was from God; irrational or not, it would come to pass.

Without realizing it, I experienced a "word of knowledge," one of the spiritual gifts listed in First Corinthians 12:8. This was significant, because our group of Baptists taught nothing about these miraculous works of the Spirit, even avoided them. Little did I know that this particular gift would someday typify my ministry. The weeks dragged by dreadfully slow and, without telling anyone, I worried constantly about the event that was facing me. On Easter Sunday, I would preach my first sermon. That was as certain as the next sunrise. This was more surprising, since I had been taught nothing about the spiritual gifts outlined in 1 Corinthians 12-14.

A month passed, and on Wednesday evening before Easter, I went to the mid-week service and waited around the pastor. He said nothing to me. On my way home, I sank into the backseat of the car more frightened. Apparently, he did not know that I was going to preach on Sunday. The next morning, I was sitting on our front porch, when his car suddenly turned in our driveway. In a loving way, he confronted me about my call to the ministry and acted as if he and the congregation knew everything God had done the month before. The church's plan, he informed me, was to "license" me to the ministry on Easter Sunday morning, and I would preach my first sermon that night. The more he talked, the more he confirmed what I had experienced the previous month, but the more terrified I became. Finally, he looked at me for an answer. I sat breathless and after a minute responded with an emphatic

"No!" My fear was overwhelming. Disappointed, he left, and afterward, I was in worse agony than before. I suffered through the night and called him the next morning, fearfully giving my consent.

Easter Sunday morning, April 17, 1949, I sat in the rear of the congregation, terrified, feeling emotionally dead and dreading what was about to happen. The course of my life and future were totally re-directed in a way I had not chosen. My only option was to submit to God's will, and I wanted to please Him above everything else. At the same time, my personal vision of a tropical garden in South Florida with acres of exotic trees, orchids, and imported plants from around the world, would never become a reality. I had been a guide at the Orchid Jungle, a tourist attraction near Homestead, and mentally planned my Garden to be similar to it. Good sites were available. I knew of water-front land with cypress and hardwood trees at $200 an acre, but I would never own any of it.

At the end of the sermon I was escorted forward, presented to the congregation, and after Brother Hartley's explanation, the official licensing took place. This was an acknowledgment by the congregation that God had called me to the ministry and their official endorsement of that Call. Simultaneously, it was a recommendation to other churches to use me, examine me, and when convinced, sanction me. Notice of the church's action would be published in the denominational magazine. Documents were signed, and afterward, I stood at the front to receive their "hand of fellowship." I was still paralyzed with fear until the first person, a tiny little woman weighing less than 90 pounds, took my hand and said, "Charles, I am praying for you ..." The instant she touched me, all my fear vanished. I felt it go. From that point on I continued the greetings with joy. When the last person filed past, the pastor announced that I would preach my first sermon that night. It was as if, in the background, I heard God say, "I told you so."

The "word of knowledge" I had been given the month before, without effort on my part, was exactly fulfilled. My time of anguished waiting was over, and that Easter Sunday night I preached with the joy of a bird freed from its cage. My text was "… Where sin abounded, grace did much more abound" (Romans 5:20). The message was prophetic about myself: Grace had begun a good work in me and grace—not me—would perform it "until the day of Jesus Christ" (Philippians 1:6). Seventy years later I am still preaching in that original assurance, that:

Charles Carrin

"Grace all this work shall crown
In everlasting days,
It lays in Heaven the topmost stone
And well deserves the praise!"

A few months later I attended youth camp in South Georgia. I was sitting in the rear of the auditorium, worried about my lack of theological knowledge when a second vision suddenly appeared in front of me. This one was at arm's length in the form of a rectangular "window." Beginning in the lower left-hand corner was a progression of steps into my future—as if I were looking up a railroad track into the distance. As my eye swept the length of the "track," each block contained the explanation to a theological question that perplexed me. Instantly I knew that every answer ever needed would be awaiting me when the need arose. God was not giving me the answer, just showing me He had them. The vision—in its flashing moment—forever ended my worry about difficult theological questions. It also promised me fresh revelation on Bible truths. I left the meeting rejoicing. Now, seven decades later, I can truthfully say God has kept His promise.

The Holy Spirit moved quickly. That summer while on my way to a Bible Conference in Indiana, I worshiped at Memorial Church in Atlanta. The pastor recognized me, called on me to pray, and as I did, three women in the congregation had a "word of knowledge" (I Corinthians 12:8). Each heard the Lord say, "The young man praying is the one I have sent to be your new pastor." Unknown to me, the pastor had resigned, and the church was praying for a new leader. No one told me what the women had heard, but the church invited me to return and preach. I agreed, continued to Indiana, returned home, and registered at the University of Florida where I planned to go in the Fall.

The invitation to preach in Atlanta came; I accepted, but when the time drew near, I faced a problem. South Florida was watching a 150mph hurricane approach the mainland. If I waited to leave as planned, I might get trapped in Miami. My family prayed and felt I should go immediately. When the bus pulled away, I was on board. As we drove north on Biscayne Boulevard, I saw people frantically boarding windows and battening-down for the storm. That Sunday, August 28, 1949, I preached my first sermon in Atlanta, not knowing I was beginning a life-long relationship with the church and city. After the service and dinner with church leadership, one

90

of the deacons, Bill Mullis, asked how I would respond if the Church called me to become the pastor. I was stunned. I had only preached four times, and quickly said "No." He was disappointed, but I emphasized the inadequacy of my age and that I was already registered at the University of Florida. He listened attentively and never mentioned the message the three ladies had received.

Back in Florida, the bus drove through miles of hurricane disaster area. The section between Stuart and West Palm Beach was severely damaged. Hundreds of telephone poles were down, huge trees were piled together, and the area was in calamity. Highway US 1 had been partially cleared, but in many areas, only one lane was open to traffic. People in Delray and Boynton Beach came out of hiding afterward to discover hundreds of beautiful old trees, broken, and piled in heaps.

Within two weeks of my returning home, Bill Mullis called, informing me that Memorial Church was extending me an official invitation to become the pastor. They had prayed and were convinced that it was the will of God. The congregation understood the uniqueness of my age and circumstance. At the same time, they were convinced God wanted me to begin ministry immediately. An older pastor, Durand Smith, would be available to assist me in any circumstance I needed support.

The invitation drove me to my knees. Never had I felt so inadequate about myself, but almost immediately I realized this was the will of God. A week later, I called back and said "Yes." Another month passed, and the same day I was scheduled to leave for the University of Florida, I shoved my suitcase onto a train in Miami and headed for Atlanta. Traveling alone, I was scared of the responsibility before me. My heart pounded relentlessly, and I slept little that night. No other congregation I knew would trust their pulpit to an 18-year-old novice, but they knew things I did not know and assured me that everything I lacked would come later. The "word of knowledge" the three ladies received was that convincing to the congregation. This was significant, as old-school Baptists, they had been taught nothing about the spiritual gifts identified in First Corinthians twelve.

The people were warm-hearted, eager to assist me, and we bonded immediately. Moving into a rented room about two miles from downtown Atlanta, my $35.00 weekly salary paid for my rent, food, college tuition, transportation, and everything else. Piedmont Park was nearby and gave me a place for recreation. The city had two Department Stores, Rich's and

Davison-Paxon, along with a popular cafeteria where I could get two vegetables and a meat for 25 cents. Much of Georgia's farm traffic was directed through the heart of the city, and one of the unexpected pleasures was the fragrance of gardenias from nearby homes and the sweet smell of truckloads of cantaloupes. Summer heat mesmerized the aroma of these two in a strange but delightful way.

On my first visit to downtown Atlanta, I stood on Peachtree Street and looked up at the blackened ruin of the old Winecoff Hotel. Broken window glass and burned drapes were stark reminders of its horrific past. Three years before on December 7, 1946, it had been the site of America's deadliest hotel fire. Flames broke out on the third floor, making it a death-trap for everyone on the twelve floors above it. Of the 304 guests in the hotel that night, 119 died, another 65 were injured. Only 120 were rescued. Among the guests were forty of Georgia's top high school students who were participating in a State YMCA program at the Capitol Building. Thirty of them were killed. Many were trapped in rooms in which the windows were sealed shut.

Thirty-two deaths were among those who jumped or fell. Some were trying to reach the ground on bed sheets tied together. Fourteen-year-old Patricia Ann Griffin, daughter of Georgia's former Governor, Marvin Griffin, was one of the 40 delegates to the Youth Assembly. She also perished. The fire was seen for miles, and spectators came from every direction to watch the tragedy taking place. Police pushed them back as far as possible, but as they looked, many hotel guests leaped from windows to their deaths onto the sidewalk below. One woman slipped from the cornice, and as everyone watched, she plunged 15 stories, landing on the hood of a fire truck.

The Salvation Army, true to their beautiful mission, hurried to the site, praying for the victims and panic-stricken spectators. To the background of sirens, screams, and mob-hysteria, their band played, and the choir sang, "Jesus Saves! Jesus Saves." The last words some victims heard were:

"Sing above the battle's strife,
Jesus saves! Jesus saves!
By His death and endless life,
Jesus saves! Jesus saves!
Sing it softly through the gloom,
When the heart for mercy craves,
Sing in triumph o'er the tomb,
Jesus saves! Jesus saves!"

As I stood there, staring at the ruin, thinking of that terrible night with crowded sidewalks, flashing lights, smoke, and shrieking victims, my only consolation was the knowledge that Jesus Saves! Today, the old building is gone, a new skyscraper occupies the site, and thousands pass by daily, not knowing the tragedy that occurred on that spot. Perhaps it is better that way. With my final stare, I walked away, regretting that I knew the building's history.

My Assistant Pastor, Duran Smith, was a gracious soul to whom I instantly bonded and whom I came to love dearly. He was a father-figure not only to me but to many in the congregation. There was a gentle saintliness surrounding him and his wife, as was also true of another older woman, Lottie Collins, who became my adoptive mother. My first task was to enroll at the University of Georgia, Atlanta Division, which, in those days, held classes in a former automobile parking garage. Classrooms had been created from parking spaces, and automobile ramps replaced the need for stairs. The University did not offer a degree, and students were expected to finish their work at the main campus at Athens, Georgia, sixty miles away. This was something I could not do.

The congregation observed me carefully, and older pastors frequently appeared on Sunday morning and scrutinized my preaching. Some expected to find doctrinal errors they could censure. That did not happen. By the grace of God, my theology was as good as theirs. We were right on some denominational views, and wrong on others. After four months of careful observation, I returned to Miami to be ordained on Christmas Day. Leaving Atlanta in the evening on the Royal Palm Express train for Miami, I arrived the next morning and was met by my happy parents.

In the few months of my absence, I had adjusted to the cold-dreariness of North Georgia. Many homes were heated by coal-burning furnaces that coated the city with a layer of soot and black dust. Days were gray; the cold was vicious, and the temperature once dropped to 3 degrees.

Back in Miami, I was shocked by the blue sky, green grass, and flowers. I felt like a tourist and kept exclaiming about the beauty surrounding me. One of my first stops was Biscayne Key, which brought back memories of my love for the tropics, but there was a difference now: I would never have exchanged my ministry for the life of a botanist. I was glad God had ignored my selfish prayers.

Chapter 11

1949

MY ORDINATION—PROMISE TO DEFEND SCRIPTURE

Christmas Sunday evening the congregation gathered at the Miami Primitive Baptist Church, as I waited nervously in the Pastor's Study. When the worship began, I was escorted into the Sanctuary and seated in a chair alone, facing the pulpit. My mind instantly went back to the previous Spring and the word of knowledge that told me I would preach my first sermon on Easter Sunday. Now, nine months later, I was here, awaiting Ordination and the "Laying-on-of-hands" that would give me the Church's official endorsement.

My parents were seated on the front pew a short distance away. A long-time family friend, Bebe Rivers, sang "Wherever He Leads I'll Go," and internally, I melted before God. In agreeing with the song, I was committing myself to follow Him in an irreversible way. The words to which I surrendered, said:

> *"Take up thy cross and follow Me,*
> *I heard my Master say;*
> *I gave My life to ransom thee,*
> *Surrender your all today.*
> *Wherever He leads I'll go,*
> *Wherever He leads I'll go,*
> *I'll follow my Christ who loves me so,*
> *Wherever He leads, I'll go ...."*

The jungles of Central America, my love for botany, my eagerness to pursue a career of my own, was now gone forever. Where I lived, what I did, would never be mine to choose. After the congregational song and prayer, Pastor Hartley examined me theologically from the denomination's Articles of Faith, reading them slowly and emphatically. Then asking specific questions, he waited for my confirmation. The first one said: "We believe the Scripture of the Old and New Testament to be the inspired Word of God and the only rule of faith and practice." Happily, I said "Yes," and he continued with the others. Those were treasured words to me. They said what my heart believed, and I happily acknowledged all of them. The Articles of Faith coincided with another document of examination that said:

"Do you take the Bible to be the Word of God, in such a sense as to hold yourself bound to believe all it declares; to abstain from all it forbids? Do you consider that Book as the only rule of faith and practice in matters of religion, and a sufficient rule, so that there is no occasion for any other judge of controversies; or for creeds, confessions of faith, traditions, or acts of Council, of any denominations, to supply its supposed defects? Do you hold that Book as your creed or confession of faith, and will you make it your directory, whether in preaching, administering ordinances, exercising government or discipline or in performing any other branch of your function?"

Eagerly, I answered "Yes!" to all of them and was finally asked to kneel before the Presbytery for the Laying-on-of-Hands. Elder Hartley prayed the Ordination Prayer, while Elder Hendricks, Deacons Joel Rivers, and Tom Adams laid-hands on me. With the final Amen, they helped me to my chair, and Dr. Hendricks delivered the "Charge." In his very scholarly way, he exhorted me to "hold fast to the faith once delivered to the saints" (Jude 1:3). When he concluded, Brother Hartley exhorted me from Joshua 1:5: "As I was with Moses, I will be with you. I will not leave you nor forsake you." I looked at my parents who were weeping, but more than that, my dad's body was shrugging with joy. Even in church, he laughed when he got happy. Mama was probably thinking of her grandfather and great-grandfather, now dead, who had been ordained Primitive Baptist preachers in Florida before the Civil War.

Afterward, as I stood at the front, the congregation sang a hymn, filed by me, giving me the "right hand of fellowship." When the last person came by, we proceeded to the fellowship hall for refreshments. The Ceremony ended, and the Presbytery officially signed my Certificate of Ordination.

My dad finally pulled me aside to compare the Presbytery to the President, who was then Harry Truman. Comparing the two, he said, "The hands that rule the world cannot do for you what the hands of these men have done. God's Ordination is permanent—forever. It is not like a political appointment that ends when the President dies." I listened carefully as he continued, "Once done, Ordination is no longer an act of men—you can never undo it. You have a lifetime responsibility to honor it." At the time, I could not realize the significance of what he said or its importance in my future—"God's Ordination is permanent." Nor, could anyone there have imagined that someday my believing First Corinthians 12,13,14, as "the inspired word of God and only rule of faith and practice," would cause the Miami Church to cancel my Ordination, repudiate my ministry, and declare me an outcast. Such a possibility never entered anyone's mind.

We finally got to the refreshment table and greeted the people, while overhearing conversations around us. At that time in 1949, the world was still recovering from World War II, and some of the discussion centered on the final actions of the Nuremberg Trial and the execution of Nazi War Criminals. Much of the private conversation that night regarded photos of Nazi executions in progress. Some of the guilty were given long prison terms, while others were put to death by firing squads or scaffold-hanging. None of the executions, however, could rectify the horrors the Nazis had brought on innocent humanity. That would come when they stood before God in the Day of Judgment. Dad returned to the Ordination topic saying, "The Nuremberg Judges are taking life. These pastors who Ordained you are imparting it!" The Nazi Trials, which he applauded, represented the kingdoms of this world. The Presbytery epitomized the Kingdom of God. It was a comparison I would never forget.

Dr. Hendricks was the first President of today's Georgia Southern University in Statesboro, Georgia. He was also independent, aggressive, and ignored conventionalities if they interfered with his needs. He was equally famous for his fast driving and sharp tongue. Once when a highway patrolman stopped him for speeding, he sat rigidly behind the wheel. Then, when the Officer approached, he snapped, "State your business, bud, I'm in a hurry!" The patrolman leaned back laughing. He knew Dr. Hendricks well, as he was the pastor who performed the wedding ceremony when the patrolman's parents were married many years before. A moment later, with no ticket to pay, Brother Hendricks sped away. On another occasion, he was a guest speaker at a church and was greeting people as they exited the building. An attractive woman stopped at the door, shook his hand, and he said, "I am Walter Hendricks, who are you?" "Brother Hendricks!," she laughed, "Don't you remember me?! You had dinner at my house tonight …." He interrupted her, "My mistake! My mistake! You've put on so much paint since then, I couldn't recognize you!"

My Miami pastor, Fred Hartley, was equally famous for his bluntness. When he talked, he spoke fast and waved his hands. Once, when the church was making plans for its new building, he laid the blueprints on a table and said to the congregation, "Come look at these plans tonight! Share your thoughts now. Don't wait until this building is half-finished and come with a complaint!" Everyone liked the plan—until the building was under construction. A woman then came with a criticism. Elder Hartley listened patiently until she said, "We don't have to do something just because others do it that way ..," He stood abruptly, "Let me tell you what to do!" He snapped, "Next time you come to church, climb in the window! The rest of us are going to use the door!"

During the Reception that night, he said to me, "Charles, the Circus Parade can't stop for every dog that barks at it! Pray and obey, then lead the way!" I listened, he continued, " … Study as if it all depends on you! Preach as if it all depends on God!" He paused, then added, "When all is said and done, you will have preached more sermons to more people if you have been considerate of their time." After the reception, when I walked out of the building, he followed me to the car, held my elbow, stared in my eyes, and said, "Ten percent of your members will cause 90% of your worry and consume 90% of your time. They're not worth it! Move on without them!" Like Dr. Hendricks, he was equally strong in his defense of Scripture. With that said, he turned and walked back into the church. A few years later he was dead, and I conducted his funeral.

After the Ordination, I remained in Miami until New Year's Eve. That evening I took the train back to Atlanta. The trip was comfortable, but I stayed awake most of the night, realizing I was heading north to a large city, not south to the jungles of Central America. Another thought interested me: I had gotten on the train in 1949 and would be getting off in 1950. More so, I had boarded in the first half of the century and would be exiting in the last. Then I realized this half would close the millennium.

Memorial Church immediately began to grow, and we soon added a new educational and fellowship Hall to the building. This provided us with wonderful space for dinners, parties, and greater fellowship opportunities. Although we were Primitive Baptists—Calvinists to the core—we experienced invasions of the Holy Spirit. I relied totally on His leadership in preaching, praying, daily routines, and everything I did. My inexperience gave me no other choice, and I tried to apply the advice Brother Hartley gave me the night of the Ordination. He encouraged me to pray and study until I experienced an "enlightenment" or "revelation" of Scripture, which today we call a *Rhema-word*. When I sensed that revelation happening during my study, I would concentrate on it, meditate, pray, close the Bible, and not read it again until I stood before the congregation.

In doing so, I would always find the *Rhema* still awaiting me. The Holy Spirit honored my reliance on Him and frequently anointed the message with His visible presence. My method of sermon preparation seemed strange to others, but it worked for me.

The church had moments of exhilaration but sometimes moments of grief. One Saturday night, a young mother in the church accidentally spilled a pot of boiling water on her year-old baby girl. The infant had second and third-degree burns over half of her body. Doctors warned the family that, if she survived, she would require a year in the hospital with extensive surgery. The next day, Sunday morning, I explained to the congregation what had happened. Everyone melted in grief as we sought God. Most were kneeling. The people prayed aloud, some wept, then standing again, we sang an old hymn containing the words:

> *"The Great Physician now is near, The sympathizing Jesus;*
> *He speaks the drooping heart to cheer, Oh, hear the voice of Jesus.*
> *Sweetest note in seraph song, Sweetest name on mortal tongue;*
> *Sweetest carol ever sung, Jesus, blessed Jesus ...."*

We had no theology for healing or understanding about it as a spiritual gift but simply believed in the love of God and the power of prayer. In Jesus, the Great Physician, was the revelation of both. Two weeks later, on Sunday morning, I asked the mother to bring the baby to the front. I held her up and lifted her dress for the congregation to see her body. She was healed, had been dismissed from the hospital without surgery and never went back. Several small scars were all that remained. We trusted God,

99

loved His Word, and relied on His grace. In a short time, the membership grew faster than any other congregation in our body of Baptists. Visitors quickly became a permanent part of the fellowship.

From the beginning, I established a pattern of preaching/teaching five times a week and maintained that practice for nearly 40 years. The only exception was when I preached 12 or more times weekly in summer revivals. This rigorous schedule of some 300 sermons yearly forced me to rely on the Holy Spirit. Frequently, I had little time for preparation between sermons and would rush to my room, pray, read my Bible until the "Rhema" came. When that happened, I also received an assurance that the message would be blessed.

The three women who had the "word of knowledge" that brought me to Memorial Church, Mary Ellen Hartley, Lottie Collins, and Nettie Lee, were saints who prayed, obeyed, and were the source of constant joy to the congregation. There was another woman, however, whom I dreaded. She was our part-time pianist. Everyone knew she was a complainer and a controller. She was never happy and never benefited by my messages. One Sunday, for the first time, she was wiping her eyes and nose, struggling to keep back the tears. Privately, I was saying, "Thank you, Lord! You have touched her heart!"

When the service ended, I went to the door and spoke to those leaving. She was in the line, and I was eager to hear her comments about the sermon. When she got to me, she did not take my hand but got in my face and said angrily, "Don't ever ask me to play again! The bouquet on the piano gave me terrible allergies! Look at my eyes and nose! Both are red and running! Don't ever ask me to play again!" With that, she stalked away. I watched her leave, hoping she would never come back.

In dealing with another of our members, Mrs. Abernathy, I needed all the wisdom God would give. This was an elderly lady who was friendly, loving and greeted everyone with open arms, but she was also a problem. "Abbey," as she was known, could be charming, but in private conversations, she would pin someone to the wall or the end of a pew and press forward until her nose was almost touching theirs. The more the person backed away, the closer she came. Abbey's hearing-aid only worked part-time, and even in short range, she whispered in a husky stage voice that could be heard across the room. Worst of all, she would pry someone for information and repeat it to others. Usually, she got the information wrong.

Abbey's middle-aged son, Lamar, inherited all of his mother's eccentric ways. He was a part-time patient at a State psychiatric hospital, and no sermon was safe from their disruption. Nor was any single woman protected from his mother's attention. Still single at fifty, Abbey wanted him married. The two always sat together at the front of the sanctuary, near the choir loft. Even at that distance, she would know if a late arriver came in the building. Lamar would then get punched in the ribs, and in her burly voice she would say, "Who just came in?" His answer, "I don't know," only brought another blow: "Look!" His reply, "I don't want to!" brought a harder jab and another command, "I said look!" Lamar would rise, twist completely around, and stare at the congregation until he identified the person. Then he'd sit down and tell her.

I will never forget the day he got punched several times before looking. He finally turned and saw the party, and replied, "It was Mrs. Philbeck." "Who? "his mother asked loudly. "Mrs. Philbeck!" Abbey still did not hear, "Who?" she demanded. Lamar leaped angrily from the seat, shoved his face in hers and yelled, "It was Mrs. Philbeck!" There were worse times if a single woman arrived. The whisper would be, "Go sit with her." His answer, "I don't want to!," only brought another blow and the instruction, "I said 'Go!'" Even if the unsuspecting woman were in the middle of the pew with others close around her, Lamar would rise, make his way to the aisle, push in beside her, give his glassy-eyed smile, and sit down. These women always fled the building and never came back. None of the deacons were willing to return him to his seat.

Abbey's most distracting feature, however, was her hearing-aid, which was a serious problem for everyone. The gadget sometimes emitted a high-pitched, violin-like squeal, that was ear-splitting and torturous. She could not hear it or know to turn it off until someone punched her in the shoulder. But stopping the "violin" was a complicated task. She kept the control box attached to her slip, and a cord went from it to her ear. This was bad enough, but she always sat where the choir of young people had an unobstructed view of her.

In the 1950's we had no microphone system, and anytime I spoke too softly she would open her blouse conspicuously, reach inside with both hands and make the adjustment. The same routine took place a few minutes later if my voice became too loud. Watching this procedure was dangerous for a group of teenagers. One Sunday morning I was at the high-point of my sermon, turned toward the choir, and realized none of them were listening. Some had their eyes shut tightly, their lips clinched, and they were gripping their stomachs, trying desperately not to laugh. I first thought the problem was something I said until I saw Mrs. Abernathy.

For the moment I could not believe my eyes. She had completely disappeared inside the neck of her dress. All that was visible was a tuft of gray-blonde hair at the top. Turning my back to her and the choir, I fixated on the distant wall; but all continuity of the sermon was lost. Nothing I said made sense. I fully expected one of the young people to lose control and have the place explode. Finally, I heard a "click" and turned back toward the congregation. Abbey resurfaced, straightened her blouse, patted her hair, and smiled at me. Holding up her hand, the mystery was explained: She had changed the battery!

Occasionally, when Lamar could endure his mother's antics no longer he would run away from home, go to the Mental Hospital at Milledgeville, and turn himself in. Unlike other patients who ran away from the hospital, he ran to it.

Not long after my arrival one of the deacons left the church without explanations, and I blamed myself for his unhappiness. To escape my depression one evening, I attended the Revival at another church. Arriving early, I sat alone near the front. My escape was short-lived. Abbey soon came in, hurried to me and sat down. Taking a long breath, she said, "I don't want this to upset you, but all of our deacons are leaving the church!" At first, I thought I misunderstood what she said. She sensed that and said again, "I don't want this to upset you, but all of our deacons are leaving the church!!" I stared at her. No words came out of my mouth. She gave me a pitying stare and left. The sermon that night was probably what I needed to hear, but nothing penetrated me. I sat stone-like, and after the benediction, I sneaked out the rear entrance and went home, walking part of the way. Back in my room, I prepared my resignation message and had it ready for Sunday morning. For the rest of the week, I battled depression.

When I arrived at church Sunday morning, one of the deacons rushed forward, welcomed me with his customary hug, and told me how thankful he was God had put me in his life. As members began gathering, they seemed more loving than ever. Every deacon was genuinely affectionate. The building was soon filled, and the people were excited to be there. No one mentioned anything about the deacons' unhappiness. After the service, Mrs. Abernathy cornered me at the pulpit, got in my face, and complimented my sermon but said nothing about the deacons' leaving. Apparently, she had forgotten it.

This may seem strange, but now, seventy years later, I thank the Lord Abbey and Lamar were there. From Sunday to Sunday, my preaching was challenged, teenagers were entertained, and the patience of adults tested, but if I had been intolerant with Abbey and Lamar, the congregation would have been disappointed with me. The test of a good preacher back then was to survive every distraction: Screaming babies, hot, unventilated buildings, old men snoring, children being disciplined, a neighborhood cat jumping unexpectedly in some lady's lap, or a dog wandering down the center aisle looking for its owner. At least, we had no cell phones.

While this was happening at church, I privately battled a crisis with a girl I met at the University who began stalking me. I could not shake her. She joined the church and made others think we were secretly in love. Her family and friends thought that. The truth was that I disliked her, distrusted her, and wanted nothing to do with her, but as a pastor, I felt obligated to treat her with equal courtesy as any other member. She pursued me at the University, changed her classes to be in mine, and made it impossible for me to share my travel plans with the church. If I had announced them, she would have been on the same bus or train.

The problem was compounded by my taking many of the young people home after church events. She lived the farthest and was the last one out of the car. Her mother worked at night, and she would go to the door, turn the knob and disappear into the darkened house. It was never locked. I warned her repeatedly it was not safe to leave the house unguarded.

During a school break, I returned to Miami. The first night I was almost asleep when my mother knocked on my door and came into the room. She turned on the light and sat down on my bed. "I have had a dream," she said, "and I don't know what it means, except that you are in serious danger." I sat up and listened. "In the dream, I was on a hill," she said, "overlooking a river, where a bridge had washed-out. Cars were driving into the river and disappearing. I was yelling, warning them to stop, but no one heard me. Then I saw your car coming, and I began yelling louder, 'Charles, stop! Charles, stop!' But you didn't hear me. Like the others, you drove into the river and disappeared. I stayed there weeping. Then, after a very long wait, you drove up on the other side."

Sitting straight up in the bed, I knew what the dream meant. Mama continued, "You are in serious danger that will take you to the bottom and ruin your ministry. In time you will recover but you will be gone a long time, and it will be a blight on you forever." Immediately, I told her about the girl, and we prayerfully discussed my actions on returning to school. The week in Miami passed quickly, and I took the train back to Atlanta. The first day in class the dream was confirmed. The girl arrived early, acted strangely, then proceeded to claim she had been raped in her garage. When I asked if she called the police, she said "No." "Why?!" I asked. She paused, then said, "It was my girlfriend's husband, who lives next door." The warning of the dream was laid-bare before me. Why I wondered, would he attack her in the garage, when the front door was unlocked every night and the house empty?

As she fumbled with other details, I realized he was the reason she never locked the door. He had free access to the house. I encouraged her to tell me more, and suddenly she admitted to having been "raped "by him many times. At that moment I saw the "river … the missing bridge … my car plunging to the bottom." If she had gotten pregnant by this married man, she would have claimed I was the father. Could I have proved my innocence? In the 1950s? Never. From that point on I was never with her privately again.

Near this time, I was invited to conduct a Revival at an out-of-state church and happily went. The pastor arranged for me to stay in his home with his wife and four teenage daughters. This was a lovely family, and I was happy to be with them, until Sunday afternoon. I was preparing to take a shower when the clouds suddenly became dark and tumultuous. The wind began swirling strangely around the house and trees. I had been in a number of hurricanes in Florida, but this was different. Watching for a moment at the window, I stared at the strange cloud formation.

Then, grabbing my clothes, I hurried to the bathroom to take a shower. I stripped and was stepping into the tub when a violent wind shook the house. Everyone yelled. I slipped and fell backward—naked, and hit the door. The door flew open, and I did an up-side-down somersault into the hall. The parents and all four girls were huddled together on the sofa a few feet away. Our eyes had a split-second meeting, mine, between my elbows and knees, and theirs from between their fingers, staring unbelievingly at me. In one miraculous leap, I was back in the bathroom, flattened against the door. That night at church I never looked at any of them.

In my early years, much of my travel was by train. One night I was crossing Texas, and I had a comfortable berth, but could not sleep. Finally, I got up, still in my pajamas, and walked through the adjacent car to the observation deck on the rear of the train. I stood there for half an hour, with the wind whipping me, and then returned to my berth; but, again I lay awake. The train was stopping, bumping, and making it impossible to sleep. Finally, I got up and headed to the observation deck again. When I got to the rear of my car, I was shocked: The car with the observation deck was gone. Mine was the end-car. Stunned, I realized what had happened: The train had divided, and the end car had gone to a different part of the nation. Reality hit me: Had I been standing on the Observation Deck when the cars separated, I would have ended up in a remote part of the U.S. with nothing but my pajamas. I hurried back to my berth and did not move again until daylight, but I was so shaken that I never went to sleep.

Once when I arrived late at a rural church, the building was packed, and the congregation was singing—waiting for me. I had no message—no anointing to preach. Franticly, I rushed to the men's restroom, locked the door and leaned my head against the wall, dropping my hands in desperation and crying to God, "Help!" That single word was the extent of my prayer. Instantly, the Holy Spirit spoke the *Rhema* into my mind, I hurried to the pulpit with assurance, preached, and the glory fell. That began a practice which I maintain to this day: Seventy years later, I still go to the restroom before preaching, lean my head against the wall, drop my hands, and say, "Help!"

In those early years, I traveled with some wonderful old men who preached in the 1800s. One of them, W.I. Dobbs, of Girard, Illinois, was a precious brother, who in his youth, went to church on horseback or in a buggy. At the beginning of his ministry in 1895, the people arrived in ox-carts, covered wagons, buggies, rode mules or horses. There were no paved roads, no automobiles, telephones, electric lights, radios, or other benefits we have today. Churches were lighted by oil lamps, and out-houses provided toilets—sometimes. Yet, people came by the thousands to hear the Word. Crowds were so large that preaching was done in open fields or the forest under shade-trees. On other occasions, they cut pasture fences to make room for the people. In one year, Elder Dobbs and his father baptized more than 1,200 new converts. I gained wisdom from him that I will carry to my grave. While the young prisoner in Atlanta imparted power to me, this old preacher imparted expectation. Today, when I stand before congregations, I can almost hear these two behind me shouting, "Impart the power!" and "Expect big results!"

1950

The Korean War

My ministry in Atlanta was still in its first year, when—on June 25, 1950—75,000 Communist soldiers from North Korea stormed into democratic South Korea. Communism seemed unstoppable and was spreading worldwide. Our greatest fear was not North Korea, but a more vicious war with Russia and China exploding into World War III. The situation in Korea was precarious, and thousands of young American soldiers were sent into battle. At our Wednesday night prayer meetings, most of the congregation got on their knees to pray. When the war ended three years later, the Holy Spirit began moving powerfully in South Korea.

One of the new converts was a fourteen-year-old South Korean Buddhist, Paul Yungi Cho, who had been attacked by tuberculosis and starvation. A young Christian girl witnessed to him about Jesus Christ. He believed and was dramatically born again. Paul experienced the power of the Holy Spirit and was healed from TB. Afterward, he began preaching under an old, army Tent. He had no chairs, and his tiny congregation sat on a dingy mattress.

Paul (who later changed his name to David) called his church the Yoido Full Gospel Church. His message spread like fire across the nation, and today the church is not only the largest congregation in the world with 500,000+ members, but has birthed scores of others in South Korea. Several of these have more than 100,000 members. When Billy Graham held an outdoor Crusade in Korea in 1973, more than 1,000,000 stood in attendance. It was the world's largest congregation. Today, South Korea is one of the most Christian nations on earth. Dr. Cho became a world-traveler, and soon after my baptism in the Spirit, I had the opportunity to meet him in Pensacola, Florida.

Chapter 12

A HISTORIC NIGHT: PAIN IN PREACHING, JOY IN MARRIAGE

In July 1951, I drove from Atlanta to a small South Georgia town to preach at a week-long revival. The weather was murderously hot, and temperatures hovered near 100 degrees every day. There were no fans in the church, except personal hand-held ones donated by the local funeral home. People kept pressing into the building until there was no more space. The singing lasted nearly an hour, and I preached forty-five minutes—sweat dripping off my face—and my clothes soaked. Everyone then visited for another hour. I knew I was over-heated, but there was nothing to do about it. Pain was part of the pastor's pay. After speaking to everyone, I drove to the house where I hoped to drop into a big chair, prop up my feet, drink a tall glass of iced tea, and rest. I found the place easily, parked, walked to the steps and stared in panic.

The house was completely dark, and a section of the porch had rotted and fallen in. At one time it had been an elegant southern home with a wide veranda that stretched across the front and around both sides. Aged Wisteria vines—wild and unpruned—wrapped about the columns and scrambled across the floor. I was so disheartened I couldn't move. In one hand I held my suitcase; in the other, I gripped a sweaty handkerchief and a small electric fan. After ringing the bell, I waited. A moment later a light came on, and an elderly, white-haired lady welcomed me. "You're the guest preacher!" Smiling, she said, "And you're so young!" Introducing herself, she took my hand and led me into the house. She was tiny. An aura of holy-sweetness surrounded her, and she seemed to glide across the floor.

Entering the hall, we passed the parlor with aged velvet drapes. We went through the dining room and the kitchen. Then opening the door to what had originally been the pantry, she said, "And this is your room ... I hope you will be comfortable." My heart sank. I could see where pantry-shelves once lined the walls. The room was just a little larger than the bed with a narrow walk-space only on one side. There was no dresser, no chair, and no iced tea. At the far end was a window that had been painted shut."Oh, yes," I assured her, "I will be very comfortable ...." We visited a few minutes, and she disappeared. I began searching the room desperately for an electrical outlet for my fan. There was none. Undressing quickly, I placed my clothes across the foot of the bed and continued looking. Finally, I found an outlet outside my door, behind a tall, old-fashioned kitchen cupboard. The cabinet's upper part was wooden, and the lower part covered with tin. It looked too top-heavy to move. At first, I knelt on the floor and tried to reach the outlet by squeezing my arm between the cupboard and the wall, but the cord was an inch too short.

Finally, in desperation, I lay down on the floor, pushed tightly under the bottom shelf, and wedged my arm below it but could not find the outlet. Several other attempts failed. In a final stab, now wet with sweat, I shoved my weight against the cabinet and thrust the prongs into the outlet. I was instantly hit with one hundred and ten volts of electricity. I screamed as if I had been struck by lightning and jerked back in pain. For a terrifying moment, the cabinet tilted, ready to crash down on top of me. With my free arm, I slammed it back against the wall. Inside I heard pots, pans, glassware, piling against the doors. For a moment I lay there—gasping, crying—unable to move. My hostess had not heard the noise.

Back in my room, sitting on the side of the bed, I prayed for help-- help to survive. Finally, in desperation, I cautiously slid the cabinet away from the wall, plugged the cord into the outlet, and retreated to my room. The fan was helpful but only stirred the hot air. I did not realize I faced a greater problem. No sooner had I gotten into bed than I was seized with a body-racking chill. I began shivering like I was frigidly-cold, but there were no blankets in the room. Piling all my clothes and a pillow on top of me I tried to get warm. The fan was whirling within a foot of the bed, but my hand was jerking so badly I could not turn it off.

I don't know how long the chill lasted, but it was followed by a raging fever. I began tossing back the covers, and my body poured sweat onto the bed until a clammy feeling spread over me. I knew my death had come, and I crossed my arms over my chest waiting to die. There was no doctor in the town. "God!," I said aloud, "I thought You wanted me for a long ministry! Why am I dying so young?!" There was no answer. At some point, I fell into a drugged-like, abnormal sleep. When I awoke the next morning, my color was strange, and the skin around my lips had chapped. To this day, I do not know what happened to me.

I do know this: That morning at church the Holy Spirit invaded the building with a burst of glory. I have long since forgotten my sermon-topic, but an indescribable presence of God fell on the people. Everyone was gripped by it. Afterward, when we began singing, people started grabbing each other across the pews, weeping in each other's arms, kissing, as a Holy Presence filled the building. Somewhere the hymn was lost. The pianist stopped playing and joined in the jubilation. Others shouted. I will never forget one elderly woman standing at the front pew whose arms suddenly shot up, with her hymn book flying to the ceiling. She fell back on the seat, clapping her hands, and stomping her feet. These were old-school Baptists who discouraged religious display, but the glory had come, and everyone knew it. That was a moment we would never forget. It was very apparent, something supernatural had taken place.

More clearly than ever before, I realized that authentic ministry is God's divine power working beyond our human ability. For the first time, I understood what Paul meant when he said, "When I am weak, then am I strong." (I Corinthians 12:10.) Standing there, my mind suddenly went back to the street corner in Miami that early morning when I saw the vision. The day I told the Lord, "I can't! I can't!" He already knew I couldn't. He never wanted my ability. All He wanted was my availability. Now, in that little hot-oven church in South Georgia, He was showing me what He could do through my submission.

Laurie and the Wedding

It was at the revival meeting that one of the most important realizations of my life became certain: I was in love. For nearly a year I had been dating our church pianist, Laurie Hancock, but had not realized how deeply I felt for her. Our contact began solely as pastor and pianist planning the worship service. At that point, I was pursuing no one, and she was happily dating a dental student at Emory University; but her maturity and levelheadedness had a surprising impact on me. She was blessed with a high IQ and had a Civil Service job with the U.S. Department of Agriculture. She did their radio announcements and was also a great pianist, violinist, and singer.

Laurie was exceptional—spiritually and academically. I began to understand why this was true.

Her hometown, Thomasville, Georgia, was surrounded by huge, Northern-owned plantations. Some contained 100,000 acres of prime-land, possessing immense wealth, which influenced the culture and academic environment. This was apparent in the town's School Board. The local system was endowed and able to import special teachers and host cultural events from New York. Laurie had four years of Latin and numerous benefits, unknown in other Georgia High Schools.

Best of all, Laurie had already learned that surviving on a pastor's salary could be a challenge: On our first date my car had a blow-out, and I had no spare tire or money. She had to buy a tire before I could take her home. But, the most important factor was that we were in love, and her maturity had stability which I urgently wanted. Younger girls in the church did not have the solidarity I wanted in my wife.

Unknown to me, Laurie dealt with a concern that was overwhelming her, and without telling me, she made secret plans to return to South Georgia. Fortunately, an elderly church-friend discovered her scheme and stopped it. At the beginning of our contact, our ages didn't matter, as we had no plans involving each other. Suddenly, that changed and the issue frightened her. I was 20; she was 28. Thinking our romance was futile, she planned an escape. That was when the friend stepped into the scene. When the Revival Meeting closed, I returned to Atlanta with a donation of $37.00 for the week of preaching, and I called Laurie immediately. We went to dinner, found a quiet spot, and I proposed. Jointly, we made the decision to obey our hearts. That same night we set our wedding date for September 1, 1951. Our engagement was kept secret until Sunday night a few weeks later when Laurie's family was present, and I had the engagement ring ready to slip on her hand.

After the evening service, the congregation crowded into the church's Fellowship Hall for refreshments. Durand Smith called everyone to attention and made the announcement of our wedding. Everyone cheered, clapped, shouted, and rushed forward to hug us. Several women were crying. The girl who had stalked me fled the building and two weeks later announced her engagement. No one ever met the groom, and the marriage apparently never took place.

One evening soon after making the announcement, Laurie and I were sitting in the porch swing at her boarding house when she snuggled against me and said, "Say something sweet." I thought a moment and whispered, "Raisin Bread." She jerked her face toward me, "What did you say?!" "I said 'Raisin Bread'—you said 'Say something sweet ….'" We both began to laugh, not knowing that expression, "Raisin Bread," would become a code-word that stayed with us until the day she died. Years afterward, whenever we were in a tense moment, if feelings were injured or explanations impossible, I would say, "Raisin Bread," and the tension would break.

Laurie was the second of four siblings—two sisters and a brother. All were beautiful people with different personalities. The two oldest girls, including my wife—like their mother—were quiet, demure, and shy. Not so with the youngest girl, Cornelia, who was a born-entertainer and a talented comedian. She had a life-of-the-party personality. The fourth and only son became a successful mechanical engineer with Lockheed Aircraft Corporation. He earned several patents for Lockheed and could adapt to any social situation.

Cornelia came to Atlanta a few weeks before the wedding to visit and shop. She was with us most of the time, including the day Laurie and I went to the Ordinary's Office to get our Marriage License. I felt a little strange, going there with two women when other men had only one.

The secretary gave me a form to complete and then pointed to benches lining the office wall where we were to be seated. Laurie sat on my right side, and—to my surprise—Cornelia sat on the other. That still was no problem, except she sat very close. When I took Laurie's hand, Cornelia put her arm around my shoulder and snuggled against me. The secretary looked at us with a frowning expression. Other couples began whispering and stealing glances our way. A few minutes later I saw a face peak in the door and stare. Pulling back, two more faces took its place. Word was out—a man and two women were applying for a marriage license.

I felt panic; my face flushed, and the longer we waited, the worse it got. Cornelia straightened my hair and played with my ear. Laurie was oblivious to everything—totally unaware of what was happening on the other side. Then—just as more faces peaked in—the secretary called my name. Laurie and I rose, started toward her as Cornelia leaped forward, grabbed my arm and cried out, "No! John! Don't!" That instant, the place fell deadly quiet and then exploded in laughter. Everyone realized I was the victim of a joke, but all I felt was a flush of heat spread across my face. This was my introduction to Cornelia—a wonderfully unique, beautiful woman who brought laughter everywhere she went. Life for her was a comedy. Tragically, she would pass away when her children were still young.

The Wedding

September 1, 1951, on my way to our wedding, I stopped in a gas station. A huge thermometer was on the wall that registered 103 degrees. That frightened me, as I knew the church would be packed wall-to-wall. When I arrived, I was correct. There was standing-room only, and like all other churches of that day, we had no air-conditioning. The Altar was ablaze with beautiful candles that melted and turned upside down. Elder Durand Smith officiated, and while Laurie and I were repeating our vows, the florist reached through the palm-decorations and straightened the candles. By the time he got to the second candelabra, the first ones had fallen over again.

As Laurie's brother-in-law, Jim Pettigrew, sang I suddenly realized I had only $4.00 left in my pocket. We were leaving the next day for Miami Beach; but, my faith in God was great, and I refused to worry. When the ceremony ended, I kissed the Bride, and we hurried down the aisle as everyone cheered. During the Reception one of the deacons slipped the church's wedding gift of $64.00 into my hand. My worry was over! That was nearly two week's pay and a huge amount of money. Unknown to me, Laurie's father had also given her a $100.00 bill. That was a huge gift! The Reception was a happy event. The Hall was crowded, and it overheated, so much so that when the frozen sherbet was put into the cut-glass punch bowl, it shattered and spilled the drink onto the table. But all went well. My family was present; Laurie's family was present, and when the photographer made pictures, Abbey, our eccentric friend, was strangely posed in the background of each photo.

Our first night I was extravagant, and we stayed in Atlanta's elegant Henry Grady Hotel on Peachtree Street—paying $8.00 for the room. The Westin Peachtree Plaza Hotel occupies the site today. From there we drove to Miami Beach and moved into a new ocean-front motel, the Chez-Paree, for $3.00 a night. That week we were on Miami's new Television Show, Meet The Bride and Groom. We were offered the free Bridal Suite at the Wofford Beach Hotel, as well as my uncle and aunt's apartment near the ocean (both, which we declined). The next day we laughed at the Miami Herald's report of our wedding. In describing Laurie's Wedding Dress, the paper meant to say, "The Bride's only ornament was a strand of pearls, a gift to her from the groom." Instead, the article said: "The Bride's only garment was a strand of pearls …." We laughed until we hurt. I still have the original clipping with that revealing description.

There were no television networks at that time, only local stations, such as Miami's, but I thought of my mother's exclamation ten years before when she said to me, "Your grandchildren may see television— but you never will!" We did not realize that the astonishing scientific progress made in those few years was an indication of the era into which we were stepping.

Midway in our honeymoon, I received a telephone call from Memorial Church that my wonderful Assistant, Durand Smith, who married us, had been rushed to the hospital in a dying condition; the church wanted us to return immediately. Cutting the honeymoon short, we hurried back to Atlanta but stopped in Jacksonville, Florida, for me to preach at Riverside Church. The next day we hurriedly returned to Atlanta. There were no interstate highways, only two-lane roads that went through the center of each town.

Rushing to the hospital, we saw Durand before he died. Two weeks after his performing our wedding, I conducted his funeral at Memorial Church and then buried him in a cold Autumn rain. The weather had changed radically in that brief period. I had the benefit of his presence only two short years, but during that time, I came to love him like a father. He brought stability and assurance to me in a way I can't describe. His presence radiated the grace of God. Years later, I wrote these words about his burial:

"Now I know that I am old
When o'er such a span of years, I can recall
How you were laid to rest in falling rain—
In that long, forgotten Fall.
Tall oaks bend that then were sapling trees
And aged men alone, remember thee …."

I Quickly Learn To Trust My Wife

Laurie and I moved into a one-room, second-floor apartment near the downtown and were very happy with our new life. We were conveniently locate near everything we needed, and Atlanta's main shopping area was only a ten-minute drive away. On one of our first trips to town, Laurie asked me to circle the block while she ran into a shoe store; she had earlier found a $3.00 pair of slippers she liked.

I pulled to the curb and she jumped out. I circled the block, but when I returned, she wasn't there. I circled again. There was still no sign of her. On the third time around, I pulled to the curb and waited. She came running out of a different store, jumped in the car and said, "I just bought us a wonderful piano!" My jaw dropped, "You bought what?" "A piano! But don't worry, it is only $300!" I held my breath: $300, was half-a-years rent. "We can pay for it monthly—I felt like God told me to buy it! It is a Knabe—one of the best!" I was shocked but did not challenge her. I had already learned to trust her judgment; that was the reason I married her. My only relief was that she had not also bought the shoes.

The church was happy and was growing. Then suddenly, the nation entered a crisis, because of heightened Cold War tensions with Russia. In the emergency, I volunteered to become an Instructor for Atlanta's Civil Defense Program. The project was overseen by a Retired U.S. Army General. We became friends, and he privately shared many details with me that were not made public. The "CD" as it was called, erected giant Billboard Signs on all of Atlanta's major highways leading out of the city. In huge red, white, and blue metallic letters, they announced, "In The Event Of An Enemy Attack This Highway Will Be Closed To All Traffic Except Civil Defense And Military Vehicles." It was impossible to avoid the signs or to remain calm in their presence.

Within a year, Laurie was pregnant, and I was numbed by the world's tension; the Civil Defense Highway Signs haunted me constantly. At night I lay awake thinking of the Bible's warning, "Woe to those who are with child and are nursing in those days" (Mark 13:17). We had all the indications that the day of crisis was upon us: Every radio-preacher proclaimed it.

A few months later I found a larger apartment with less steps, more space, and better parking. We moved, and in the icy, predawn hours of

January 24, 1953, Laurie grabbed my hand and squeezed it. I leaped out of bed, knowing her delivery-time had come. We dressed quickly, and I bundled her in a blanket and rushed her to the car, which was frigidly cold (we had no heater). We raced to Atlanta's Baptist Hospital a few miles away.

Parking in the Emergency Entrance, I hurried her inside, only to be told a minute later that I should go home to wait. She was nowhere near delivery-time. I went back home, proud of the fact that I was calm, not panicking like other men. I rearranged all the furniture, removed and polished the brass knobs on a desk, did the laundry, and was preaching to an imaginary congregation about being good parents, when the phone rang.

The nurse, who was a member of our church, shouted, "Pastor if you want to be here when this baby arrives you better come now!" With that, she hung up the phone. I raced back to the hospital and was met by her in the hallway, as she said, "Congratulations! You have a six-pound baby girl!" Considering Laurie's weight-gain, I said to her, "Go back! There's one more!" But, the nurse was right. Cecile was our only one and became the joy of our lives.

We discovered quickly that, like her mother and grandmother, she was musically talented and had a high I.Q. Like me, she, possessed a sanguine personality. She met strangers easily, approaching them if they failed to approach her. Controlling her in department stores was a real challenge. She climbed onto displays, went behind counters, talked to strangers, and happily entertained everybody. One Sunday morning when she was four years old, we were driving to church and stopped at a traffic light. A moment later another car pulled beside us with cane fishing-poles sticking from every window. The windows were down, and we waited. Then Cecile called loudly to the driver, "Why are you taking those fishing poles to church?" He stared, sank in his seat, and sped away. She was puzzled by his unfriendliness.

Chapter 13

THE HOLY SPIRIT'S LONG-RANGE PLANS

1954—A Year Of Historical Kingdom Power

That year, while our attention was focused on the threat of the Cold War, another event that would impact Christianity worldwide was taking place in South America. Unknown to me, the incident radically involved phase two of my Miami-vision. It was this: An American Evangelist, Tommy Hicks, walked up to the Palace of Dictator Juan Peron in Buenos Aires, Argentina, and asked to speak to the President. The guard laughed at him. Tommy had no credentials except the claim God had sent him. The purpose for his visit with Mr. Peron, he explained, was to request use of the 15,000 seat Atlantic Stadium for an Evangelistic and Healing Crusade. The soldier was not interested in the Stadium or the Crusade—but he was very interested in healing. At that moment he was in serious pain and interrupted Tommy to ask, "Can God heal Me?" He then explained his need. Without hesitating, Tommy took the young man's hands and prayed. Immediately the power of God went through him. Every evidence of his disease, including pain, disappeared. He was healed. Wide-eyed, the soldier gasped, "Come back tomorrow!" He assured Tommy, "You will see the President!"

The next afternoon when Tommy returned to the Palace, he was quickly escorted into the spacious Presidential Office and stood facing Mr. Peron. A large desk was between them. Mr. Peron asked him to be seated, and Tommy immediately explained that God had sent him to Argentina to hold a Salvation-Healing Crusade. They needed a large stadium. He also needed free radio and press coverage. President Peron listened intently. Suddenly, he interrupted the evangelist, rose to his feet, and said, "Can God heal me?" He stared at the young American, asking again, "Can God heal me?"

Although the Argentine public did not know it, President Peron suffered from a dangerous eczema that was slowly disfiguring his body and causing a serious threat to his life. Doctors had been unable to help. Tommy quickly reached across the desk and said, "Give me your hands." Mr. Peron responded, and as Tommy prayed, the power of the Holy Spirit went through the President's body. With everyone in the room looking on, Juan Peron's skin suddenly became as soft and clear as a baby's. "Dios mio! Estoy cuardo!" Peron exclaimed, "My God! I am healed!" And he was.

Tommy Hicks had no difficulty getting the Atlantic Stadium, or free news-coverage or the people. The Holy Spirit began to move. Enormous crowds packed the Stadium until there was no more room. Ushers soon worked twelve-hour shifts. Bleachers were filled half-a-day before services began. Parking lots around the stadium were jammed, and additional loudspeakers were installed to broadcast sermons to the crowds outside. Peasants walked for miles from the surrounding countryside and camped under trees. Trains and buses were overcrowded. Visitors flew in from other Latin American countries. President Peron attended and told of his own healing, and he was photographed with Tommy—photographs which I personally have seen.

Although it was winter, every available seat, including the aisles and ramps were filled. In many cases, people stood for hours. Others slept all night on the metal walkways to be sure of getting a spot. Their effort was well rewarded. The Holy Spirit fell in power, and thousands upon thousands were healed. Many thousands more were saved, as God began revival in Argentina that has no parallel in modern times. When the crowds out-grew the Atlantic Stadium, they moved to the 180,000 seat Hurricane Stadium, the largest in the country, and immediately overflowed it. No sporting event or political rally had ever been able to draw enough people to fill it. God changed that. He turned Catholic Argentina upside down and planted the Tree of the Gospel deeply into its soil. God's hand "was stretched out upon the nation, and there was no turning it back" (Isaiah 14:26).

In a short time, every available Bible in Argentina was sold out— 55,000 copies. New ones were ordered from other countries. An English newspaper in Buenos Aires reported that the congregation grew to more than 200,000. The Vice President of Bolivia's sister brought her children to be healed. One of the nation's Provincial Governors was healed. A nationally-known Spanish publisher who had spent his life in a wheelchair leaped from it and ran around before an astonished crowd. The Argentine Vice President's wife began prayer meetings and Bible studies in her home. This was in South America, where a few years before, heretics had been tortured to death for owning a Bible. Now thousands of Bibles were being distributed across the land. Catholic hierarchy went into panic.

By the end of the century—less than 50 years later—the spiritual face of Latin America would be totally revolutionized, and I would be traveling, preaching from Argentina to Mexico to huge congregations. My part began when Omar Cabrerra, pastor of a 250,000 member church, Vision del Futuro, in Argentina, had me minister to his congregation. In the 1950's I could never imagine such radical events happening.

The Year of the Argentine Revival, 1954, Americans at home were terrified by the worldwide spread of Marxism, and Senator Joseph McCarthy enhanced our fear with his creation of the House Committee on Un-American Activities. The purpose was to discover and destroy Communists in every area of American life. His intentions were noble, but his ambitions exceeded his ability. In the end, he caused damaging fear on the home-front. Everyone became suspect, and the noose of fear tightened around us. In time, the Senate condemned his conduct as "unbecoming to a senator" and President Eisenhower, whom we all trusted, publicly denounced his tactics. McCarthy kept his job but lost power and died in 1957 at the age of 48.

December 1st, 1955, racial-crisis exploded in Alabama. There, the law not only forced black people to sit toward the rear of the bus but ordered them to surrender their seat to any white person who demanded it. Rosa Parks, a black woman, who was on her way home from a working-day, got on a bus in Montgomery, Alabama, and took her seat. The bus soon filled, and a white woman demanded Rosa surrender her seat. She refused. A scene erupted, but Rosa remained quietly seated. The police were called, and Rosa was arrested.

Two years later, September 9, 1957, President Eisenhower signed the Civil Rights Act into law. This provided federal prosecution of those who interfered with another's right to vote. Slowly, Constitutional Law came to the defense of black Americans.

The Atlanta Jewish Temple Bombed

The 1950s were frightening. Laurie and I were having breakfast one morning when I turned on the radio in the kitchen. The news was terrifying. We put down our forks to listen. In the predawn hours that day, October 12, 1958, the Jewish Temple on Peachtree Street became the target of a terrorist explosion. Fifty Sticks of dynamite placed by the front door exploded and severely damaged the building. Thankfully, no one was injured, but great damage was done to the structure.

This was a terrifying replay of Kristallnacht in Germany and what Hitler had done to Jews in Europe. I felt wounded for the Jews and humiliated for gentiles. Worse than the physical damage to the Temple was the reality of violent anti-semitism among Georgians. Atlanta had identified itself as the "city too busy to hate," and while that was true of most citizens, there was a violent presence of the Ku Klux Klan and White Supremacy groups in the State. In part, the bombing was retaliation against Rabbi Jacob Rothschild, the Temple's leader, for having supported Dr. Martin Luther King's demand for racial justice. The Civil Rights Movement was shaking the conscience of Americans, arousing violent reactions. To me, the Temple bombing was an attack against every American, Jew and Gentile alike.

Later, that year, I was standing at a curbside on Memorial Drive east of Atlanta and realized a parade was approaching. A string of flatbed trucks, convertibles, and other vehicles with blaring music was slowly coming my way. I waited, and to my horror, I discovered it was the Ku Klux Klan. As their cars passed, I saw the Grand Wizard approaching—riding in an open convertible, elevated on the rear seat, and waving to the crowd. The Klan's bloody past, their hatred of Jews, the incredible violence they had done to Blacks, and using the Cross of Jesus as their burning-sign of evil, angered me beyond description. Years before my arrival in Atlanta, a mob of them lynched an innocent, young, Jew Leo Frank, for a crime he did not commit. My anger against them was overwhelming.

As the Wizard's car came in front of me, I ran into the street toward him, pointing my finger, and yelling "Khrushchev! Khrushchev! Khrushchev!" He fully understood my message. He leapt to his feet, shook both fists at me, and started screaming threats. Nikita Khrushchev, then Premier of the Soviet Union, was a blood-thirsty killer, God-hating, monster of a man, who starved millions of Ukrainians to death, destroyed thousands of churches, and vowed to "bury" America. To me, the Klan and Khrushchev represented the same monstrous evil. It was this Klan-hatred that bombed the Jewish Temple, and they dared to parade in the streets of the same city?! How insufferable! Whether my anger could be called "righteous indignation," I don't know— probably not—I only know one thing: If need be, I would do it again. In all my preaching, books, and articles, I have consistently defended the Jews and will not be silent when they are defamed. With Paul, I say, "My heart's desire and prayer to God for Israel is that they might be saved …" (Romans 10:1).

I hold the same defense for black people, and if I were a pastor, I would never again serve a segregated church. I have discovered a potential of greater spirituality in racially-mixed congregations that is not achievable in an all-white or all-black congregation. I am not speaking of sociological factors. What I have realized is that the Body of Christ reaches a higher-level of potential when the Body of Mankind is more fully present. In my early ministry—before the Civil Rights legislation—all southern churches were segregated by law. A white pastor who accepted black members could have been jailed.

Memorial Church continued to grow, and we welcomed everyone eagerly. Soon after the parade, I opened the Atlanta Journal one morning and on the front page was the photograph of a man who, on rare occasions, attended our church: Larry Lord Motherwell. As I read the article I was speechless. He had been captured at the Atlanta Airport by the FBI and was one of America's Ten Most Wanted desperadoes. Motherwell was a cold-hearted serial-killer who murdered eight women, one of whom he buried alive. He slew his afflicted infant-son and had the body buried in a dog cemetery. According to the article, he preyed on wealthy, older people, and had numerous convictions against him. I dropped the paper and stared unbelievingly into space: He had recently rented a room from one of our senior-couples in their elegant Druid Hills home and it was at their insistence he attended church. What might he have done to this couple? I pushed the paper to the floor, raised my hands, and thanked God for his capture.

In 1960 I was preaching a Revival in central Georgia. On Sunday night after the meeting closed, I received a call, telling me my father was dead. The news was shocking. Still holding the receiver in my hand, I dropped into a chair. At first, I could not believe it. In spite of his long illness, in my mind, he was indestructible—invincible. This was the end of a long struggle for him. I was only three years old when his health was destroyed. To his dying day, he fulfilled the neighbor's warning who met us that historic moving-day and said, "You will always regret having lived in this house." His final hospitalization had been the longest: One year, one month, and one day, at the Veteran's Hospital in Coral Gables, Florida. He was only 68 years-old the night he died.

When I went to my room, sitting in the dark, my grief turned to gratitude, then to grief again. I was glad he was gone, but desperately wanted him back. He was my rock, my source of wisdom and guidance. I was thirty years old. Cecile was only seven, and I had hoped she too would grow up under the benefit of his wisdom. Many times, he jokingly said he wanted to die "with his boots on"—meaning he did not want to die in bed. I learned later that the night he died, he was in bed when the doctor came in, spoke with him briefly, and then turned to the adjoining patient. Daddy got out of bed, put on his shoes and died. The doctor heard a muffled noise, turned around and he had slumped over in the chair, dead. It was that quick. I flew to Miami the next day, conducted the funeral at his Church, visited with my family, and returned to Atlanta. It never occurred to me that as an old man, I would still weep when I thought of him.

Smith Wigglesworth's 1936 Prophecy Begins

In April that year, 1960, I read an article in Newsweek Magazine which was destined to change my life and ministry. It told about an Episcopal Priest in Van Nuys, California, Fr. Dennis Bennett, who claimed he had experienced the baptism in the Spirit and spoken in tongues. Reading the story, I was shocked and genuinely embarrassed that he had made such a foolish claim about himself. His church had responded angrily and forced him to resign. I agreed with their action. But why an Episcopalian and why was it in Newsweek Magazine? The event was not that newsworthy. Later, I learned that the story had gone nationwide. Nearly every news-media in the U.S. had told it. I had no idea that the same experience which cost Bennett his church, his friends, and his reputation, would someday do the same for me.

Unknown to any of us, Smith Wigglesworth's 1936 prophecy had begun. Soon afterward, every denomination and thousands of pastors were experiencing the Holy Spirit's invasion: The "Charismatic Renewal" was underway. In the meantime, Memorial Church had great happiness. The congregation was growing. People were excited. God was blessing, but in 1960, I realized my ministry there was ending. Where I would go, I did not know, but I enrolled at Columbia Theological Seminary, a Presbyterian school not far from our home. My emphasis was New Testament Greek. I felt greatly benefited but encountered the same problem with dyslexia that had harassed me earlier in life.

In the summer of 1961 we moved to a small town in south Georgia. We continued to get the Atlanta Journal newspaper. One morning, we read headline news about one of the members of Memorial Church. An attractive young woman who joined while I was there had become active in the single adult fellowship and endeared herself to the congregation. Her father was a pastor. She was quiet, sweet, and in a short time married a young man with a professional career. Their home was comfortable and blessed with four beautiful children.

The Newspaper report was this: While the family slept one night, she loaded her husband's gun and methodically killed each member of the family. Shooting him first, she moved from bed to bed, murdering each child. Afterward, she took her own life. It was a bizarre murder that numbed the city of Atlanta, and to my knowledge, it still holds the record for the worst murder-suicide in the city's history. At the time I was her pastor I knew nothing about the gifts of the Holy Spirit or Deliverance Ministry. The concept of spiritual warfare was foreign to me. Like most denominations, we taught nothing about the believers' authority over demons and our ability to expel them. Unknown to us, this young wife and mother had a demon of murder hiding inside her. Laurie and I were numb with grief. She was the last person we would have suspected of such a crime. Not her! Not this quiet, shy girl!

My anguish is this: The spiritual-gift, "discerning of spirits," could have identified the demon hiding in this young woman and driven it out. (Luke 10:19; I Corinthians 12:10). Kingdom power could have delivered her and saved the family. Jesus said, "I give you power to tread on serpents and scorpions and over all the power of the enemy" (Matthew 12:28; Mark 16:17). It was our spiritual ignorance that allowed the devil to destroy this innocent husband and children. I can think of no grief so terrible as that which came to the grandparents when they were told their son, his wife, and all their grandchildren were dead. That happened to them. Had my loyalty been more to Scripture and less to religious tradition, she might be alive today and that family well and happy. Have I seen such demons be cast out? Yes! Absolutely.

After a brief two years, I received a preaching request from a church in Delray Beach, Florida, that I knew was looking for a pastor. I refused the invitation, explaining that I understood their circumstance, but I was not available. My family and I loved where we were and wanted to stay. Soon, they called again, with the same request, believing God had directed it, and again, I refused. As I hung up the phone, I distinctly heard the Holy Spirit say, "You did not even ask Me if you should go." I was gripped with guilt, called the pastor immediately and said, "I will come and preach, but please let the congregation know that I am not available for their call." He agreed, and with that understood, I took the train to Delray Beach. I preached and knew instantly God was sending me back to Florida. That same night I accepted their invitation. All the while my heart was breaking that my family and I would be making another change. We had fallen in love with Georgia's small town and wanted all my pastorates to be like the first one—at least ten years long.

Chapter 14

FAITH AND FEAR IN DELRAY BEACH, FLORIDA

In the summer of 1962, Laurie, Cecile, and I moved to beautiful Delray Beach, Florida, to a wonderful Primitive Baptist Church that welcomed us with open arms. We quickly fell in love with the congregation and were delighted with the accommodations. Both the church and school were in walking distance of the pastorium. Cecile was in the fourth grade, and there were numerous children her age in the church. Best of all, we were accepted like family. While my ministry was strongly denominational and my theology Calvinistic, we were well received by other pastors and business people in the community. The congregation was active, eager to be involved, and it was a wonderful place to be.

Delray Beach was a winter-gathering place for many of America's "rich and famous," and we met significant people in the community. Christmas, 1964, I had a private visit with Senator Ted Kennedy and his wife, Joan in their ocean-front estate in Palm Beach. His brother Jack, the President, was not with them. Ted had been in a plane crash earlier that year, and this was his first Florida-visit after the accident. Both he and Joan were very gracious to me and he, particularly, asked me to assist his walking. He still wore a metal brace that added to his handicap.

While reading the newspaper at breakfast one morning, Laurie learned that Catherine Marshall LeSourd, with her husband Leonard, and their family, had moved into the community. Cecile recognized the name of their son, Chester, as the new student in her class at school. For years, Laurie and I had known of Catherine, author of numerous best-selling Christian books and movies. The newspaper explained that she was still on staff at *Guideposts Magazine* in New York and Leonard would continue serving as Executive Editor.

Catherine's book that catapulted her to fame was *A Man Called Peter*, the life-story of her Presbyterian preacher-husband, Peter Marshall who served as Chaplain in the U.S. Senate. When parts of the movie were filmed at Agnes Scott College near Atlanta, Laurie, Cecile, and I had gone and watched from afar. It never occurred to us that someday we would become friends with Catherine and Leonard, spend quality time in their home and they in ours.

We soon met and became friends. They attended our church on occasions, and Laurie took Catherine to the organic farm to buy vegetables. They became interested in my writing, and Len asked me to prepare a story for Guideposts Magazine. I did, and it was published in their International Edition, which was the first of my articles to be circulated worldwide. It was their encouragement that pushed me into my writing ministry, which, if counting translations into Japanese, Spanish, French, and Chinese, resulted in ten books and more than one thousand scriptural articles.

When Catherine felt a special need for prayer, she would come to my church office, and several of us sought God's direction together. At that time, she was writing her now-famous book, *Christie*, for McGraw-Hill in New York. Bill Goyen, Senior Editor, came to Florida to assist with the work. Catherine was very eager for Bill and me to become acquainted and asked that I meet him at the Palm Beach Airport. I was then writing *Island In The Sun*, the true story of my grandmother's Florida family during the Civil War.

Bill became fascinated with this true history and accepted it for McGraw-Hill. He spent daytimes working with Catherine on "Christie" and evenings with me. During that time, he said to me, "Charles, I don't want you to take my offer lightly. I am taking on only four new American authors this year—and you are one of them." I could not believe my ears. This wonderful man was the top editor in the nation, a lover of Jesus and was offering to become my personal publisher and guide.

That never happened. Three days later—in the midst of my excitement and celebration—the New York office notified Bill of a shake-up in their top Staff, and they were moving him to a managerial position. He refused, wanting to work with writers, not finances. They insisted, and he declined. They demanded, and the crisis continued. In the upheaval, he sent my book to David McKay Publisher in New York. Soon after Catherine's book was published, Bill left McGraw-Hill and joined the faculty at Princeton University. My dreams for Bill's editing my book ended forever.

We stayed in contact, and he periodically consulted me about a "Jesus" book he was writing. The McKay Company kept my book one year—then tragically, sent it back. I put the manuscript in the closet where it stayed for nearly forty years. To this day, I remember Bill saying, "I don't want you to take my offer lightly. I am taking on only four new American authors this year and you are one of them."

The Cuban Missile Crisis

The afternoon of October 16, 1962, Laurie and I had just returned from a long trip, undressed, fallen across the bed when someone began banging on our front door. I threw a robe over my shoulders and rushed to answer it. A neighbor, a divorced mom with three children, pushed into the house, "Have you seen the TV News?" she yelled. Not waiting, she rushed by me to the television and turned it on. President Kennedy was speaking. He warned that Russian Missiles, apparently armed with nuclear warheads, had been discovered in Cuba. These were in striking distance of the U.S.—especially Florida. The woman was frantic.

Laurie was up, peering from the cracked bedroom door. I steered the neighbor to our dining table, gave her a slice of cake, offered to make coffee, and hurried back to the bedroom to dress. Returning to the TV, we saw aerial photographs of the weapons in a Cuban jungle-clearing. Crisis grabbed the nation and people held their breath worldwide. Nikita Khrushchev, one of the most dangerous men of all time, was Premier of the Soviet Union and had vowed to bury us. The missiles were his project. America was the principal opposition to the spread of Communism worldwide. If we were removed, there would be no other resistance to Marxism's dominating humanity with its godlessness.

Unknown to us, President Kennedy and his Staff in Washington were battling each other about the best defense to take. Wrong choices could destroy us. The President prevailed and immediately ordered a "blockade" around the island that prevented outside help from reaching it. None of his Staff approved this measure. They wanted him to take a more aggressive position against the Soviet Union. The next day, photos of the Missiles were on the front page of every paper. Televisions, radios, spoke of nothing else. Nationally, we were terrified. Everyone in South Florida was urged to prepare a "fall-out" shelter under the house or some other safe place and supply it with drinking water, non-perishable food, blankets, and tools. For most, this was impossible, as Florida has no basements.

Charles Carrin

Our house was a split-level with one end slightly elevated above
ground. I was able to make preparations under that section, but I had a
serious problem: The only access into it was an air-vent just large enough
for a person to squeeze through. To do that it was necessary to climb
over a retainer-wall and push through the narrow opening. The site was
claustrophobic. I went back and forth with supplies, but Laurie and Cecile
never tried to get in it. That would only happen if we heard sirens.

The next day I went into the crawlspace with canned food and was
part way out, struggling to twist my body through the opening, and I
stopped. Looking up at a beautiful Florida sky, I propped my elbows
on the retainer and said, "Lord, in coming back to Florida, this is not
what I had in mind!" Even so, life went on, and the next day I attended
a Kiwanis Club meeting at the Columbus Hotel in Miami. The dining
room was at the roof-top with a glass wall overlooking the ocean and
Biscayne Bay.

When I entered the room, the tables were empty, and a crowd of people
was pressed against the glass, staring at the sea. I joined them, and in the
distance, we saw a convoy of American Battleships heading to Cuba. The
sight was sobering. Everyone realized World War III could break-out at any
moment, and Khrushchev hungered for the attack. The Pope, in an address
on Vatican Radio, pleaded with Khrushchev to spare mankind from an
atomic war. There was no response: Moscow remained silent.

The next day the anxiety increased: I approached a bridge over the
Intra-coastal Waterway near our house when suddenly, red stoplights
began flashing, the gates came down, and I was unable to cross. What I
saw was sobering: Dozens of slow-moving tug-boats and barges, loaded
with huge artillery and weapons of every sort, were approaching. I waited
several hours; finally, the bridge opened, and I went home.

President Kennedy's tactic worked, and war was averted: Rather than our
attacking the Soviet Union, which most of his Staff wanted to do, Kennedy
ordered the blockade. On Sunday, October 28, 1962, the Soviet Union
agreed to remove the missiles from Cuba, and on November 20, Kennedy
announced, "I have today been informed by Chairman Khrushchev that
all of the IL-28 bombers in Cuba will be withdrawn in thirty days ... I
have this afternoon instructed the Secretary of Defense to lift our naval
quarantine ...." Few Americans, then or now, knew how perilously close
we came to an nuclear-missile attack.

128

The missiles were dismantled, and the U.S. was saved from desolation. The sudden terror bonded people together. A sense of comradery and the need for each other replaced an attitude of divisiveness in churches and races. Historians have called that crisis "The most dangerous 13 days in the history of the world." Thankfully, the Blockade worked, and Russia backed down.

President Kennedy Is Murdered—1963

One year after the Cuban Crisis, November 17, 1963, President Kennedy was at his family home in Palm Beach. On Sunday he worshiped at St. Edward's Catholic Church. Later that week he went to Dallas for a Presidential Parade. Saturday, November 23rd, I was crossing the street in downtown Delray Beach when a car screeched to a stop near me, and the driver screamed, "President Kennedy has just been shot!!" Saying nothing more, he sped away. I was stunned and ran to a nearby store where a group had already gathered to watch the news on TV. Pictures showed Dallas in chaos; the parade-route was in a panic, and hundreds of people were running and screaming. Newscasters were in confusion, and terror was rampant.

Minutes later we learned the President was dead. Panic struck the nation, and we instantly feared his death was related to the Cuban Blockade the year before. Everyone had the same anxiety: Was this the beginning of a Communist takeover of America? Would other government-officials be killed? Was Khrushchev getting revenge for the Missile Crisis? Everyone had an opinion. Traffic across the nation gridlocked in some areas as the news spread from car to car. Many schools dismissed early, and students were sent home. People were weeping publicly.

Within minutes, Lyndon Johnson was sworn in as President, and an intense, national grief gripped the land. A strange-looking man, Harvey Lee Oswald, was captured and identified as the killer. The hours following the President's assassination were terrifying. Chaos and disorder were rampant. Millions of TV viewers, including me, saw a stranger (Jack Ruby) run out of the crowd in the Dallas Police Station and shoot Harvey Lee Oswald in the belly. All of us watched Oswald's face grimace in death-pain as the bullet tore into his body. Ruby was jailed but died of cancer in 1967.

It was a long time before we resumed life in a routine way, but, like it or not, we had to adjust to the crisis and return to normal. That took effort. My church responsibility increased at the same time. I became more active in civic affairs and was made President of the Kiwanis Club. Soon, I served with the Beautification Committee that widened and landscaped Atlantic Avenue, was elected Chairman of the Ministerial Association, assisted in a number of Garden Club events, and other causes. I wanted to help spiritually, civically, and any other way I could. The church was stable, and as much as a Primitive Baptist Church could thrive, we did.

Chapter 15

A CHALLENGE BEGINS: MY INTERNATIONAL TRAVEL AND THE WAR IN VIET NAM

Israel and the Holy Land

The next year, 1964, I was in the pastor's office at First Baptist Church, Delray Beach, and I picked up a Holy Land travel-brochure from his desk. He said excitedly, "Come! Go with us! We are visiting ten countries—also Israel! This will be a great experience … You can even finance the cost and pay for it monthly!" I was instantly intrigued and showed Laurie the brochure when I got home. She was thrilled and insisted I go. She was playing the piano for a local ballet school, and her weekly salary was enough to cover the monthly finance charge. Thankfully, I went. This tour with a delightful Baptist group included visits to England, France, Italy, Switzerland, Greece, Egypt, Lebanon, Jordan, and Israel. It was a turning point in my life, and in the years following, I escorted a dozen groups to that part of the world.

On that first trip, I climbed the inside-tunnel of the Pyramid of Khufu to the burial chamber, visited a number of historical sites, and spent time at the University of Cairo. While we visited a number of other countries, our great delight was being in Jerusalem. We stayed in the American Colony Hotel that had originally been the private family-estate of Bertha Spafford Vester. It was Bertha's father who wrote the famous Christian hymn, "It Is Well With My Soul" in 1873 after his four daughters were drowned at sea.

We visited the Garden Tomb, Gethsemane, and the "place of a skull," the probable site of Jesus's crucifixion. Natural caves in a cliff here created the distinct appearance of a skull (John 19:17). Suddenly, the dirt and squalor disappeared, and I returned to the time of Jesus. He was there at the pool of Bethesda, the Garden of Gethsemane, Jericho, and hundreds of

131

unexpected places we went. Several times when the Biblical-reality hit me of where I stood, I bent over weeping.

Unexpectedly, I met a Jordanian, Kalil Kando, who first acquired the Dead Sea Scrolls after their discovery in 1945. These were considered one of the greatest archaeological finds of modern times. Kalil talked excitedly, sharing much information about the scrolls. In eleven years, 1945-1956, some 981 ancient scrolls and fragments were removed from caves northwest of the Dead Sea. I later visited the cave where the original find was made by Juma, a shepherd-boy. The most famous scroll is the complete Book of Isaiah, which is on display today in Israel's "Shrine of the Book Museum."

One night in Jerusalem I was in bed asleep. I awoke after midnight, dressed quickly, and returned to the old city through the Damascus Gate. Then I climbed to the ramparts and walked halfway around the city wall in the moonlight. I wanted to recapture Nehemiah's experience when he had done that (Nehemiah 2:12). It was probably a dangerous thing to do, but I was unaware of that, and I am glad today I did it.

There were numerous situations that were more dangerous: Many of our bus drivers were Muslims who passed on curves, hills, blind turns, and took many dangerous chances. We were aghast and screamed frequently during a trip. Only later, we learned that Muslims are fatalists and believe death is unavoidable. When your "time comes," you will die, regardless. No one can live beyond that assigned moment—no matter the precautions you take—you will die.

Viet Nam War 1965

On March 8, 1965, I was at home in Florida, spiritually renewed by my trip to Israel. The church was thriving, and Lyndon Johnson was President. Tragically, he was a man with a vulgar mouth who shamed both his High Office and the American people. The Nation was slowly recovering from Kennedy's assassination, but that day we heard more troublesome news: American combat troops had invaded Viet Nam. This action was one the U.S. would always regret. The Vietnamese were our ally, and we had protected them in the past, but not with a direct war action against the Communists. The Marine attack changed that policy, and Americans were immediately divided over the issue. Tempers were hot; opinions were strongly spoken.

More than 58,000 Americans were killed in Viet Nam and another three million Vietnamese civilians and military lay dead. President Richard Nixon ordered the withdrawal of U.S. forces in 1973, and our veterans began coming home—ten years after the Marine invasion began. That day, April 30, 1975, with the war un-won, American troops and personnel retreated from the Capital, Saigon, in humiliating defeat. There were no parades in welcoming the soldiers home, no applause and celebrations as veterans in other wars received. South Vietnamese troops continued to fight, but the Communist forces finally seized control in 1975. The cost to America, according to the Defense Department, was 168 billion dollars, which in today's finances, would be nearly one trillion dollars.

Sadly, the end of the War did not bring peace to American Troops who came home: Thousands of them suffered from Post-Traumatic Stress Syndrome, night-terrors, alcoholism, and personal defeat. All were victimized by guilt, humiliation, shame, and other war-effects which only the Holy Spirit could have remedied. Few American churches and pastors, myself included, understood these veterans could benefit by Deliverance Ministry and other Spirit-empowered care. Derek Prince was teaching it, but few were listening. None of us realized our returning troops were victims of Buddhist curses and could be radically helped by authentic Christian Deliverance Ministry. My own spiritual-awakening to this truth did not come until two years later in 1977.

Family Trip to the Holy Land

In December 1966, I directed another Holy Land trip, and took Laurie and Cecile, and several of our Primitive Baptist friends with us. We spent several days in Beruit, Lebanon. The next day we flew south to Cairo. While we were still ascending, suddenly, the plane made a U-turn and proceeded to head north. I was startled at that unexpected change and pressed my face against the window, seeing the Lebanon Mountains in the distance. That was a frightening sign, and I wondered if we were being hijacked. The flight-engineer suddenly rushed into the cabin, swearing in Arabic, and removed a section of carpet in the aisle. Dropping to his knees, he opened a compartment and began hammering on equipment below. Still swearing, he closed it and ran back to the cockpit. A moment later the pilot announced that we were returning to Beirut for an emergency landing. The landing gear had malfunctioned, and he did not know if it had retracted and locked.

Again, my face was pressed against the glass, and as we approached the landing strip. I saw a string of fire trucks and ambulances chasing along beside us. Thankfully, there was no incident, and when we touched down safely, passengers began cheering. Several hours later we continued to Cairo. During the delay at Beirut Airport, we learned that King Saud of Arabia and his harem of wives were staying in our hotel in Egypt. Hearing that, one of our widows said, "Do you think he wants one more wife?" Everyone laughed, and we assured her we would find out.

Several days later in Cairo, our group gathered in the hotel lobby waiting for our tour bus. Everyone was present except this widow; she was outside the building. Suddenly, the elevator doors opened, and a large group of handsome, well-dressed men marched out to form an honor guard at the main entrance. These were Saudi Princes, and we realized their father, the King, was arriving. A few minutes later he stepped out of the elevator, walking with a cane. He was white-haired, stooped, and wearing the traditional Muslim thawb. The men suddenly stiffened into military position. Everyone else stepped back. Saud was walking painfully slow toward the door when suddenly, our widow came rushing in and collided with him face-to-face. She was horrified and leaped back. He was angered—insulted, and he shook his cane at her. The Honor Guard flinched angrily. We could see their furor, but they never broke rank. If looks could have killed, she would have died on the spot. After everyone was seated on the bus, someone said to her, "You had a perfect chance! Why didn't you ask him?!" Without looking up, she said, "I changed my mind!

The Six-Day War

On June 5, 1967, Israel and the United Arab Republic—Egypt, Jordan, and Syria, exploded in battle. Worldwide, everyone watched the war and a short, six days later, June 10th, it ended with Israel's decisive victory. The war established Israel as the dominant military power in the Middle East, and the Arab world was horribly demoralized by their defeat.

Immediately, Jewish troops stood before the Western Wall of their ancient city and shouted in the joy of victory. This huge stretch of stonework had fortified Jerusalem's Temple which Titus and the Roman Legions destroyed in the year 70 AD. Some of these stones weigh 570 tons, are forty-five feet long, fifteen feet wide, and twelve feet high. It was in reference to blocks similar to these that Jesus shocked the disciples when He said, "Not one stone shall be left upon another" (Matthew 24:2). Anciently, it was called the "Wailing Wall" but today has become the Western Wall. Jewish days of wailing are over. Immediately, Israeli soldiers bulldozed the hovels and shacks that filled the area and opened the huge courtyard for worshipers.

After the War, I returned to the Middle East and escorted a group of 20 Americans with me. I named my travel company the "Three Continent—Holy Land Tour," and worked with Wholesale Tours, International, in New York City. I found this Company to be extremely reliable and helpful in every way.

While I was away, Laurie sang several times with a professional choral-group at the Breakers Hotel in Palm Beach. One of the events was the National Governors Convention when Ronald Reagan was Governor of California. After the Concert everyone gathered for hors d'oeuvres in the Ball Room. There, Governor Reagan approached Laurie, took her hand and complimented their performance. When she later told me about the event, I said, "What did you say to him?" She explained, "I was so overwhelmed at meeting him that all I could do was stare. I tried to speak, but nothing came out of my mouth."

While these were joyous times, there were also frightening moments during our trips. In Israel, I had the most frightening incident of all. While escorting groups to the Middle East, I always carried a large amount of cash to tip those handling baggage and doing other services for us. On this particular trip, I had more than $1,000 with me—which in the 1970s was a huge amount of money—which I kept safely hidden in a money belt under my clothes. No one knew I had it. One afternoon in Jerusalem I rushed to my room, took a quick shower, and was in the process of dressing when suddenly I missed the belt. My last memory was placing it on top of my suitcase near the door. I looked, but it wasn't there. Glancing about the room and not seeing it I rushed to the door and found it unlocked.

I panicked—fearing someone had entered the room and taken it while I was in the shower. Searching madly about the area I realized the belt was nowhere to be seen. Hurriedly, I dressed, raced to the hotel office and explained to the Manager what had happened. He returned to the room with me, stripped the bed, removed the mattress, dumped my suitcases and dresser drawers onto the floor, examined everything but found nothing. He was as frantic as I was since the hotel had a reputation for excellent security and theft would greatly damage its record.

In desperation, I called the Travel Office in New York and told them what had happened. "Don't go to the police!" They cautioned me, "Keep searching!" That evening I met my tour group for dinner but told no one what had happened. I pretended to be happy and enjoying events of the day, while inside I was screaming for God's help. Paying the men who served us was vital; they had wives and children to feed—money from tips was their only income. Now, I had nothing to give them, and the tour had just begun.

That night I delayed going to bed but stayed up late, dreading a sleepless night. Finally, in exhaustion, I went to my room and undressed. Tossing my pajamas on the bed, I pulled down my underwear. To my shock, there was the moneybelt! I had it on! My eyes bulged. I could not believe it! After the shower, I had unconsciously strapped it around my waist and put on my shorts. Seeing it, I began shouting, dancing, and clapping my hands! People probably heard my "Yahoos" all through the hall. I rushed to the hotel desk, shoved the manager into his back office, pulled down my pants and showed him the money-belt. "You found it!" He shouted in broken English, "Where you found it?! Where you found it?!" Embarrassed, I explained, and he happily believed me. Another factor of my gratitude was that I had not gone to the Police. Had I done so, they would have strip-searched me, found the money, thought I was lying—trying to defraud the hotel—and arrested me. Thank God, that did not happen! I stayed awake a long time that night, laughing, shouting, praising God and thanking Him that the trip would continue as planned.

Chapter 16

A FEARFUL RETURN TO THE US

A Trip to the Yucatan Peninsula and Aruba

The next year, April 4, 1968, I went to Mexico's Yucatan Peninsula to visit the Mayan ruins at Chichen Itza, fulfilling a life-long desire to explore this historic site. I had seen the pyramids in Egypt several times and wanted to compare those in Mexico.

This was an exciting and educational trip in every way, though one in which I did no preaching. Taking advantage of the opportunity, I explored the jungle and found beautiful orchid plants of *Shomburgkia Tibicinis*. This was probably my favorite of all orchids and one which I desperately wanted to take back to Florida, but I had no plant import permit.

Several days later on my flight back to Miami, a newspaper lay on the seat between a woman by the window and me. "May I read your paper?" I asked, picking it up. "You may," She answered, quickly adding, "But you don't want to!" Unspeaking, I stared, and she continued, "Martin Luther King was assassinated two days ago, and there is rioting in Miami and across the nation!"

I dropped my head in grief—not just from fear of the rioting—but because America needed to hear the message Dr. King brought. Racial prejudice was wrong, and everyone suffered because of it. I immediately thought of the Jewish Temple in Atlanta that had been bombed because of hatred against both Jews and Blacks. Memories of Hitler and his violence flashed through my mind. Tragically, this was "Holy Week," the seven days preceding Easter when humanity focused on Jesus, Who had come to deliver us from the evil of racism.

The woman continued, "Riots have broken out in more than 100 cities across the United States. Hundreds of buildings have been burned; thousands of arrests made, and more than 40 people have been killed." For the first time, she looked straight at me, "We whites are wrong! Blacks have been treated unfairly! That must stop!" I heartily agreed with her and laid the paper aside. I did not want to read it. After a worrisome flight, we arrived in Miami and found the airport with a heavy presence of police and security officers, but quiet and safe. Once outside, I hurried to the parking deck for my car.

Thankfully, I saw no violence and an hour later was back home in Delray Beach. What followed was a wave of civil disturbance which swept the United States in the greatest outburst since the Civil War. Some of the biggest riots took place in Washington, D.C., Baltimore, Chicago, and Kansas City. Dr. King was buried in Atlanta, just a mile from where my ministry began in 1949. It is now a pilgrimage-site for visitors from around the world.

Pastors Beware

Probably, the most serious threat that can come to a pastor's reputation happened soon after I was back in the U.S. A woman whom I knew remotely called, explaining that her husband was dead. She was ill and unable to get out of bed, and in need of food. She asked if I would please bring a sandwich to her house? Her invalid uncle was there and would be in the front room. It would be unnecessary to knock. I naively agreed, found the address, went in and spoke to the uncle. Then I carried the food—salad, sandwich, bottled drink—to the her room. The woman had the blanket pulled up under her chin. Thanking me profusely, she asked me to pray. When I said "Amen," she threw the blanket off her body and showed me she was completely naked. I dropped the tray on top of her and ran out of the house—not even speaking to the uncle as I raced out.

Aruba and My Most Embarrassing Moment

In the 1960s and '70s, when I conducted tours to Israel and the Middle East, I always flew the Royal Dutch Airlines—KLM. In appreciation for my work with them, KLM invited me to be their guest on inaugural flights to new destinations. In July, 1967, they flew me to the Dutch islands of Aruba, Bonaire, and Curacao, off the coast of South America. These bits of land are close to the Continent, and on a clear day, it is possible to see the mountains of Venezuela.

Laurie was not free to go with me, so I went alone and met other KLM guests on the plane. My plan, when the event in Curacao ended, was to fly to Caracas, Venezuela, and visit Angel Falls in the country's interior. Angel is the highest waterfall in the world, splashing down a spectacular 3,211 feet. It had been my ambition to visit this waterfall since I was a teenager; that was the period which I planned to live in the jungle.

Our group was met at the airport and driven to the other end of the island to a luxurious hotel. The dining room was elegant, the food superb, and we were treated royally. We had no responsibility but to swim, relax, and enjoy the beauty of the island.

Friday evening our group of twenty-five was invited to a KLM pool-party at a hotel on the opposite end of the island. I dressed to swim, hurried to the bus, jumped on, and we left immediately. After I took my seat near the driver, I looked back at the other guests and was shocked: The women were in evening gowns; the men wore suits, and a few had on tuxedos. Aghast, I asked why? They explained, and I realized I had misread the invitation: It was not a "pool" party but a "poolside" party—this meant a formal dinner, music, dancing, and all the glamour. In horror, I looked down at my swimsuit, gaudy-cabana shirt, bare legs, and sandals. All I had was my room key, no wallet, no money—and no way to go back.

When our bus arrived at the dinner-site, other KLM guests from South America were hurrying out of their buses. The Latin women were elegantly-gowned. All the men were in tuxedos, and before I knew what was happening, our group was escorted to a beautiful poolside patio with candle-lighted tables, orchid centerpieces, a full orchestra, and formal staff of waiters. The scene was extravagant. I was terrified and looked desperately for a place to hide. There was none—I was trapped! Finally, I spotted a table at the far end of the dining area and grabbed a chair where I could partially hide in the shrubbery, and that is where I stayed for the entire evening, with a palm frond pulled across my lap to obscure myself in the landscaping. Three hours later our bus returned to take us back to the hotel, and I was first to get on and first to get off.

The next night, Saturday, our hotel lobby was crowded with wealthy Venezuelans who had come to Curacao to gamble. Casinos were a big attraction in the Dutch islands, and the people were partying, dancing, and celebrating. After dinner, I went back to my room, read Scripture, and went to sleep. Sunday morning, I darted to an early service at the Dutch Reformed Church and hurried back to the hotel to eat. When I entered the lobby, I was shocked to find it filled with the same people from the night before—ladies were still in their evening gowns and men in their tuxedos. Obviously, they had been up all night; none had gone to bed. What struck me most was the frightened expressions on their faces. Then I noticed a group gathered at the bar where a small radio was giving news. The broadcast, in English, explained:

At 8:00 PM, the night before, a devastating earthquake had hit Caracas. Measuring 6.5 on the Richter Scale, it had toppled buildings, killed an uncounted number of people, and buried countless more in the rubble. Another 80,000 were homeless. Communication lines were down, and the airport was closed, severely damaged. The Venezuelans in the lobby were trapped in Curacao with no way to get home and no contact with loved ones. My heart hurt for them in a way I can't describe. Some parents had left children in the care of others, while they enjoyed a weekend away. All of them had friends and loved ones in the city. I tried to be of comfort, but my Spanish was too inadequate. KLM agents did their best to console the people, but this was a situation in which nothing could be done but pray and wait. Another alarming fact to me was that these Dutch Islands where we were—Aruba and Curacao—sit on "stems" in very deep water. I wondered if an earthquake could break the stem and topple the islands into the sea.

My original plan to fly to Caracas the next day and visit Angel Falls never happened. Instead, I caught a plane back to Jamaica and met a flight attendant who told me her experience that fatal Saturday night in Caracas. She checked into the hotel, and as she was getting on the elevator, the door closed in her face. Annoyed, she was waiting for the elevator to come down when the quake hit, shaking the building and trapping all the elevators between floors. There was no one to help and no way to rescue the passengers. She fled the building and never learned what happened to those caught in the elevator—or thousands of similar incidents across the area.

God Comes to Our Rescue

The church in Delray Beach thrived and grew in the years of my ministry, but in 1970 God made it very clear that my time there was finished. I resigned—with no income, no savings, and no place to go. A friend helped financially for a few months, and then his support ended.

Laurie, Cecile, and I moved five times in the following few months, eating 10-cent canned-mackerel and other cheap food. I felt like Elijah at the brook Cherith when "the brook dried up," and the ravens brought him scraps of meat to eat (I Kings 17:5).

During that time, Dr. James Lockhart, a wonderful man I had met several times, sent word for me to visit him. His family was the founding owner of the Lockhart Steel Corporation in Pittsburgh, Pennsylvania. Like my father, he was partially paralyzed, and though a multi-millionaire, he had gained a medical degree so he could benefit humanity. I went to his house, and as we chatted, he said, "My wife and I are leaving soon and will not be back for many months. You are welcome to live here as long as you like. We will be returning north shortly." I was speechless at his offer—and the goodness of God. The joy on my face showed him how grateful I was—and I immediately accepted the offer.

The house was an ocean-front estate near Delray Beach with several hundred feet of private beach, a huge swimming pool, putting-green, rose garden, beautiful landscaping, and a tennis court. A full-time gardener cared for the grounds. Electricians came each month and replaced all the light bulbs inside the house. My only responsibility was to call the interior decorator if a household item needed repair. With that blessing, I was able to continue writing, and Laurie got a part-time job paying $10.00 a week. That bought a lot of mackerel.

Len and Catherine and others came for dinner, and we lived luxuriously—on cheap food. On one of their visits, Catherine gave me more than 100 books from her personal library. Our friend, Bill Goyan, occasionally called from New York.

Chapter 17

ATLANTA: WAR AND A NEW MINISTRY BEGINS

Return To Atlanta

In June 1970, I was in the garden early one morning when the Holy Spirit spoke distinctly, saying: "Do not leave the house today." The message was so clear, so definite, that for a moment I was perplexed. There was no mistaking what I heard, and in obedience, I never left the estate. About 8:00 o'clock that evening I was standing at the double-doors facing the ocean when the phone rang. Before I could turn toward it, the Holy Spirit said: "That is the church in Atlanta calling. They want you to become their pastor. Tell them you will go." Again, I was shocked. There was no mistaking the "word of knowledge." When I answered, the voice on the other end greeted me and said, "Brother Charles, this is Ollis Elton, a deacon at the Atlanta Church. We have just had our pastoral-call conference and are extending you the invitation to become the pastor." I listened as he kept speaking: "We want you to pray, and as soon as you have God's answer, please let us know." I interrupted him and said, "Brother Elton, I can tell you now …." There was a pause.

"Oh! You can?" He replied, sounding disappointed that I could answer without prayer. I said, "Yes, I can tell you—if you want it now." "Yes," he answered despondently, "Yes, go ahead, tell me now." He assumed I was declining the request. Without waiting, I said, "I accept your call." There was a pause; he then spoke, "You do?!" "Yes," I said again, "God already told me to accept your call …." He interrupted me, said, "He did? I'll call you right back!" and slammed down the phone. I stood holding the receiver, puzzled at what appeared to be rudeness. He could at least have acted like he was glad and said goodbye. Ten minutes later he called back, out of breath, happily explaining, "The people were leaving—driving out of the parking lot—I stopped them, and we are now re-gathering to thank God for His wonderful reply! Thank you! God bless you!" Without another word, he hung up.

The following September, Laurie, Cecile, and I returned to Atlanta where my ministry had begun over twenty years before. Interestingly, my first pastorate at Memorial Church in 1949, was only one mile from my new location. We were back in familiar territory. The new church was in one of Atlanta's elegant old neighborhoods, Druid Hills; and the pastorium, in Decatur, was just a few miles away. Our situation was ideal. The congregation received us warmly, and they were eager for my ministry. The first Sunday new members joined.

Cecile was in her Senior year and enrolled at Druid Hills High where she excelled. She made many new friends and represented the school in Atlanta's "Junior Miss" Pageant where she won the Talent Competition and placed 1st Runner-up. She played a medley of classical and popular songs, including the song "More," which she improvised. The girl who won the Title also won the State title, and the Atlanta Crown was given to Cecile. Later, Cecile won the Talent Award and was First Runner-Up in the Miss Atlanta Pageant. Afterward, she graduated Cum Laud in music at the University of Georgia. For one of her Piano Recitals, she played with the Atlanta Symphony Orchestra. In every instance, God's grace prevailed in astonishing ways.

Best of all, we loved the people at the Atlanta Church, and they loved us in return. Newcomers began joining; many were baptized, and the church thrived. We were located on a main drive and exposed to a lot of drifters. These were a challenge. One wintery Sunday evening, the congregation was singing the final hymn before my sermon when the doors to the foyer opened. There the tallest, most gorilla-like man I had ever seen, stumbled into the building. He was almost seven feet tall and was wet with rain. He had a huge body with ragged clothes, bushy, uncut hair, and a heavy stubble of beard. Worst of all, it was apparent he was mentally deranged. In one arm he carried a large, burlap bag, and in the other a portable radio with the antenna towering over his head. At the top of the antenna, he had attached a metal pie pan and glass mirror.

As he came down the aisle, stumbling toward me, I could not believe what I saw. His feet were so large that he had cut the tops off the shoes and appeared to be walking barefooted. Most frightening of all was the fixation in his eyes—staring malevolently at me. Slowly he made his way forward with people in each row stopping their singing, staring wide-eyed as he came into view. At the front he stumbled to a seat and dropped down— the radio antenna swinging overhead and the mirror rattling against it.

The hymn ended and the congregation was seated. I tried to proceed as if he were not present, but it wasn't possible. People were watching him, not listening to anything I said. In a spastic way, he kept moving the radio from the seat onto his lap and back again. I continued with the Scripture reading and the sermon, but I kept my eye unflinchingly fixed on him. So did everyone else. Ten minutes passed, and then with more erratic-actions, he began reaching into his coat pocket, obviously searching for something. Not finding it, he did the same thing with the other pocket. The process then repeated. All the while, his eyes were locked in an alarming stare into mine.

I was frightened, wondering what he was doing when suddenly, it hit me: He was searching for matches—he had a bomb! He was going to blow up the building! Slamming the Bible shut, I clapped my hands, pronounced the shortest benediction of my career and yelled, "Service is dismissed! Everybody! Leave the building!" Most everyone jammed the entrance as they fled. The good news was he had no bomb. There was no apparent danger, but, after calling the Police Department, I learned that even in his demented state, he capitalized on his frightening appearance. One method was to push into an elevator crowded with women and tell them "I'll get off if you'll give me money!" It worked every time.

We had been in Atlanta two years when Bill Goyen and his wife, Doris Roberts, visited us. We escorted them around the city, showing its most famous sights, and then took them to the Airport for their return to New York. That was our last time together, though Bill and I stayed in touch by phone. He soon joined the Staff at Princeton University, teaching creative writing, and she continued her stage and television career. Later, Doris became more famous as "Marie," the sarcastic mother-in-law on the "Everybody Loves Raymond" TV comedy series. Occasionally, I see re-runs of those old telecasts and remember our happy times together. I will always be grateful to God for this couple and the impact Bill had on my life. "His works follow after him" (Revelation 14:13).

Catherine died in March 1983, leaving more than 18,000,000 books in circulation. Bill died six months later, in August, that same year, with Doris outliving him more than thirty years. She passed away in 2016 at age 90. Len survived Catherine until 1996, remaining a loving devotee to me to the end. I outlived all of them. Catherine's signed photograph is still on display in my home where I see it daily. In the ten books and more than 1,000 articles, I have since written, Catherine's, Len's, and Bill's influence have been profoundly present.

UNEXPECTED PANIC

We had a guest speaker at church, a delightful British scholar Dr. Charles Alexander from Liverpool, England, who stayed in our home. One morning at breakfast we were having a delightful meal together when suddenly a big, ugly roach flew onto the table between Laurie and our guest. For a split-second, no one moved—staring in unbelief. Then my wife slammed her hand down on the invader so hard she rattled dishes on the table. In the same instant, she froze—as if paralyzed—unable to move. Her eye's and Dr. Alexander's locked together, staring at each other in unbelief. When I realized she needed help, I rose, went around the table, lifted her hand, and wiped away the remains of that hapless bug. Embarrassing as it was for my wife, the pastor and I suddenly broke into laughter that we could not stop. We hooted until we wept and lost our breath. This poem, "The Uninvited Guest," (with embellishment) grew out of that experience.

THE UNINVITED GUEST

It was a fancy dinner! The company dressed up grand!
And the Madam of the Manor held out a diamond-studded hand
To all the guests who entered and were seated in the Hall
Where banquet tables waited between candle-lighted walls.
The silver shone so brightly it nearly burnt the eyes
Beneath a crystal chandelier of most enormous size.
A staff of well-dressed waiters served goblets of champagne
But when the toast was offered a guest–unwanted–came.

It was a haughty cockroach that crawled out from the lace
And wiggled his brown bottom in every startled face!
No ordinary fellow—not easily shooed away—

For when the butler grabbed the plate on which the culprit lay
He flew onto a lady's neck to hide down in her dress
And golly-whiz what happened then—was anybody's guess!
A shriek that shook the chandelier and snuffed ten candles out
Drowned out the background music in a most un-lady-like shout.

Well! The Madam of the Manor was embarrassed beyond all words
'Cause in all the Social Season nothing else like this occurred.
So the only gracious thing to do was just to swoon away
And hope when she revived again, the guests would leave, and say:
"My what a lovely evening! The dinner was just grand!
You'll make the front-page stories in the papers 'cross the land!"
But that ain't the way it happened, 'cause the papers later showed
The grand-dame laid out on the floor like someone knocked her cold.

What else had also happened, she couldn't rightly tell
But strangely it resembled all she'd heard of Hell.
A chair was on the table and from the chandelier
A mink stole hung like Tuesday's wash, drip-drying in the air.
Now don't giggle 'bout that party and in yourself feel smug,
Remember, the best-made dinner plans are vetoed by a bug!
And you ain't no exception, a roach may come to you!
And when you least expect him, he'll pris' right into view;
He wants to join your party with its aristocratic antics,
But wonders why—when he appears—folks create such a panic!

Soon after that, Andy Sparks, editor of the Atlanta Journal Sunday Magazine, and I had lunch together. He was more interested in publishing the story of my great-great-grandmother's arrival in Florida. She, her husband, and son were immigrants from France,. They came to the U.S. by way of New Orleans, and then traveled northward to Illinois. Immediately after the Civil War, she put her wounded soldier-son, his pregnant wife, their son, in an ox cart and drove them to Florida. Loren Wilson, an artist-member of my church and later a pastor, painted a beautiful scene of the family's Florida log-cabin. This was included in the Sunday Magazine story. The article was given a prominent place with pictures and through that article, I was introduced to many of Atlanta's well-known writers. One of them was fifty-year Atlanta Journal writer, Celestine Sibley, who worked for the paper from 1949 to 1999. In time, I became part of their "Writers Club" that sometimes met at mine and Laurie's house. This was a fun-group of intellectuals. Several were committed Christians, and all of them were well-known in the publishing world. They encouraged my own writing career in a significant way. When the book, *Word, Spirit, Power,* which I co-authored with Jack Taylor and R.T. Kendal, won the "Best Book" Award in 2013, by the Christian Retailing Association, I thought of these friends and the impact they made on my life.

The Haiti Mission

In 1974, I made my tenth visit to Israel and wandered alone one day inside the Muslim sector of Jerusalem's "old city." Gunfire and fighting suddenly broke out. People started running, screaming, and colliding into each other as they tried to escape. A light rain had fallen, and the cobbled-stone streets were slippery as oil. I bolted into a small Arabic store and hid behind the counter. The owner slammed the shutters down and crouched beside me. Finally, when the shooting stopped, a loud-speaker declared safety and ordered everyone to open their shops. We came out slowly, looked around and found Israeli tanks blocking the streets. The area resembled a war-zone, and the terror was severe. Later when I got back to the hotel–which soldiers raided–I learned that students in the school next door had been killed. The remaining days of the trip were frightening. I have been in other war-zones, but this was the most frightening of my life. My assistant, Emerson Proctor, and I had responsibility for some twenty American tourists.

When we finally flew out of Tel Aviv, I dropped into my aisle-seat on the plane, leaned back against the cushion, closed my eyes, and said, "Lord, Thank You for getting me out of there! Thank You, Lord!" I had never been more grateful and continued thanking Him, but what happened next was shocking: God's answer, a severe rebuke, changed my life forever. In anger, He said, "What do you think about those who cannot pack their bags and run?!" I was speechless, and for a moment I could not move—could hardly breathe. The message was frightening. I had heard the Lord's rebuke before, but this was the most extreme, ever.

Specifically, I was rebuked for my abstinence from foreign mission work. In Israel and numerous other countries, I visited missionaries but had remained uninvolved. During the 1830s my denomination of Baptist Churches rejected mission work and numerous other needed practices. In our perverted form of Calvinism, we emphatically denied that the gospel was "the power of God unto salvation to everyone who believes" (John 1:12, 3:16, 8:24; Romans 1:16). As hyper-Calvinists who placed more emphasis on the doctrine of personal-election than on personal-belief, we were blind to other scriptural truths. We never gave an invitation for anyone to accept Christ and be saved. If a person were God's elect—be he, Muslim, Hindu, Buddhist, Sheikh, etc., he would be saved—regardless of missionaries or other evangelists. If one were not the elect, forty missionaries could not save him. In our Calvinistic-mindset, the doctrine of salvation began and ended there; but that was not the end of God's expectations. Specifically, there on the plane, He was telling me: "Begin Missionary work! Do it now!"

My answer was, "Lord, I don't know how to start! If you will open the door, I will obey, but I don't know how to begin!" Within five minutes, a friend on the plane, Herb McComas, stood in the aisle beside me and said, "Charles, if you will go to Haiti and consider starting a Mission, I will pay your way ...." He had not gotten the words spoken before I stopped him: "Yes!" I answered quickly, "Yes! I will go and take Emerson Proctor with me!" Herb immediately agreed. When we landed in Amsterdam, I shoved Emerson onto a bench in the airport and said, "You and I are going to Haiti to begin a Mission!"

We went in January 1975, believing that God would connect us to some young pastor who would oversee the ministry. We would direct the construction and financial needs from the States; but, when we arrived in Port au Prince, and I saw the living conditions and incredible poverty, my hope totally collapsed. Never had I imagined such mental and physical dearth. We were besieged with beggars—children, old people, all ages—whose pain was enormous—so great as to be beyond anyone's help. We had been in the city only a few hours, were making our way through roadside-trash when we came upon a deep pit in the middle of the sidewalk. There was no barrier, no warning of danger, nothing to prevent someone from falling into it. This was typical. Haiti was hopeless. I grieved that we had told friends and churches at home that we were beginning a Mission here.

Haiti was beyond help—regretfully—I turned to Emerson and said, "Even God can't do anything here!"

By Tuesday evening I wanted to go home but couldn't. Wednesday I was scheduled to preach at Second Baptist Church in Port au Prince. Pastor Cenofah Pon-du-Jour was expecting me. At that service, when I watched people cram into the building, line the walls, sit on the floor, and stand on the hood of cars so they could see through windows, I was rebuked. Clearly, I heard the Holy Spirit say, "What was it you said I could not do in Haiti?!" The voice was the same I heard on the plane in Tel Aviv; I immediately repented. Emerson and I had five days to find the local person through whom we could work. We traveled widely, met many wonderful Haitian people but not the special one. Finally, the last day came. We were packed, ready to return to the Port au Prince Airport and fly to the U.S. We had not met our special man. With my suitcase beside me in the motel patio, Emerson and I awaited our taxi to take us to the airport—and home.

People were passing on the dirt road, women with baskets on their heads, others carrying flowers. A man with Elephantidis, whose leg was swelled five times its normal size, shuffled along, and in the distance, a young man walked briskly our way. At the motel he turned in, came to the patio, calling my name. In that moment I had a feeling like the Prophet Samuel must have felt when he met young Saul. God's words to the Prophet were, "Arise and anoint him; this is he" (I Samuel 16:12).

When I saw this young Haitian, I suddenly knew he was the man God had sent. With only minutes before leaving for the airport, the one we had come to Haiti to find, stood before us. His name was Enoch Deroseney, and he had just graduated from the Evangelical School of the Bible in Port au Prince. Quizzing him, I learned that because of his high grades and academic ability he had been awarded a full scholarship to a University in the U.S. To a Haitian, the opportunity to study at an American University and live in the U.S. is unspeakably great. That he would give up such an opportunity would require a definite work of God in his heart.

In our few minutes together, I quickly explained our purpose in being there, urged him to pray about remaining in Haiti as our local pastor and assistant for the project. He agreed to pray. I gave him a cassette player which Loren Wilson had given me. I explained we would communicate with recorded messages. With that done, Emerson and I hurried to the airport and home. Enoch prayed God said "Yes! Stay in Haiti," and he obeyed. One of our American pastors and wife, Jerry and Dot Lee, moved to Haiti to oversee the work.

Our site for the Mission was on a beautiful hilltop overlooking the sea at Grand Guave on the southern peninsula. It was donated by a wonderful Haitian businesswoman, Carmel Herreaux, who operated an ocean-front resort on the beach below. Work on our facility was slow, but when completed, we had a two-story building, constructed of concrete-block that provided a church, school, dormitory, kitchen, medical clinic, and an apartment for the pastor. Jerry and Dot Lee were our first American missionaries on-site and were perfect for the task. They were skilled in different ways and devoted their energy, time, and strength, to the work. Other churches have since grown from this original Mission. Best of all, since opening day it has housed, fed, and taught the Word of God to more than 1,000 orphaned children.

January 12, 2010, fifty students were playing on the soccer field. Only one student, a boy, was in the building on the second floor when suddenly the structure began to shake horrifically. Frightened, he ran to a window and leaped out unharmed. At that moment, a 7.0 earthquake slammed the area, and the building collapsed. In one second's time, the labor of years was lost. Everything was buried in a pile of rubble. Thankfully, none of the children or adults were harmed.

Today, the Mission is being rebuilt, and Enoch lives part-time in Haiti and the U.S. Wonderfully, the work that began one scary day in Jerusalem and later on a flight out of Tel Aviv, had served long and well. On that historic flight when the Lord said, "What do you think of those who cannot pack their bags and run?!," He began a monumental and permanent work. Enoch has remained the Mission's Pastor-Overseer since the day we met, and now, more than forty years later, he and I are still devoted brothers.

One of the young men who took part in the Haiti Mission, Pat McCoy, has since become both an American pastor and successful Missionary in the Ukraine. Pat went with us on our trip to the Holy Land in 1966 and was ordained under my Primitive Baptist ministry.

Chapter 18

OUR NIGHT OF
FAMILY DARKNESS FALLS

From 1949 to 1977, I enjoyed a successful ministry and remained contented in my denomination. I was editor of the denominational magazine, wrote Bible Study literature, served as Chairman of the Ministers Schools, assisted with the annual Bible Conference, and other areas of need. That changed. The visions, unusual blessings in preaching, and joyous church-life of my youth, slowly disappeared. I knew this was happening, but I did not realize I was moving from spirituality to religion. Nor did I have the wisdom or solution to make the correction. It was in the midst of my concern for our dying churches and my own declining ministry that Laurie and I plunged into a "dark night of the soul."

In August 1977, Laurie was invited to go to lunch with several of her close friends at church. The car in which she was riding was hit by a speeding truck, and they were slammed into a telephone pole. She received all the crushing impact, leaving her with thirteen broken bones, a collapsed lung, a concussion of the brain, and so many injuries she could not be safely removed from the vehicle. At the time of the wreck, I was several hundred miles from home and knew nothing about the accident. We had no cell phones in that day. I had just concluded the funeral of a dear friend, Marian Agan, the wife of my favorite pastor, Virgil Agan, and at that moment was standing near her grave. Everyone turned away, and I had a private moment alone. Raising my wrist, I looked at my watch; it was 12:00 noon. Strangely, my mind "photographed" that setting on the dial. The effect was powerful—so much so—that now, many years later, I can still see that 12:00 on my watch.

Grabbing a quick bite of food, I returned to Atlanta. Stepping into our empty house that night, I found a note on the living room floor. Cecile had written, "Mama was in a little accident today. They are keeping her in the hospital overnight, so come, but don't hurry." The language was purposely deceptive; if she had told me the truth, I might have panicked. When I entered Laurie's room, I discovered how gravely she was injured. It was doubtful she would live. I stood there, staring at her, unable to move or speak. The accident had occurred at 12:00 noon, the same moment my memory "photographed" the setting on the dial. That day Laurie and I descended into a darkness that defies description. All the lights in our lives went out.

Standing there at her hospital bed, my confusion became overwhelming, and my feelings flashed from anger to grief, grief to anger, and back again. I was bewildered—absolutely numb. My mind was paralyzed with fear. She had already been in a frail emotional state as she suffered with Depression. Sometimes it was severe. Now her frailty had been overwhelmed with a broken body and a future of incredible suffering. Turning away from the bed I walked back to the corridor, fell against the wall and gripped my face in my hands. My insides were screaming. Praying seemed futile. I was angry at God, at the truck driver, at my own sense of helplessness, and everything around us.

Later, I called Laurie's aunt on the hall telephone to tell her what had happened, but she interrupted me to say, "Charles, God is going to bring something good out of this ...." I cut her off and was so angered at her statement, that I wanted to jerk the telephone off the wall and smash it on the floor. If God cared–or had any capacity to care–He would have done something before the tragedy. It was too late now to look to Him for help. Physically, I felt helpless; emotionally, I felt abandoned, and spiritually, I felt betrayed.

For years I had read about pastors going through such agony, but I had never imagined how horrendous it was–or that it would ever happen to me. There were two distinct aspects to my darkness: It was physical and spiritual. The spiritual aspect was that for a month before the accident happened, I had a terrifying premonition that such a tragedy was going to occur. It was stalking my wife. Seemingly, it waited for an opportune moment to seize her. I wrongly blamed God for the threat and frantically begged Him to spare us. With my background of fatalistic-Calvinism, I thought He was the threat; I wept, fasted, but nothing seemed to penetrate what I assumed was His emotionless sovereignty.

Little did I realize that I had probably "opened the door" to that horrendous calamity by bringing home several voodoo masks from my most recent trip to Haiti, one month prior to Laurie's accident. At that time, I had no knowledge or teaching about the real dangers of owning objects, such as voodoo masks, that had been used in satanic rituals. I thought they were just a unique novelty, with no danger attached; however, it was right after I brought the voodoo masks home and mounted them on the wall of our stairwell to the basement when I began having "premonitions" of an evil attack against Laurie's life. As it was, I was plagued for a month by the knowledge that something horrible was going to happen to Laurie; however, I did not know what to do about it. When I looked at my watch that day at Marian's funeral, I knew it was a significant moment.

Cecile had already graduated from the University of Georgia and had moved back home. She was devastated but not as profoundly as I was. She had had a genuine encounter with the Lord while she was still in college through Josh MacDowell's ministry, and the Holy Spirit's work in her was a source of great strength. Yet sadly, Laurie's life hung by a thread. Two nights after the accident, her right lung collapsed suddenly, and there was no time to get her to the operating table. The inflation had to be done in her hospital room. She survived by seconds, but a few days later, still in that terrible state, a church friend visited her bedside and said, "Laurie, God could have prevented this if He had wanted to." That statement–destructive as it was, fitted perfectly with our theology.

Doctrinally, our view of God's sovereignty affirmed that He was answerable to no one; He could kill, maim, destroy, and violate His own Covenant if He wished. He did not protect Laurie because He did not want to: On hearing the woman's statement, Laurie's last flicker of hope went out. Why–she wondered–should she pray now asking Him for mercy, when He had already shown what He thought of her? Unknown to me, she quit praying and abandoned all hope. In her mind, God had no more mercy for her, than He did for Judas Iscariot. In effect, He had turned His back on her.

We were both under spiritual attack: During that time, I thought I heard a voice mocking me. It was bizarre. My first reaction was that I was losing my mind. Then the voice became specific, saying: "You knew this was going to happen!" It said, "You even knew the exact moment it happened. You were looking at your watch. But you were powerless to stop it!" Nothing in my theological training, or years of ministry, had prepared me for anything as bizarre as this. While I knew the voice was real, it was too unbelievable to share with anybody. I considered myself a sincere student of Scripture, but I had avoided preaching about demons and their activity in the Bible. Those verses made me uncomfortable. My remedy for church members' strange behavior was secular therapy. Jesus's statement, "I give you power to tread on serpents and scorpions and over all the power of the enemy" had never been part of my belief-system (Luke 10:19). Denominationally, we did not need those Scriptures, any more than we needed the spiritual gifts listed in First Corinthians 12.

Of one thing I was certain: My pastor-friends did not have the answer I needed, nor did I know anyone who did. At night I could not sleep and longed for the daylight. In the day, the feeling reversed, and I longed for the night (Deuteronomy 28:67). Cecile and Laurie both needed me, but I no longer needed myself. Suicide suddenly became very appealing. With that death-plot hidden deeply in my mind, my world got incredibly black.

Forty days after the accident, Laurie was discharged from the hospital; but she could not lift herself from the bed and was confined to a wheelchair. With her constant battling pain, I could not tell her about the hellish depression that was gaining control of me. Nor did I ask any of my brother-pastors about the strange spiritual experience that preceded the wreck. Theologically, they knew what I knew. I knew what they knew, and I knew we didn't know. Overwhelmed by that ignorance, I felt abandoned, worthless, helpless. I tried to resist the idea of suicide, but it became an inescapable bear that pursued me constantly.

During that time, I came out of a Sears Department Store building and unknowingly stepped into the path of a speeding truck. In that split-second, someone grabbed my collar from behind and snatched me out of its path. If it had been one instant later, I would have been killed. I was astounded that someone behind me saw the danger when I could not. As I caught my breath, I turned to speak to the person, but no one was there. I looked around. The area was empty. For the moment I was angry at being rescued; this would have been an ideal escape from my pain.

The anguish increased, and one afternoon when I could endure it no longer, I drove out the Stone Mountain Freeway, floorboarded the accelerator, took both hands off the wheel and screamed at God, "What are You going to do about it?!" Bridge abutments, concrete posts, traffic, flashed past me. Only God could have saved me—and did; how I do not know. My only consciousness of that terrorizing event is being back in my driveway, staring at the hood of my car—angry that I was still alive.

Without telling Laurie, I consulted the hospital psychiatrist who prescribed medication. Instead of helping, it made me severely worse. At my request, he changed the prescription, and I hurried back to the pharmacist who had filled the original one. He was on a raised platform where he could look down at me. When I told him why I was unable to take the original prescription, he paused, cupped his hands together on the counter, leaned forward, staring intently at me. After a pause, he said in a warning voice. "This is the same stuff you've been taking–only its twice as strong!"

"Don't fill it!" I snapped, staring at him in unbelief. Hesitating a moment, I walked away. Medication was the only hope I had, and I felt betrayed by the doctor. The pill would have put me in a worse psychiatric trauma. That night I lay awake, staring into the dark, saying, "God, if You don't kill me, I am going to do it for you!" Two hours later I was still awake. Then it was three hours. Four hours passed. Sometime later, for what seemed like a few tumultuous minutes, I collapsed into sleep with my fists clenched. A month passed with no change.

One of my escapes was to take long walks in a heavily wooded area near our house. My favorite spot was a deep, forested ravine where I could find easy places to hide. But even this site lost its appeal. One morning I went a different direction, walking along a busy thoroughfare near Agnes Scott College. With no forewarning, the Lord abruptly announced, "Here in the city of Atlanta you will meet your 'Ananias.'" I was shocked, and stopped on the sidewalk: The message was puzzling. What did it mean? "Me, Ananias?" Saul of Tarsus was blind; I was not. Why would I need an "Ananias?" Whatever he might do would be no help to me. Perplexed by the message, I kept walking.

My religious-bias prevented my understanding of God's announcement. It never occurred to me that, like Saul, I needed to be "filled with the Holy Spirit." Such an idea had never entered my Baptist-brain. But neither could I shake Ananias from my thoughts. Nor could I hide from the terrifying mental despair that was intensifying inside me. Regardless of whose aid I might have sought, I was not wanting sympathy. My only desire was to get off the planet. If God did not do it for me, I would show Him how. Ananias made no difference to me. With that thought hidden deeply in my mind, my world grew darker.

An Unexpected Revelation Prepares Me for the Future

Near that time the Holy Spirit began bringing old lessons back to mind. These included events where I had failed to receive His instruction in the past. One of my favorite places was Lookout Mountain in northwest Georgia. Two years before, I had been on the mountain on a bright October morning when maple trees were in their full glory. That day I parked near the western bluff and was standing where I had a hundred-mile view of the valley and the Cumberland Plateau in the distance. The scene was magnificent, but what really captured my mind were the beautiful maple leaves in my hand. The pink, red, and gold, seemed to be alive, pulsating with color and vitality. There was no deadness about them.

I had learned a few days earlier that these beautiful colors had been present in the leaves all summer long. That fact amazed me. Although the red and gold are not visible in the summer, they are still there. During hot-weather the green chlorophyll overpowers them. When shorter days and cooler nights begin, the chlorophyll fades, and the more beautiful colors appear. In that instant, I understood what Paul meant when he said: "There is a natural body and there is a spiritual body" (1 Corinthians 15:44). Like the leaves, I had two identities: Summer green and Autumn gold. The green represented my visible body and natural life; the gold represented my spiritual person or "hidden man of the heart" (1 Peter 3:4). The outer man had the power to obscure the spiritual man the same way the green obscured the gold.

While standing there on the bluff, the Holy Spirit spoke to me in a very short but commanding voice: "Charles," He said, "Your green has got to go!" I was stymied. The Voice was very kind but very strong: "Your green has got to go!" What did it mean?! What about me was 'green?'" The maple leaves were still clutched in my hand. A few minutes later I dropped them and walked away. I didn't understand. The real truth was I did not want to face the challenge.

Then came another test: During my early pastorate in Atlanta, I read about a local family who owned an antique European mirror. For years, it hung above their mantle, until the frame came apart; and they took it to a shop for repair. To everyone's shock, the repairman discovered a valuable painting by the famous French artist, Jean Baptiste Corot, hidden behind the glass. At some time in the past, probably during the war, the painting had been concealed to protect it from thieves. When the original owners died, the mirror was sold, and knowledge of the painting was lost. It would have remained unknown forever had not the frame come apart.

At the time I read the story, I was strangely moved. "Charles," I sensed the Holy Spirit saying, "You read my Word like those people looked in their mirror. They saw only an eighth of an inch of glass—nothing more. It wasn't until the frame came apart that they discovered the lost work of art." He was saying to me, "You study my Word the same way those people looked in their mirror. They never discovered what was behind the glass until the frame was broken. You read to learn doctrine. I want you to see beyond doctrine and discover Me." Did that rebuke–stern as it was–open my eyes to deeper truths in Scripture? No.

At that time, I was religiously-devoted to denominational-dogma and did not know how to implement the change ––at least, I claimed not to know. Like many other pastors, I would not yield until tragedy tore my frame apart. While I realize God did not cause the wreck, I also know He can "make all things work together for my good." That included the wreck (Romans 8:28). More than I understood, He wanted me to see beyond doctrine and into the glory of eternal-truth (Luke 24:31). I had refused. At that point, I still did not understand what He meant by saying, "Your green has got to go …" and the message of the art hidden behind the glass.

PART TWO OF
THE MIAMI VISION BEGINS

Chapter 19

ATLANTA FEDERAL
PENITENTIARY:
I MEET MY ANANIAS

Not long after that, one of my church members dropped in for early morning coffee. Sitting at the kitchen table, he said, "Charles, I teach at the Atlanta Federal Penitentiary and have a young prisoner in my class I would like you to meet. He's a Christian ...." "I'll go tomorrow!" I interrupted him. He looked surprised at my immediate response but did not realize how eager I was for diversion from my pain. If I were around other hurting men, perhaps it would help me. The next morning, I arrived promptly at the Penitentiary. First, I met my church friend, the Chaplain, who introduced me to "Tom," the special prisoner.

I quickly realized this stranger was the most authentic Christian I had ever met. In that dismal, oppressive place, he seemed unaffected by the spiritual darkness that permeated it. There was a calmness and serenity about him that I had never seen before. My most devout Christian friends did not have the inner light he displayed. Somehow, he was unaffected by the prison life that swirled about him. Quietly, Tom told his story. He had grown up in a gangster family, was a convicted felon, a hopeless addict, a failure, and was sent to the Federal Penitentiary at Fort Leavenworth, Kansas. There, with drugs smuggled from the outside, he was committing suicide and had enough heroin in the syringe to kill four men. The needle was in his arm, and he was ready to shove it in when Jesus stopped him.

Clearly, Tom heard Him say: "I died that you might live. It isn't necessary that you die also. Trust Me!"

Tom was speechless—overcome by what he heard. His moment of truth had come: He could end his life or trust God to redeem it. For a moment he hesitated. Something inside shouted, "Shove it in!" The other Voice said, "Trust Me!" Suddenly, he jerked the needle out, threw it to the floor—and was instantly born-again. Not only so, but he was delivered from addiction and suicide. In that awesome moment, the Holy Spirit flooded into him. That happened one year before we met, and in the interim, he had read the Bible through, saturating himself with Scripture. His testimony astonished me—and I knew every word of it was true—even the part about his being "filled with the Holy Spirit." Theologically, I knew nothing about this experience—but I dared not deny it.

That day I officially became Tom's Chaplin, and I had the privilege to visit him as often as I wished. In a short time, we bonded on a deep level. Spiritually, he excelled everyone I have ever known. A week passed before I returned to the prison, checked in, and waited for admission. Huge as the Penitentiary was and with no way for him to see out its massive walls he was waiting for me. Two huge electric doors, ten feet apart with sentries to inspect me, had to be entered. That day as I went through the second electric gate and passed Tom's cell-block I saw his face pressed against the bars. I was shocked. "Tom!" I exclaimed, "What are you doing here? They have not called your name!"

"Charles!," He laughed, "I'm waiting on you! The Holy Spirit told me when you came in the parking lot!" As an old-line Baptist, I had no training for experiences like this and was mystified by his behavior. Later, he read First Corinthians 12:8, to me, explaining that the Bible called such information a "word of knowledge" and that every Christian should experience this miraculous gift. My mind immediately went back to the message I received nearly thirty years before when I knew a month in advance that I would preach my opening-sermon on Easter Sunday. That was my first "word of knowledge," but I did not know to call it by that name (1 Corinthians 12:8). Slowly, I began to remember other times the "word" came to me. How sad, I thought, that I spent all those years being taught nothing about the Holy Spirit's miraculous gifts.

Time passed, and we visited often. If he were working in the yard when I arrived, it would require another hour for him to shower before getting to the Visitor's Room. One day when he was working in fresh cement in the yard, he stopped abruptly and said to the guard, "I have a visitor coming. May I go to the shower and clean up?" The guard replied, "They haven't called you, Tom …" "No," he explained, "but they soon will, and it will take me a long time to get clean." The guard gave him permission, and he was in the shower when they summoned him to the Visitor's Room.

I was magnetized to Tom, desperately wanting what he had; and I knew that my freedom could be gained only in the same miraculous way he had gained his. But, I was also afraid of him. He relied on Scriptures about the Holy Spirit which my denomination denied, and he experienced other spiritual "gifts" which we claimed no longer existed. I desperately needed his wonderful wisdom but did not want to change my theology to get it. Only one thing was certain: I could not continue to live as I was.

May 3, 1978, was a day I will remember forever: While I waited in the Visitor's Room, I randomly opened the Bible and read Psalms 35:1-3: "Plead my cause, O Lord, with those who strive with me; Fight against those who fight against me. Take hold of shield and buckler, And stand up for my help. Also, draw out the spear, And stop those who pursue me. Say to my soul, 'I am your salvation.'" Reading the passage, it helped me believe that God would someday rescue me from the depression that stalked me. A moment later I closed the Bible and pushed it to a corner of the table. Tom soon joined me, opened to the same Psalm I had read and said, "Charles, God wants you to hear this!" He then emphasized the same Scriptures and preached an encouraging message about my future. I was overwhelmed—even though my depression remained unchanged. Why he chose the same Scripture I had just read was beyond my explanation.

The next week when I returned to the prison I was still puzzling over the incident. As I waited, I read Matthew 10:1-2: "When Jesus had called His twelve disciples to Him, He gave them power over unclean spirits, to cast them out, and to heal all kinds of sickness and all kinds of disease." Unknown to me, this passage revealed the final half of my ministry as the Miami Vision had foretold. Suddenly, I closed the Bible. "Lord," I said, "Last week Tom read the same passage back to me that I had just read. Was that coincidence or was that You? If that were You, do it again!" With that, I closed the Bible and pushed it away.

A short time later, Tom dropped into his chair, took the Bible and immediately began reading Matthew 10 aloud. His voice was emphatic,

"Charles, God wants you to hear this! He is describing your future ministry! Benefit by it!" I could hardly hear what he said for astonishment at what God had done. This seems strange, but something in my mind fought desperately to keep me stoic, unmoved by the experience. I was not interested in the future; I wanted God's help immediately. If He really cared about me, He would do something helpful now. I needed more than entertainment.

Later that day, when I left the Penitentiary, my brain was still grappling with what had happened. Outside, on the prison steps, I stopped abruptly, changed my attitude, and said. "Lord, I am grateful for these little evidences of your speaking through Tom. But I want a big one!" For a moment I waited, my mind searching for something suitable. "Next week when I come back," I said, "I want Tom to tell me that all week long he has been studying the 'Book of Joshua' and Lord, I want him to read to me from the first of the book." With that said, I hurried to my car and left the prison.

When I returned the following week, I never opened the Bible. Nor would I let my mind think about Joshua. Tom soon rushed in, and without sitting down reached over my shoulder, picked up the Bible. "Charles," he said, "all week long God has had me in the Book of Joshua for you!" I held my breath. "Hear what He says to you!" He then read aloud from chapters one and three: "Only be strong and very courageous … Have I not commanded you? Be strong and of good courage; do not be afraid, nor be dismayed for the Lord your God is with you wherever you go" (Joshua 1:6:9). I closed my eyes, bowed my head in astonishment. In the background–I could hear God saying, "Do you need more proof? I am speaking to you through this man! Hear what he has to say! Believe him! He has your answer!"

One would think that such miraculous signs would have blasted me free from my religious stronghold, but they did not. A huge, monster-sized opposition dominated me from within. I desperately wanted the "new wine" of the Spirit, but I wanted to keep it in my "old wineskin" (Matthew 9:17). Too, I knew if I ever experienced what Tom had, I would lose my church, my home, my income, my friends, and everything I had worked thirty years to achieve. My loss would be huge. But if I rejected it, there was no other solution to my crisis. One thing was certain; I could not continue to live as I was.

The spiritual gift that terrified me most was the gift of tongues. I wanted nothing to do with it. It was undignified. Worse still, it seemed senseless and strange. I even told God that He should have left tongues out of the Bible. "More people would have believed the New Testament," I reprimanded Him, "if You had not included the gift of tongues at Pentecost. People don't like it!" When I shared my opinion with Tom, he looked me straight in the eye and said, "Charles, you hate the gift of tongues because it is already doing its work in you. This is the only gift that exposes your pride, your egotism, and your conceit; it is for that reason, religious people hate 'tongues.'" I stared at him; he was right on every point, and I knew it. He continued, "This offender-gift protects the other gifts. Unless you humble yourself to the embarrassment of tongues, the others will remain locked inside you forever."

I changed the subject, hoping to defend myself in a different way. "Tom," I said, "In New Testament-doctrine a person cannot get saved without the Holy Spirit! When you receive Him, your destiny needs nothing more. He is in you and remains! Jesus said, 'He will abide with you forever!'" Tom answered graciously, "Yes! But, the Holy Spirit's work in us is continuous—on-going—and we will not experience His final work until the Resurrection!" I wanted to argue but listened. "Jesus is our example," he said, "He was not only conceived by the Holy Spirit in the womb of the Virgin but 30 years later was anointed by the Holy Spirit. The first took place in Mary's womb; the second took place during His baptism in the Jordan. One could not replace the other." I agreed. "In His first sermon at Nazareth," Tom continued, "He specifically said, 'The Spirit of the Lord is upon Me because He has anointed Me …' (Luke 4:18). Conception by the Spirit equipped Him for the work of Redemption—Anointing equipped Him for public ministry (Luke 1:34,35; 4:16-18.). If Jesus needed two very definite works of the Holy Spirit, how can you say you don't? Like Jesus, we need both! We need to be born-again by the Spirit and anointed by Him for ministry!"

I wanted to interrupt but listened as Tom continued, "Scripture gives us five examples of people who experienced the Spirit's dual-works: Jesus was the first. The other four, in the Book of Acts, are of believers being born-again and later filled with the Spirit." He went on. "The first example is the original disciples. Jesus came to them the night of the Resurrection, breathed into them and said, 'Receive the Holy Spirit' (John 20:22). Until then they were 'Old Testament Jews.' That day, they were "born again" and stepped into the New Covenant. Later, on the Day of Pentecost these same disciples were baptized in the Spirit (Acts 1:5-8; 2:4). This equipped them with the Spirit's miraculous gifts for world-evangelism (Matt. 28:18-20; I Corinthians 12). These two operations of the Spirit are not the same. Jesus did no miracle until the Spirit came upon Him at baptism." I listened intently, knowing he was speaking truth but becoming more fearful of the decision it forced on me.

Tom then gave other examples of people in the Book of Acts who received salvation and spiritual-baptism at separate times. He then challenged me to study them. They were: Saul of Tarsus, who was saved on the Damascus Road and filled with the Holy Spirit in the Damascus Room (Acts 9:1-6; 10-18); Cornelius, the Gentile Centurion, a believer on whom the Holy Spirit later fell (Acts 10:1,2; 44-46; 11:15,16); the disciples at Ephesus on whom Paul laid hands and were filled (Acts 19:1-6, Acts 1:5-8).

That week at home, I studied all the Scriptures carefully. One special day, I put down my Bible, sat staring into space and wondered how I could have spent so many years studying Scripture and failed to see this obvious truth. Tom was right! For years, I had missed this reality. Even so, the effect this could have on my future terrified me. Three days later I was back at the Penitentiary, eager to learn. Tom arrived quickly, we hugged, and prayed. Opening the Bible, he read from First Corinthians 12: "Now concerning spiritual gifts, brethren, I do not want you to be ignorant" (12:1). Tom looked at me, "Charles," he said, "this appeal that we 'be not ignorant' appears seven times in the King James New Testament; once by Peter, six times by Paul. In spite of that plea, there is no topic about which the modern church is more ignorant than of spiritual gifts.

Scripture talks about the operation of nine miraculous works of the Spirit. All are the direct result of the Spirit's baptism. Having said that, Paul seems to shout, "But if anyone is still ignorant, let him stay ignorant!" (14:38) In other words, he says, "After this careful explanation of spiritual gifts, if anyone refuses to learn, I have nothing more to say to him. Let him stay illiterate!" Tom looked at me, "Charles," he said, "As a pastor, what will you do about your ignorance of spiritual gifts?"

I agreed and realized the change had to take place in me: The Holy Spirit demanded my full, public endorsement of all Scripture—including spiritual gifts. That was a frightening confrontation. Admitting this is painful, but there were numerous Bible passages I had never included in my preaching. Though I believed them, knew they were true, they did not fit my denomination's belief-system, and it was easier to ignore them than confront them. As Calvinists, my group denied that the "gospel was the power of God unto salvation to everyone who believed." A person might live and die a Muslim, Hindu, atheist, or something else, never hearing the Name of Jesus Christ. If he were God's elect, he would be forcibly saved. At the same time, we insisted that First Corinthians Twelve through Fourteen were invalid. How blind! For me, that had to change.

If I said "No" to God, my peril would continue. If I said "Yes" to Him, my Ordination would be canceled, and no church would accept me. The question of "tongues" would be the firing pin. In that setting, I began praying for the Holy Spirit to fill me, but with one specific condition: I did not want to speak in tongues. Specifically, I would kneel in our empty bedroom, grip the cannonball foot board and say: "Lord, I want to be filled with the Holy Spirit. I need to be filled with the Holy Spirit! My only conditions are these: 'I do not want to speak in tongues, shout, or be spectacular.' With that understood, You may go ahead." I would wait expectantly, assuming God would eagerly comply. When there was no response, I prayed again. Still, nothing happened. It never occurred to me that I, myself, was the hindrance. Instead, I interpreted God's silence as being His rejection of me personally. He no longer cared if I lived or died.

Finally, on Wednesday before Thanksgiving Day, 1977, I went to the prison and found myself weeping uncontrollably. Suicidal depression had a stranglehold on me. My brain was in chaos. At least four times I went to the men's room to wash my face and blow my nose. It must have looked strange to others in the Visitors Room. The pastor in his dark suit, white shirt, and dressy tie was being consoled by the prisoner in government-olive-drab. I could feel the eyes of the mafia inmates and their gawdily dressed women staring at me. But it didn't matter. That day I was literally going over the falls and could feel my body getting sucked into the undertow.

Praying frantically, I begged God to rescue me, but there was no response. Without His deliverance, there was only one solution left for me: When I left the prison that day, I would crash my car into a bridge, kill myself, and stop the pain. No one would know it was suicide. With that decision made, I dropped my face onto the table and broke into deep, deep groaning. I wanted to live, someday see my grandchildren, care for my invalid wife, but my pain was beyond words and hopelessness beyond help. Conversations at other tables hushed and—except for me——the Visitors Room became deathly quiet. It was a strange scene: Something vital, life-changing, was finally happening inside me: Self-will, religious pride, ego, was gasping and dying.

The next moment, I felt Tom's hand resting gently on my head and heard him quoting Ananias' words to Saul of Tarsus: "Brother Charles," he said, "The Lord Jesus who appeared to you on the road as you came has sent me that you may receive your sight and be filled with the Holy Spirit" (Acts 9:17). Surrounded by Mafia godfathers, felons, mobsters, the gangster world's most notorious criminals, and hardened prison guards, the Atlanta Federal Penitentiary became my "House on the street called Straight" (Acts 9:17). Unknown to me, the final half of the Miami Vision that appeared that early morning in 1948, had begun.

Still in pain, I went home, dropped across the bed as a dying man, and prayed the most historic prayer of my life. My exact words were "Lord, I can't go on. If You're ever going to help me, it has to be now! Next week, next month, a year from now will be too late!" What happened next cannot be described in human terms: The Holy Spirit fell on me (Acts 11:15). God's presence literally flooded the room. A tangible glory covered me. Demons of depression and suicide were jerked out of me like the roots of a giant oak. I felt them go. Then consciously, I felt myself being filled with the Holy Spirit. It was as if I stood under Niagara Falls and all the water of that huge cataract was pouring into me. At the same time, my body was caressed more lovingly than my mother had cuddled me the day I was born. All depression was gone forever. There, on the bed:

"I bathed my weary soul
In seas of heavenly rest
And not a wave of trouble rolled
Across my peaceful breast."

For a long while, I lay motionless—absolutely still—in shocked unbelief that such a God-encounter could happen to me. It was beyond all my theological knowledge. I remained unmoving, staring at the ceiling, not wanting to disturb the Holy Presence. When I finally rose from the bed, I discovered that all depression, despair, suicidal thoughts, were totally gone—never to return. My mind was free as a soaring-bird, and my spirit was singing the Lord's "new song" (Psalm 40:3). The best description I can give is in Charles Wesley's old hymn. He said:

> *"Long my imprisoned spirit lay*
> *Fast bound in sin and nature's night,*
> *Thine eye diffused a quickening ray,*
> *I woke, the dungeon flamed with light.*
> *My chains fell off, my heart was free,*
> *I rose, went forth, and followed Thee!"*

To my utter amazement, two things had happened: I experienced an exorcism from a demon of depression and was "baptized" in the Holy Spirit (Acts 1:8; 2:4; 8:14-17; 9:17; 10:44,45; 19:1-6). The impact was so life-changing, so powerful, that for two years I never picked up a newspaper, watched TV, sang a secular song, or did many other customary things. My new-found love for Jesus was so great I would not allow anything to distract my mind and heart from Him. This required no discipline and no effort on my part. Instead, like a flowing stream, it was the most natural, peaceful era I had ever experienced. Some attitudes in me disappeared completely, never to return, and certain denominational errors that had blinded me from my youth vanished. For the first time, I saw the Kingdom of God in its Glory and the Church in her beautiful but subordinate role. This was a radical change. Previously, I had no concept of the Kingdom. All my focus was on the denominational church. Now, I saw the Church as the "Bride!" She was Glorious, Magnificent, Grand! Best of all, She, was Universal, Heavenly, Flawless. My sleepless nights were gone forever! Unknown at that moment, my ministry would soon impart authentic, Holy Spirit power and see thousands impacted by it. A new world lay before me.

Chapter 20

THE HOLY SPIRIT BEGINS DRAMATIC CHANGE IN ME

Six weeks later, January 13, 1978, around 3:00 a.m., I was asleep, dreaming that I was reclining on an outdoor porch with my left arm resting on the banister. Suddenly, the dream changed to a vision, and an incredibly beautiful dove, white and glistening, flew from behind my head and suspended Himself above my wrist. The feathers, beak, and every detail of its body were as distinct as if a jeweler had etched them in porcelain. He shimmered with indescribable brilliance. I remember saying, "Isn't that amazing! That dove is not afraid of me!" Instantly, he landed on my wrist and turned into a sunburst of blinding, silvery light. When that happened, my body was electrocuted. Seemingly, ten million volts of power hit me. My only conscious thought was that I was dead. When the Light stopped, the dove was gone, I awoke, but my body was still vibrating from the jolt. Nothing in my past, experientially or theologically, prepared me for such an encounter with God. Finally, I shared it with Tom, who fully believed me and rejoiced in it. After that, I kept it secret for years; it was too sacred, too unbelievable, to tell anyone.

In the months that followed, our relationship deepened. I was his only contact with the outside world, and he was my only contact with the spiritual world. We eagerly looked forward to the future when we would be traveling and ministering together. With that thought in mind, I hurried to the Penitentiary one morning, and we sat at our table in the Visitors Room, laughing, talking excitedly about our future. Suddenly, the Holy Spirit spoke an identical message to both of us. We stared wide-eyed at each other. I knew what Tom heard; he knew what I heard. In a commanding way, the Holy Spirit said, *"Tell each other goodbye!"* I stared at Tom; he stared back at me. With no more conversation, we rose, stepped away from the table, hugged, said goodbye, and in separate directions walked out of the room. I headed to the visitor's door and never looked back. I couldn't. Behind me, I heard a heavy metal gate slam shut behind him. That was the end of our contact. Getting in my car, I drove away and never returned. The year was 1978, and it was a long time before I was reconciled to the loss of my best friend.

In another way, however, the Holy Spirit's ministry through Tom would continue: The power God released through his hands to me would soon be released through my hands to others. Since that incredible day at the Penitentiary, God's gift has been passed to thousands more around the world. From Russia to Argentina, Africa to Alaska, Kazakhstan to Canada, wherever God has sent me, Tom has always been in the background. The parallel was similar to Elijah's bestowing his anointing on younger Elisha—except in our case, the younger ministered to the older (Titus 2:2-4). Probably, this is what the Apostle Paul had in mind when he wrote the Romans, "I long to see you, that I may impart to you some spiritual gift, so that you may be established" (1:11). Paul's impartation was not mere instruction which he could have included in the letter. He had to be present for the gifting to take place. However, it is explained, I only know that when Ananias finally stepped into my dark night and laid–hands on me, I received an impartation that was undiminished forty years later. Jesus said, "He who believes into Me, out of his belly will flow rivers of living water;" I experienced both the inflow for myself and the outflow for others (John 7: 37,38).

Crisis In The Atlanta Church—I Shout

The first instruction the Holy Spirit gave after my spiritual renewal was to resign the church. I obeyed, waiting until the Christmas holidays were passed and then informed the congregation that I was not available for recall. I would keep my commitment to stay with them until summer. Immediately, I began preaching about the Holy Spirit in every sermon, and the congregation happily received what I taught. Two Sunday nights later, my topic was a continuation of the Spirit's personal work in us; the message was good, anointed, and special guests had come that night to hear me. Afterward, they were planning to take Laurie and me to dinner. When the sermon ended, and the final prayer said, I went to the front door to speak to the people as they left. For a moment I stood there alone, and then two men approached me, held out their hands, and I reached toward them. But we never touched:

Suddenly, I shouted at the top of my lungs, "We need God! We need God! We need God!" The building almost shook. The voice had the power of a freight-train and rattled the windows. It was not mine. The volume was not possible for me. The men paled, jaws dropped, and they turned and ran. I watched the entire congregation rushing out the rear door, with my wife and the special guests among them. Instantly, I lost all sense of weight or gravity, and my body felt like it was swirling into another dimension. I grabbed the tract-rack and held on. To me, it was a fearful moment, one out of my control. Thankfully, someone's arms wrapped around me, holding me up. Without him, I would have dropped to the floor. Had that happened, the deacons would have called 911.

When I finally looked to see who was gripping me, it was the same man who had repeatedly tried to get me to attend meetings of the Full Gospel Business Men's Fellowship. I had refused him persistently because I knew the Full-Gospel people were crazy. They shouted, spoke in tongues, and fell to the floor. Significantly, he was the only one in the room who understood my shouting was a "God" event. He was still gripping me when I suddenly felt normal again. It was very strange. I was not out of breath; my heart was not racing, and there was no after-effect of what happened. It seemed as if it had not occurred.

Though humiliated beyond description, Laurie and I went to dinner with our friends, but I could hardly face them as we ate. And inwardly, I was angry at God. When we got home, I yelled at Him, "I told You I did not want to shout! –People now think I'm crazy!" I also knew at that moment every church member was on the phone talking about my strange behavior. Their explanation for the shouting was that the emotional strain from Laurie's wreck was finally pushing me into a nervous breakdown. Most everyone was glad I had resigned the church and spared them the pain of firing me. Though angry at Him, I knew the shouting was God's way of exposing my ego and pride; I had specifically told him, "I don't want to shout …." Now I feared He would also deal with my having said, "I don't want to speak in tongues or be spectacular." That was another scary thought.

Time passed, and in spite of my horrendous outburst, church members recognized good changes in me. Many began asking questions. One young man grabbed my hand and said, "You've changed! I want what you've got!" This was especially true of some twenty members who could no longer remain in the denominational lock-up. They began meeting weekly for prayer. While they were sympathetic with me, there were others who detected a charismatic-element in my sermons that they rigorously opposed. Serious antagonism began arising, and one man who wanted to destroy my credibility was plotting irreparable harm. I realized he was capable of bringing great damage to me personally and the Kingdom publicly.

In the emergency, I went to the wooded ravine near our house to pray. No sooner had I climbed down the slope than I heard the name "Ahithophel!" shouted in my ear. There was no mistaking the name, but I had no knowledge of reading it in the Scripture. It was totally unknown to me. Scrambling out of the ravine I ran all the way home saying "Ahithophel, Ahithophel, Ahithophel." I was afraid I would forget it. When I rushed in the house, read the Scripture, I was shocked: Ahithophel attempted but failed to overthrow King David (2 Samuel 17:14). God was saying that my attacker was another Ahithophel who would fail. But the Scripture had more to tell: "Ahithophel … hanged himself and died" (2 Samuel 17:23). From that point on, I knew God would defend me. Unfortunately, the man who plotted my defeat—though youthful—was soon dead of natural causes.

In the months that followed, the church functioned without crisis. I made a final study-tour to Western Turkey, retracing the missionary journeys of Paul and visiting sites of the Seven Churches of Asia (Revelation 1:4). This was a cruise-ship event, and our last stop was the ruins at Ephesus, Turkey. We were trying to get ashore at Dikili but were handicapped by a storm at sea. Waves were high, there was no gang-plank, and passengers boarding the tenders had to step directly from one boat to the other.

This was hazardous as the two vessels rose and fell independently of each other. When my turn came, I miscalculated the step and fell about three feet, landing on my knees with my elbows in another man's lap. I was not harmed, and we both laughed. When I learned he was an American, I asked which state he was from. "Georgia," he answered. "I live in Georgia too!" I replied in amazement. "Where in Georgia?" "Atlanta," he continued. "I'm from Atlanta!" I half-shouted. "Where do you work in Atlanta?" I asked. "I'm a pastor ...."

By this time, I could hardly believe my ears. "I'm a pastor too," I answered, "Where is your church?" He was in the process of answering, "My church is at Ponce de Leon Avenue and Oakdale Road ...," when I interrupted. "My church is on Ponce de Leon Avenue and Oakdale Road!" I shouted.

There were only two churches at that intersection—mine and a Lutheran congregation. He continued, "I am pastor at the Lutheran Church at that intersection." I was aghast! My office was on the second floor, and every day I looked out the window at his handsome granite building.

When we both recovered from the shock, he said to me, "I think the Lord wants you to know that no matter where you go—anywhere in the world—He can have someone there to help you." And he was right. The Holy Spirit is our "paraclete," the One who travels beside us to give guidance and direction. Thank God! The pastor's advice was well-timed, and he had no way of knowing that in the following months Laurie and I would desperately need that assurance.

In mid-summer, I preached my final sermon to the congregation, emptied my office, and drove away. Cecile quickly established herself at First Baptist, Atlanta, sharing an apartment with a girlfriend and pursuing her career in music. The adjustment was harder for me than Laurie. We moved into a low-rent apartment near the Emory University campus, had a small savings but no income. No denominational church would invite me to preach. Every door was tightly closed. The prayer-group helped sustain us and a church member allowed us to store our furniture in his empty warehouse. Two weeks later he called to tell us all of it had been stolen.

My denominational pastor-friends disappeared. Word quickly spread about my heretical "baptism" in the Spirit and numerous falsehoods began circulating. One of them was that I believed the Bible was still being written; another insisted I had lost my mind. Overnight I found myself abandoned. Where I had been an appreciated minister, editor of the denominational magazine, writer for its Bible Study literature, and had served on numerous committees, I was instantly ostracized. Laurie and I faced fierce and total rejection. On our first Sunday without a special church to attend, we wandered aimlessly about Atlanta trying to decide where to worship and what to do with ourselves. We felt purposeless, ate an early lunch and went back to our apartment, sat in chairs staring at each other.

We liked our apartment, except for one major problem: The woman across the hall, "Betty," was a prostitute-bartender in a topless Go-Go Bar, who ran advertisements in the newspaper for overnight "guests." Her cursing and violent outbursts were the foulest I had ever heard. The woman terrified me on our first meeting. She winked at me and said, "… I sleep with my doors open!" After that, I avoided her as much as possible and would not use either door without peeking out first. If she were outside, I waited, then ran to my car. Even so, avoiding her was difficult. At times, she lured yard-men off their mowers and into her apartment. I was more afraid of her than Elijah was of Jezebel.

Early one morning, I was up at 5:00 a.m. praying, when the Lord suddenly interrupted my prayer and said, "Witness to Betty!" I held my breath! His word, unmistakably clear, was not a request but a command. She was the last person to whom I dared speak about the Lord. I hesitated, then replied, "I will Lord if You prepare the way, but only if You prepare the way!" I was not going to approach her without God's specific help. Beginning that morning, I prayed earnestly about witnessing to her.

Laurie and I had no special church at that time but were attending First Baptist, Atlanta. We were especially eager to hear Dr. Leonard Ravenhill, the English Evangelist who was preaching there nightly. Laurie was recovering well from the accident and had joined the choir. That day she left early for rehearsal. I stayed indoors until late afternoon when I peeked out to see if Betty were inside. Unknown to me, she was standing on the steps, out of view, and when I closed the door, she heard the lock click. Spinning around she burst into tears, saying, "Will you please pray for me!" There was panic in her voice.

I was aghast! Never had I expected a prayer to be answered so quickly. "I have already prayed for you, Betty!" I answered. "When?" She half-shouted, "This morning I was praying for you at 5:00 a.m!" "That's the reason! That's the reason!" She broke into hard sobbing, "You don't know what God has been doing to me today! My life is a wreck! I need God!" Immediately, I explained Paul's instruction in Romans 10:8-11 about believing in her heart, confessing with her mouth, and being saved. Standing there on the steps, crying loudly, she believed, confessed, repented, and was saved. Within a minute, her voice, countenance, and appearance changed, and a totally new woman stood before me. The topless Go-Go bartender-prostitute had disappeared, and a new Jesus-disciple was in my presence. Everything about her seemed new. I was shocked at the transformation.

Strangely, God wasn't finished. He wanted her conversion to be as public as her prostitution. That night she went with me to First Baptist and heard one of the most shocking sermons ever preached in that huge building. Everyone was stunned. Dr. Ravenhill pretended to reach into the congregation, pick up a prostitute, hold her up to God and say, "You are going to look at God!

Look at Him! And He is going to look at you! Look at her God!" His words thundered and could not have been more explicit if he had been told who she was and where she sat.

I was next to the aisle, Laurie beside me, and Betty was on the other side of her. All I could see were her hands shaking frantically all the while Ravenhill preached. At the sermon's end when he gave an invitation for people to come forward for public confession, she shoved Laurie and me out of the way so hard that I was almost thrown into the aisle. At the front, she fell across the pulpit steps wailing loudly in repentance. Everyone in the building knew "This is the one God was speaking to."

Betty immediately quit her job at the bar, found respectable work, started tithing her income, and donated her free time to pushing wheelchairs at a nursing home. Her countenance changed! Everything that identified the old Betty was gone. The "mantle of darkness" I had seen on her in the past was no longer there. She had become a "new creature in Christ."

An interesting proof of her conversion came in a strange way. One day she got locked out of her apartment when she had a pie baking in the oven. Her only key was inside. In desperation, she tried to locate the building superintendent, but he could not be found. She called the office, but it was closed. Other employees in the area had no key. Finally, she sat calmly on the rear step as black, burning-pie smoke came under the back door and onto the step beside her. Not only was the pie ruined but the kitchen was covered with sticky-black soot. Betty, in her former days, would have kicked the blankety-blank door off its blankety-blank hinges and torn the place apart to get in. That never happened. For her, old things had passed away, and all things had become new. The part of Betty's story that amazes me most is that it began one morning at 5:00 A.M., when the Lord said, "Witness to Betty!"

Chapter 21

GOD COMMANDS:
"RETURN TO FLORIDA,"
MIRACLE BEGINS

Laurie and I learned to love our Atlanta apartment. Betty became a good neighbor, and we could have stayed there forever, but God had other plans. Cecile interviewed for a musical position at a Baptist Church in West Palm Beach, Florida, and Laurie and I went with her.

We visited my former pastorate, the Primitive Baptist Church in Delray Beach, and I preached for their Wednesday evening meeting. The congregation was eager for a fresh word from God. Holding nothing back, I shared my full testimony. I told about the prisoner in Atlanta's Federal Penitentiary who had "laid hands" on me to be filled with the Holy Spirit. I also shared how I was delivered from a demon of depression and how God had totally changed the direction of my ministry. No one challenged me doctrinally or objected to anything I said. They were open to Bible truth and listened intently.

Using Paul's treatise on spiritual gifts in First Corinthians 12,13, and 14 as an example of my failure, I explained how Scripture begins with the exhortation, "Concerning spiritual gifts brethren I would not have you to be ignorant." He then concludes the 84-verse instruction with the stern rebuke, "But if anyone is ignorant let him be ignorant," (12:1; 14:38). I confessed that I had not only been ignorant of spiritual gifts, but I had kept others ignorant with me. Tragically, I had refused to learn these vital truths. The church was very enthusiastic about the message, wanted to learn more, and asked if I would become their pastor again.

When our visit ended, Laurie, Cecile, and I returned to Atlanta. Cecile declined the music position in West Palm Beach and continued to teach music in private schools until 1981, when she became a flight attendant with Delta Airlines.

I accepted the invitation to return as pastor in Delray Beach. Back in Atlanta, Laurie learned about a "Charismatic" Christian event at Georgia's Rock Eagle Campground, and we attended one afternoon. She got out at the entrance, and I parked the car. When I stepped into the building, I was almost knocked back by a blast of music. Dozens of tambourines were in the air, and I saw a melee of hands raised in worship. People were dancing in the aisle. The sight was surreal, and I stepped back, fearful to go inside the building.

Finally, I went inside and saw Laurie on the back row, with both arms waving overhead. I froze in unbelief. "She's only been here five minutes!" I said to myself, "and has already become one of them!" I felt like I had lost my wife, but I pushed my way to her and was instantly enveloped by a "Presence" that isolated me from everything else around me. God was there. My only thought was of David's dancing wildly before the Lord (2 Samuel 6:14). The speaker who directed the meeting seemed very sane, very capable, and real. Everyone else was genuine, sincere, and I instantly felt safe in their midst.

The name of Derek Prince was mentioned a number of times in highest regard and admiration. Little did I know the enormous role this stranger would later play in my life. In the afternoon, I met Oliver and Joanne McEachern and went to their mobile home, where he prayed for me. As I knelt beside an ottoman, he started to pray. Then he began "prophesying" over me, saying flattering things about my future. I became very suspicious. He was too complimentary and too confident. According to him, God was going to use me mightily. I would meet great leaders, travel with them, preach to thousands with signs and wonders. Kneeling there, I said to myself, "I'll bet this Joker says that about everyone he prays for!"

Oliver concluded the prayer, and I started to get up, but to my terror, I could not move. My eyes would not open; I could not raise my arms, nor could I feel myself breathing. I was frozen to the ottoman like a piece of stone. Terror gripped me. After a moment the Lord spoke, quietly asking, "What was it you said about this "Joker?" I got the point, repented for scorning Oliver, and immediately I could move again. That was in 1978. Today, more than 40 years later, I have experienced every detail of which Oliver prophesied. What I thought was flattery, was the plan of God for my life. Derek Prince, whom I heard about that morning, would be the one who would impact my life and ministry in incredible ways.

After that prayer time, I was destined for another huge surprise that afternoon: I attended a "Group Deliverance" Ministry directed by Frank Hammond. For the first time, I saw others experiencing Deliverance exactly as it had happened to me in my bedroom. Little did I know that "Deliverance Ministry" would become a major feature of my new life and work.

That Autumn in 1978, we moved to Delray Beach, and I resumed the pastoral role at the Delray Beach Church. Moving back into our former house, it was like being home again. We loved it! This time, I emphasized to the congregation what our Articles of Faith claimed: "All Scripture is given by inspiration of God and is the only rule of faith and practice." I promised God and the people that I would never again ignore certain Scriptures because the denomination disapproved, nor would I support the claim that First Corinthians 12, 13, and 14 were invalid. Unknown to me, that decision would ultimately create a firestorm that would destroy my traditional ministry and push me into a totally new world.

Visit By Oliver McEachern

I was called away from Delray for a week. Upon returning, I found several of the church youth in crisis. Immediately I asked Oliver to come to our aid. He and Joanne came and ministered to the young people. Many were delivered from personal crisis, filled with the Holy Spirit, and radically transformed. He preached on Sunday with "signs and wonders" that both astonished and converted the congregation (I Corinthians 12,13,14). In Oliver's first service he laid hands on me. I crashed to the floor and was powerfully swept into a fresh God-encounter. When I fell, the congregation panicked and a Deacon jumped over two rows of pews to come to my rescue. I remember opening my eyes and seeing the faces of two young girls only inches away, staring at me in terror, and screeching loudly. They thought I was dead. Oliver assured everyone that I was OK. He explained that this was a "God-event." Oliver later gave the invitation for others to receive prayer ministry and many responded.

Probably twenty people were laid out, resting in the Lord's Presence that first night as the Holy Spirit flooded into them. Shocking? Yes. Alarming to Calvinistic-Baptists? Definitely! Was it real? Absolutely! Unknown to us, that "sign," disturbing as it was to those who had never seen it, had appeared throughout the church's past and in all of America's historic revivals. Many modern Christians have opposed the miraculous works of the Holy Spirit because they challenge their ego and pride.

Charles Carrin

After Oliver's visit, God began moving more obviously and verified much of the Scripture that our official doctrine denied. Youth meetings became exciting; other young people began attending, and a vitality ignited them that they had not known before. Harold and Suzi Kilpatrick, Bob and Peggy Stogdill, Tom and Betty Hatcher, and many others joined us. They began promoting excellent ideas for ministry in the community.

Many of the church youth had previously been captivated with "hard-rock" music. When they became convicted of its danger, we had a "Hard Rock" burning service. Young people, some we didn't know, brought their albums, tapes, disks, and everything related to that culture and threw them into a bonfire. Some came with arms full of material. That event proved to be a time of great liberation for many. The devil was no longer just a scary name in the Bible—he was their greatest enemy—and they knew how to defeat him.

A few years ago, one of the girls who was active in the youth group at that time said to me, "I have no idea where I would be today if I had not been filled with the Holy Spirit when Oliver came. Although I was attending church, I was also running with a crowd of wild young people who would have eventually led me away from the Lord. Being filled with the Holy Spirit stopped all of that!" She has remained a committed believer to this day.

A stream of strong, new people began uniting with us, Church membership boomed, offerings doubled, then doubled again. The scene became reminiscent of John Wesley's statement: "When the church gets on fire people will come for miles to watch it burn." The congregation was eager to help those in need, and we installed a giant TV system in one of Florida's Penitentiaries to provide Christian programs for the inmates.

We were also blessed with great outdoorsmen who directed us in buying six Grumman Canoes, a trailer, tents, cooking gear, everything necessary, and took unchurched young people on camping trips. Building bonfires, we fed them, led them in worship-songs, witnessed to them about the Lord, and saw many come to Christ. This was the day of TV-satellite communication, and we installed a big TV dish in the church's back-yard where we could receive direct telecasts from other ministries.

Though I was new in the Spirit's work, He began moving visibly, and the local Christian bookstore spread the word that the Primitive Baptist Church in Delray Beach had come alive and was experiencing "signs and wonders." One young man came to the office and reluctantly explained he was confused about his sexual identity and wanted to change. Sitting there in the chair, he broke into hard sobbing. "I want a wife, family, and children!" He wept, "I don't want to be homosexual!"

After a brief time of Scripture teaching, I anointed him with oil, laid hands on him in the Name of Jesus and commanded all demons to go. I did not rush but ordered, "Every spirit contrary to the Holy Spirit must leave!" Suddenly, he began bellowing like a bull—-louder than I can describe—-until the walls seemed to vibrate. Then suddenly, he leaped from the chair, threw his arms into the air, and ran through the office shouting, "It's gone! It's gone! I'm free! I'm free! I felt it go!" And, thank God, he was free! I then prayed for him to be filled with the Holy Spirit. Excitedly, he told others what had happened. It was events like this that quickly spread through the community.

The church in Delray Beach continued with its commitment to the truth of Scripture. One Sunday morning, Elwood Holley brought his son David forward for ministry; the boy faced a threatening condition in his eyes. When I laid hands on both of them, Elwood was instantly slammed to the floor; no one caught him. David sensed nothing. Glancing first at his father on the floor and then to me, he seemed to say, "I am the one in need! Not him!" There was no visible manifestation; however, he was healed.

One of our church ladies who had been imprisoned in a Nazi Concentration Camp in World War II and wore a hip-to-neck brace came forward for prayer. Like David, she experienced nothing visibly. That night when she was in bed asleep, the power of God suddenly went through her like an electric-surge, and she was healed. The brace was never worn again.

Another woman for whom I had a specific word of knowledge regarding pain in her wrist, stood below the pulpit, saying, "How did you know?! How did you know?!"

An older woman in the congregation Ruth Redd developed a severe case of shingles. She was confined to home and called, asking for prayer. The doctors warned she would be months recovering. I went to her house, anointed her with oil, prayed, and left. There was nothing significant about our time together. At five o'clock the next morning she got out of bed, removed her gown, and all the scales fell off. She was healed. The shingles never returned.

The congregation doubled, then doubled again. Barry Roon, an ordained Baptist pastor, and his wife Suzanne joined. People were happy,

183

and the Holy Spirit continued moving in power. Homes were restored; addicts were delivered, and lives were changed. New believers were sometimes taken to the ocean after the night service and baptized in the dark. A wonderful young couple Wendel and Jan Hollingsworth, who were both musicians, joined our staff and ushered us into anointed worship and praise. New faces appeared in every service; Catholics, Lutherans, Episcopalians, and others came to experienced the Holy Spirit's miraculous power. The "word of knowledge" became a powerful tool of direction on which I relied. Without it, I would have been hopelessly crippled.

Baptism In The Ocean

One weekday a handsome young man, who was a professional basketball player from Norway, appeared at the church office. He was anxious to speak with me about salvation. Wendel Hollingsworth was present, and we explained Paul's instructions on the new birth. (Acts 16:30; Romans 10:8-10). He eagerly responded to the Scripture and was genuinely born-again. Immediately, we provided him with clothes for baptism and took him to the ocean. The water was calm and clear as glass. Every shell was visible on the bottom. After immersing him in the Name of the Father, Son, and Holy Spirit (Mathew 28:19), I explained that I would lay hands on him to be filled with the Holy Spirit. His response was, "I want it! I want it!"

The second I touched him on the forehead, he fell backward with a splash, with his body vibrating electrically, and his lips chattering in tongues. I quickly got my shoulder under his head to keep him above water. Never had I seen anyone more overwhelmed in the glory of God and quaking in the power of the Spirit. After supporting him for a long time, I backed away and let him sink.

As Wendell and I watched, he went straight to the bottom. Stiff as an iron bar, he rose again to the top. As his face came through the surface, he broke ecstatically again into tongues. Spiritually, he was out of our dimension. Then, taking a breath, he sank again. This sinking and rising continued for half an hour. I thought of the early church father Tertullian (160-220) who said that "Christians should rise from the water of baptism expecting the gifts of the Holy Spirit to come upon them." It was the practice of Tertullian's day to "lay hands" immediately on the newly baptized. This happened with this young Norwegian-brother, and the gift had come! It also helped me realize how "signs and wonders" in the early church had convinced unbelievers about the truth of Jesus's resurrection and the power of the Holy Spirit. In early Christianity, there were no Bibles to study. Only later were Scriptures written and circulated among believers.

Finally, Wendell and I went back to the beach, sat down on the sand, and watched our new convert floating in the ocean alone. Periodically, he stood, threw up his arms, shouted, fell back to the water and disappeared. As we watched, I said to Wendell, "If he floats to Bermuda he will make a great missionary!" Later, we physically carried him across the beach and put him in the car. Back at the church, he re-dressed and disappeared. I never saw him again. This I know: That young man had a baptism encounter with God he never forgot. Even in the ocean, he discovered what it was like to be filled with the Holy Spirit.

The Lutherans Attend

A large group of Lutherans began attending our meetings, and their pastor became very disturbed when he learned they were being "filled with the Holy Spirit." He did not believe it and angrily announced he, too, would attend. He would also prove their "falling under the power of God" to be fake. The night he came he wore no clerical collar and did not introduce himself, nor did I know he was there. At the end of the message, when I gave the opportunity for personal ministry, he was first to spring to his feet and rush down the aisle. The back of the building was filled with Lutherans anxiously watching. As he neared, I reached out my hand but never touched him; he was slammed to the floor as if hit by a prize-fighter. No one caught him, and he landed on the carpet with a crash.

As he went down, all the Lutherans sprang up, wide-eyed and astonished. When he regained his strength, he sneaked out, never to return; but most of his members united with our congregation and became happy "charismatics." Later, I said to them, "My warning to skeptics, religious, or otherwise, is 'Don't dare God!'" At that time, a four-generation Catholic family joined us and proved to be great supporters of the church. All of them, including the great-grandmother, were "buried with Christ" in baptism and raised into great, reliable service in the Kingdom. This was the family of Herbert and Linda Johnson. She later became my wonderful secretary.

Suicide Victim Delivered

Another young woman, vivacious and happy, came to my office and chatted light-heartedly. Her grandfather was one of the most high-ranking clergymen in South Florida. As we prayed, the Holy Spirit said, "Take command over the spirit of suicide." I was shocked. This girl seemed the most cheerful and happy person I had met, but the same instruction came again. This time I obeyed. I stopped the prayer, looked at her, and in a quiet, authoritative voice, I commanded the spirit of suicide to go. She looked at me in astonishment. "How did you know?!" Then she jerked up the long, cupped sleeves that hid ugly scars, where she had already slashed her wrists. "The Holy Spirit told me," I explained, "He loves you and will set you free."

Pray For Mildred!

One Wednesday evening at our mid-week prayer meeting, I was kneeling at the front pew, with my head down, when I received a word of knowledge to "Pray for Mildred." For a moment I was puzzled. There was no one by that name in the congregation. In obedience, I looked up and said aloud, "Pray for Mildred." As I closed my eyes again, I received a second instruction, "Mildred is Jewish." Without hesitating, I spoke out again, "Mildred is Jewish." Obediently, everyone prayed for this unknown Jewish lady named Mildred. During the teaching that followed, nothing more was said of her.

At the end of the service, a distinguished looking matron rose quickly from the rear seat. She hurried down the aisle, and in a breathy voice she said, "May I speak to the congregation?" I handed her the microphone. "I have never addressed a church before in my life, but tonight I must! I am a visitor, and I came because of a telephone call I received from a friend in Pennsylvania. The caller and I were sorority sisters in college fifty years ago, and we have remained close friends ever since. She is seriously ill in the hospital and asked if I would have my church pray for her." The woman paused, trying to maintain her composure, "This was the church I felt impressed to come to. I arrived too late to make the request, but it didn't matter anyway, because the Lord told you for me. My friend's name is Mildred, and she is Jewish."

The visitor went home, called her Jewish friend and told her what had happened. The result was that Mildred was healed! She was so impressed with the Holy Spirit's speaking her name to a congregation more than a thousand miles away, that she went to a Baptist Church in her community, heard the gospel, and got saved.

Observe that the Spirit's grace gifts were revealed that evening in a three-step progression: First, as a word of knowledge, secondly, as healing, and finally, as salvation. Salvation is always the destination of grace.

Healing Stories

Healing from Multiple Sclerosis

One Sunday morning, a young Jamaican woman came forward for healing. She had Multiple Sclerosis, and her vision was 20/75. She was healed of M.S., and her eye-sight became 20/25. Her husband, we learned later, was one of the biggest drug-pushers in Palm Beach County. He too was born-again, delivered from an infestation of demons, and became a powerful witness to addicts and pushers in the area. Another young woman, blind in one eye, who had come from Brazil for surgery in the U.S., was healed during worship. She discovered her sight had returned when she placed her hand over the good eye, looked up, and saw all the lights overhead.

At a meeting in Tennessee, there was a young woman who had been injured in a horse-back riding accident. She was dependent on crutches, and her doctors had told her that day that she would never recover; she was doomed to be an invalid the rest of her life. In a moment's time, she was totally healed; and she left the meeting walking normally, with her mother waving the crutches over her head. The mother was still in contact with me nearly forty years later, and the daughter remained healed.

Alzheimer's Patients Healed

A nurse in my congregation asked if I would pray for a patient she was tending in a home nearby. When she told me the address, "Gulfstream," I knew this was one of the wealthiest communities in Florida. The patient, she explained, was an elderly Jewish lady who was an Alzheimer's patient, comatose and unable to speak. Another church-brother, Carter Miller, went with me, and together, we stood at the bedside of this tiny little woman, curled unconsciously in a prenatal position. Gently, we anointed her with oil in the Name of Jesus, laid hands on her and prayed. It was that simple and brief. Within a few minutes, we were gone.

187

About a week later I was in my office when the secretary called and said, "Pastor, someone is here to see you." I stepped out and was greeted by an attractive, elderly woman in a silk pantsuit, hair nicely styled, standing very erect. "You don't recognize me, do you?" She asked. "No." I replied puzzled. "I am the Jewish patient in Gulfstream you prayed for!" I was astonished. Her transformation was incredible. She went on to explain that she heard us that day as we prayed. Mentally, she was locked into paralyzed silence, but her hearing was unaffected. As we prayed, she joined with us, accepted Jesus and was born-again. I learned from that experience that those who are comatose may still be listening and comprehending. Later, the nurse explained that while she had been in her silent condition, family-members stood at her bedside, quarreling about her estate and will. After being restored, she returned to the Attorney and had the will changed.

Have I experienced failure? Yes. Many times. But, failure will not control my future. I will continue ministering, believing Jesus's words, "These signs will follow those who believe, they will lay hands on the sick and they shall recover (Mark 16:17, 18).

The Ministry of the Laying-on-of-Hands

It is very important to note that there is absolutely no power in the human hand—none. The Holy Spirit releases power from the "Temple of the Holy Spirit"(I Corinthians 3:16-19) which is inside the human body. The hand has value only because it is an extension of the Temple. When a ministering Temple touches a receiving Temple, there is a power-transfer from one Temple to the other. This move by the Holy Spirit can be restricted by "insulating" factors in either party. By "insulation" I mean: attitudes of jealousy, anger, fear, pride, or other "works of the flesh." Carnality grieves the Holy Spirit and restricts His ministry. Additionally, where there is no humbled devotion and reverencing for the full New Testament truth, there will be meager results.

Chapter 22

WEALTHY WOMAN AND CATHOLICS EXPERIENCE THE HOLY SPIRIT'S POWER

A group of local pastors invited me to attend a prayer meeting at one of their homes. We visited for a few minutes and then began to pray. Suddenly—in a vision—I saw a Catholic Priest at St. Vincent de Paul Seminary in Boynton Beach. He was bending over a maple table, praying urgently, facing north with his face almost touching his hands. The vision was photographically-clear. I raised my head, told the other pastors what I had seen, and together we prayed for this unknown priest at the Seminary.

When I left the meeting, my intention was to go to St. Vincent's, but the Spirit clearly stopped me. Several months passed. I had almost forgotten the incident when my church hosted a community meeting for local pastors. A Monsignor from St. Thomas Moore Catholic Church attended. Afterward, he came to my office, strangely bonded to me, and asked that I pray for him. During this personal ministry, he experienced both deliverance from a spirit of oppression and was filled with the Holy Spirit. Physically, the power of God was upon him. It was a point of radical change in his life. Elated with what had happened, he asked me to preach to his congregation at St. Thomas Moore. I agreed but was confused as to how he fitted into my vision of the priest at St. Vincent de Paul Seminary.

A moment later he rose to leave and was out the door, saying goodbye, when he stopped abruptly. Turning back, he said, "I forgot to tell you! St. Thomas Moore does not have a building of its own. We meet in the Chapel at St. Vincent de Paul Seminary!" I was stunned, knowing he was the same priest I had seen in the vision. I never told him about the incident at the prayer meeting; instead, I visited him at the Rectory, looking for the maple table.

A number of Priests shared the same facility, and he took me through his quarters and all the public rooms: To my disappointment, I never saw the table. Later, as I was walking to the parking lot, he stopped me, "Come back," he called, "I did not show you our Board Room!" Taking me by the hand, he led me to another room, opened the door, and in front of me was the maple table. It was exactly like the one in the vision. Still not telling him, I studied the room carefully as we chatted. He mentioned the spiritual-renewal he experienced in my office and wanted his congregation to experience the same. "Monsignor," I said, "The Holy Spirit may move radically!" "I want it to happen!' He answered quickly, "I want it to happen!"

The first night, the Catholic congregation was a mixture of laymen, priests, and Professors from the Seminary. Many of my congregation were also present. Speaking to the Priests, I cautioned them in two ways: "First of all," I said, "Know that you are truly born-again and filled with the Holy Spirit. You must not live in presumption about these vital questions." I was aware some of the Priests might have only a religious-concept of Jesus and not a truly authentic relationship with Him. I told them about my twenty-seven-year delay between my new birth and baptism in the Spirit.

When I announced that the Monsignor wanted me to lay hands on them, everyone obediently filed to the front. Both nights, the Holy Spirit moved in power and members of the congregation, the faculty, and young seminarians encountered the power of God. No one was more surprised than I that Catholics who embraced so many non-Biblical concepts would experience the Holy Spirit's visible manifestation. But that happened in mass—wholly because of the grace of God. One little woman was startled to see her friend drop to the floor and exclaimed, "Mildred, dear, get up! Get ..," She never finished the sentence. When I touched her, she dropped to the floor beside her friend. All of them arose that night refreshed and revitalized in the Spirit. Before leaving, plans were announced for my return visit.

Immediately, a group of young priests encircled me. They had experienced the power of God and were so excited they were literally dancing on their toes. When I exhorted them not to make my mistake of lost time between salvation and anointing, one of them interrupted me. "Father!" He said, "You are what we want to be!" I was stunned. Young Catholic Priests were telling an evangelical preacher he was what they wanted to be! Incredible.

I Met One Of God's Amazing Converts: Jennifer

One morning I read in the newspaper about a woman in Boca Raton, Florida (whom I will call "Jennifer") who lost her bank envelope. It contained more than one-half million dollars in cash, jewels, and negotiable bonds. Several newspapers carried the report. Finishing the story, I dropped the paper, not knowing she would soon appear in our congregation. Nor did I know she would face a loss far greater than the diamonds and cash. The next Sunday morning her Rolls Royce appeared in our parking lot. No one knew who she was. She sat alone, listening intently to the sermon, weeping throughout the service. God was dealing with her about a lifetime of personal issues.

A few days later she called, invited Laurie and me to lunch, and we quickly realized she was the most spectacular person we had ever met. She was by far the most beautiful and glamorous. She was wearing two rings with diamonds as large as marbles. Laurie filled a need in her life for a Christian friend, and the two quickly bonded. After that, they spent much time together. Jennifer lived part-time in her lavish home in the Boca Raton Yacht Club and her mountain top estate in North Carolina. She also maintained an apartment at the Waldorf-Astoria in New York. Sometimes she flew from Florida to New York in her private jet, had lunch at the Waldorf and flew home. Before her husband's death, they owned ocean-front mansions, yachts, race horses, millions of dollars in jewelry, and everything money could buy. There were times when she and her husband went to Miami Beach Nightclubs, and she wore more than $1,000,000 in diamonds.

It was after one of their night club visits, they returned home to their oceanfront estate and almost immediately heard a knock on the door. Foolishly, her husband opened it and faced a man with a gun. Jennifer, not knowing what was happening, came running, still wearing her diamonds. Too late to escape, the robber, tossed her a bag, ordered her to remove all her jewelry and give it to him. She obeyed. He then ordered them to lie face down on the floor. They submitted and he slammed the door and was gone. That man was "Murf The Surf," the most famous jewel thief in America.

Those were Jennifer's "old days." She was now a widow, still youthful and glamorous but out of touch with God and feeling very much alone. Spiritually, she was empty and abandoned. That first Sunday at our church she experienced a presence of the Holy Spirit that she desperately wanted.

191

Two weeks later, on Saturday morning I was working in the churchyard with Bob Stogdill when I turned suddenly and hurried into my office. The phone was ringing, and when I answered, it was Jennifer. As she spoke, her voice was trembling. I realized that something tragic had happened. "Pastor," she said weeping, "I learned at three o'clock this morning that my only child, my daughter in California, had killed herself. She was a single-mom and left two young boys."

Jennifer was gasping, struggling to talk and then said, "Since the call, I have been sitting with a gun in my lap. I don't want to kill myself, but I have nothing else to live for. Please help me!" She broke into hard sobbing. Putting the telephone down I ran back to the churchyard, got Bob out of a tree, put him on an extension line, and we ministered deliverance to her on the phone. Taking command over the spirit of suicide in the Name of Jesus Christ, we commanded it to go. Within five minutes Jennifer was delivered—she even knew when the demon left. We then prayed for her to be filled with the Holy Spirit. That also happened. In a few minutes time, a total transformation took place, and the death-threat was ended forever. Where there had been panic, near-hysteria, there was peace. It was not an ordinary peace that came upon her—this was different. Jennifer tried to explain but could not. A holy calmness enveloped her. From that moment on she was a new, Spirit-empowered woman.

A few days later the daughter was buried in North Carolina with a huge congregation of mourners' present. Their grief was overwhelming, compounded by the daughter's two orphaned boys. They were close to 8 and ten years old. It was not the pastor who brought hope and strength to the family that day. It was Jennifer. The anointing of the Holy Spirit covered her, and it was she who upheld everyone else. She had experienced life and hope in a way she could now share with others. What the family saw and heard at the funeral was a woman totally transformed. No longer was she the self-indulging person who flew around the world in her private jet, flashing her diamonds, or carrying $100,000 cash in her purse. That woman was now gone. She was only a memory in the past.

Jennifer gave her most expensive mink coat to a pastor's wife. She disposed of her floor-length Chinchilla fur and traded her Rolls Royce for a used Cadillac. She drove it for the rest of her life. Best of all, she only wanted to talk about God's love and how she had been radically delivered and filled with the Holy Spirit. A few months later, at lunch, she shared privately with Laurie and me the real significance of the bank envelope. It contained much more than half a million dollars. One of its contents was a huge diamond, the largest, most expensive she had ever owned—a gift from her husband.

The morning she lost the bank pouch, she put it on the automobile roof, unlocked the door and drove off. It was not until she reached the bank that she realized what she had done. That special ring was in the pouch. Frantically, she called the police, retraced her route but never found the bag. Nor was it returned. It was shortly after that she appeared in our Sunday morning worship. Later, she told me that she did not know where to go to church: She simply got in her car, started driving, and to her surprise came to Delray Beach. Here, she pulled into our parking lot.

Time passed. Jennifer never missed church, and one Sunday morning when I gave the opportunity for hands-on ministry, she leaped to her feet and rushed forward. I reached-out but never touched her. Instead, as everyone in the congregation witnessed—she was thrown back to the floor so fast that her beautiful blonde wig flew off and landed about three feet behind her in the aisle. An usher ran, grabbed it, and was trying to replace it when I signaled him to stop. Jennifer never knew the wig was gone. She was bathed in the glory of Heaven.

Today, years later, a huge marble slab covers the daughter's grave in North Carolina and next to it is Jennifer's. She too has been gone a number of years. The daughter's stone contains a lengthy poem I once quoted to Jennifer, and she immediately wanted it on the girl's grave. It begins and closes with these lines:

"Do not stand at my grave and weep,
I am not there; I do not sleep ..,

Do not stand at my grave and sob,
I am not there—I am with God!"

There is more to tell: After robbing Jennifer and her husband, "Murf The Surf" committed what was called the "Jewel Heist of the Century." On October 29, 1964, he and two accomplices broke into the American Museum of Natural History in New York City and stole more than twenty gems. One of them was the world-famous "Star of India," a 563 carat

Star Sapphire—the largest gemstone in the world—valued at more than $300,000,000. He also took the 16+carat Eagle Diamond and the 100+ carat De Long Ruby. Interestingly, the Star of India was later recovered from a bus station footlocker in Miami.

Murf was caught and sent to prison for nearly twenty years. While there, he was born-again, baptized in the Spirit, and became an Ordained full-gospel Minister. I met him in the 1990s, telling him about my friend, Jennifer—but he would not talk about her robbery. There was much he wanted to forget. After his salvation, Murf's ministry expanded, and he was the keynote speaker in Jerusalem at the World Conference on Crime Prevention and Rehabilitation through Religion. He also gave his testimony on CNN's, Larry King Live broadcast. After visiting more than 1,200 prisons to share his salvation testimony, the Florida Parole Board canceled his lifetime-parole. When I told Jennifer about meeting Murf, of his salvation and ministry, she was glad but insisted she never wanted to see him again. The memory of that night at gunpoint, seeing his glassy-eyes staring at her was too painful. She could not face him again.

Murf was a strange but amazing man. In his youth, he was a National Surfing Champion, a tennis pro, movie stunt mania high-tower circus diver, and an accomplished violinist who played with the Pittsburg Symphony Orchestra at age seventeen. He had an unusual combination of talents. Thievery was one of them.

Now, forty years after meeting Jennifer, I think of the Saturday morning I walked into my office and heard the phone ringing. Bob and I ministered deliverance to her, while she held a gun in her lap. Without question, she was the most spectacular, most amazing, and the wealthiest person I have ever known. She wore the biggest diamonds I ever saw. Best of all, she experienced God's greatest gift: Eternal life. Having witnessed the work of grace in this remarkable woman I could never go back to my days of powerless preaching.

Chapter 23

POLICE OFFICERS WITNESS A "SUCCESSFUL EXORCISM"

One of the first Spirit-filled ministers I met in South Florida was Fr. Richard Bass, a priest at St. Joseph's Episcopal Church in Boynton Beach. We met, bonded, and within one minute were on our knees praying together. It was an astonishing union between two strangers, but God knew how quickly our relationship would be needed. Soon after that, Laurie and I were in bed asleep. It was one o'clock in the morning when the phone rang. I answered, and the Priest shouted an address in my ear, and yelled "Get over here!" and slammed down the receiver. In that split-second, I recognized demonic noises in the background and knew Richard was involved with a heavy-duty deliverance ministry.

When I arrived at the house, the yard was filled with police cars, fire trucks, a paramedic wagon, and neighbors huddled together. Rushing inside, a woman grabbed my arm and hurried me to a bedroom, "It's my son," she said, fearfully, "he's gone crazy! The Police want to take him! Please help!" I stepped into the room where a slender, teenage-boy was pinned to the bed by three large men. The 200-pound father lay across his chest facing me. A fireman sprawled across his legs the other way, holding onto the bed frame, and the priest was gripping his feet. The youth was roaring lion-like, trying to get up. Immediately, I knew we were dealing with a spirit of witchcraft and told the men that fact. I had access only to the boy's face, and when I anointed him with oil in the Name of Jesus, commanding the demon to go, the youth raised all four of us to a standing position. He stood erect on the mattress, and his roar was heard across the neighborhood.

I learned later that the police were at the door demanding the mother let them take him to the hospital. They were tired and wanted to leave. She stood, arms and legs stretched, barricading the entrance, insisting they give me time. When she refused, the officer in charge said, "We are Christians too, but we don't believe in hocus-pocus." An hour passed. I was commanding the spirit to go and encouraging the men to pray, expecting the youth's deliverance. Suddenly, it happened. The boy fell limp—motionless. We backed away, and a moment later he slowly sat up. Looking around the room, he hesitated, then spoke, "Where am I?" Turning to his father, he said, "Dad, what happened! What's going on?"

A few minutes later, when he stepped out of the room, perfectly normal and sane, the expression on the Police Captain's face was one of utter shock. The other officers were equally astonished. I thanked them for coming but explained the crisis was over, and they could go. To the family, I said, "Please do not give my name to anyone—tell no one who I am." Fr. Bass and I hugged, and I went home and crawled back in bed. A few days later the *National Enquirer* published the story on their front page, quoting the Boynton Beach Police Officer who officially reported, "We witnessed a successful exorcism." True to the Enquirer's sensationalism, they described me as a "mystery man who arrived after midnight and disappeared into the room carrying a strange black bag." Fortunately, they did not know my name. Unfortunately, they did not know the "strange black bag" was my Bible. In a short time, other tabloids carried their version of the story, and it went nationwide.

While I thanked God for setting the youth free, I was deeply grieved for another reason: Such a Biblical event—rescuing a young man from the powers of darkness by Jesus Christ—would quickly be published by secular papers, while Christian publications wanted nothing to do with it. How up-side-down can the church get?! This was a Jesus-event! It was His Name that brought deliverance to that teenager! (Acts 16:18) If that young man had been taken to a hospital and drugged into submission, he might never have been normal again. He could have been locked in a psychiatric ward for the rest of his life—but that did not happen because Jesus Christ set him free! True to what I told the father, the boy later confessed that he and another teenage-friend had secretly studied books on witchcraft and Satanism.

Years later a stranger came to my office, and asked if I remembered that night. When I said I did, he held out his hand and said, "I am the fireman who helped hold him to the bed!" He went on to explain, "That made a believer out of me! At that time, I was a nominal Catholic. Now I am a 'Bible-thumping' Christian!'" Thousands more like the fireman could be converted and changed if the church preached a full-gospel and let them see the power of God in action.

The conversion of pagan Rome could never have been accomplished by modern preaching. It is also important to know that radical "signs and wonders" occurred in early America in various ministries. One of them was Jonathan Edwards, a young pastor in Massachusetts, and later President of Princeton University. He, George Whitfield, John Wesley, others from England, became fire-brand revivalists in the hands of God. Through them, America experienced its first Great Awakening.

Spiritual gifts are fundamental to Christianity. They are real. They are needed. Best of all, they are available to any believer who will accept them. Many times in my early ministry my members perished in alcoholism, violent anger, depression, and other demonic symptoms because I did not preach a full gospel. Their marriages, homes, children, were destroyed, as a result of my depriving them of full Bible truth. Would I ever surrender to the half-gospel of my former ministry? Never! An old hymn writer expressed it this way:

"For this, let men reproach, defame, And call me what they will,
I will follow Christ the Lamb, And be His servant still!"

Occasionally someone says to me, "Pastor, you are over-emphasizing the importance of `Deliverance Ministry!'" If I am over-emphasizing it is because I have been on both sides of this theological fence and know the consequences each side has to offer. In my early years some of my church members died from suicide, alcoholism, were killers, addicts, because I failed to provide them with the full benefits of the gospel. Please hear this carefully: Gifts of the Holy Spirit are vital! God gave them for our benefit. The pastor who teaches against them is committing a terrible sin against God and his congregation. We desperately need all of God's provision!

During that time, a woman in Atlanta telephoned who had been a severe alcoholic for eighteen years. She lost everything. Her husband divorced her, her children avoided her, and her grandchildren were growing up without knowing her. She was the neighborhood "drunk." Combing her hair, wearing clean clothes, caring for her appearance, were concerns she ignored. Years earlier I had been her pastor, but as a *cessationist*. I had been unable to help her. My solution to such problems was secular therapy. I had nothing else to offer. That wonderful day in a ten-minute telephone "deliverance ministry," the woman was totally set free. Why? I had received the power Jesus promised. He said, "These signs will follow those who believe: In My name, they will cast out demons." Mark 16:17. On that authority, the demon of addiction was cast out. Alcohol never bothered her again. Not only so, but she was also filled with the Holy Spirit.

For the first time in years, her life was normal. Excitedly, she told her church about the Holy Spirit freeing her. The alcoholism was gone. She was a new woman, and she anticipated how thrilled they would be to hear her good news. But her testimony frightened them. The pastor (a cessationist) had no theological explanation for her miraculous Deliverance" and did not want to be challenged by it. Such an experience was not itemized in their "Articles Of Faith." As cessationists, they did not want to talk about such things. Church friends soon began avoiding her.

The frightening truth is this: The church could accept her alcoholism because it did not challenge their theology. They would not accept her deliverance, because it severely disproved their cessation theory. In effect, they were willing to let her, and others like her, drown in addiction before they would correct their denominational error. In time, the woman was forced to leave the church where she had been a member for twenty-five years. Thankfully, she found another congregation that could rejoice in her Holy Spirit-rescue. To her dying day, she lived a happy, fruitful–sober–life.

I soon discovered that her Deliverance would become typical of my new ministry. More amazingly, the action of her church only motivated me to love the unbelievers more. I wanted them to experience everything the Holy Spirit had done for me. My experiencing Kingdom-power fortified my love for the local congregation and enabled me to serve them better. This fact became supremely clear: I could properly minister to the church only if I fully identified myself with the Kingdom.

Everything the church possessed, believed, taught, or received had come through the Kingdom. Jesus said, "If I cast out demons by the Spirit of God no doubt the Kingdom of God has come upon you" (Matthew 12:28). He never said that about the church. For the first time I saw the church in her universal reality and beauty but in subordination to the Kingdom. I realized the gospel was the "gospel of the Kingdom" (Matthew 24:14). The parables of Jesus were illustrations of the Kingdom. More importantly, He instructed us to "seek first the Kingdom." The list of Kingdom instructions goes on and on.

Near that time, a pastor came to me at a Conference in Florida and asked if I would minister deliverance to him. I agreed and taking three other men with me went to a private room. This gentleman was a well groomed college graduate with a successful ministry and family life, but he confessed he had a serious problem. "My ancestors have practiced Druid worship and psychic-powers for generations," he explained, "and I experience torment from its presence. I am not participating in any way with witchcraft, but I feel that darkness constantly hovering over me. It torments me." He paused, then continued, "I explained the problem to my Presbyters and asked them to minister deliverance to me, but they refused. Our doctrine denies that Christians can have demons in their bodies or minds." I reminded him that none of us have been through the Resurrection, our mortal has not yet "put on immortality," nor our corruptible "put on incorruption" (I Corinthians 15:53,54). Because of that fact, demons can go anywhere sin and disease go.

In the next few minutes, astonishing things happened. Demons began speaking out of him in guttural, dog-like growls, contorting his body, changing his appearance into something ugly and grotesque (Mark 1:26; 9:26). Four major spirits were identified—one of those was the spirit of "idiocy." When we challenged it in the Name of Jesus, the man's eyes suddenly crossed; his hands became spastic; his tongue thickened and turned sideways in his mouth; and he began slobbering with senseless jabbering. In a split-second, he became a full-blown idiot.

The good news is that he was totally delivered. The mental pain was gone forever, but please be aware of this frightening truth: Had this young pastor not received Deliverance, the spirits hiding in him would ultimately have destroyed his sanity, ruined his family and ministry, and had him locked away in an asylum. Could that happen to a born-again pastor? Yes. Absolutely. I have no doubt that asylums contain many such Christians. If believers were immune to demons, we would also be immune to wickedness and illness. Like it or not, we are still vulnerable to powers of darkness and must fight as Jesus taught. Spiritual warfare is a constant, on-going battle (Ephesians 6:10-18).

The Hidden Danger of Psychic Information

A few days later I returned to Delray Beach, and Ginger Hendricks, one of our members, called to tell me that a Psychic Fair was being held in the local Mall. She wanted us to share the gospel with the psychics and their victims. I prepared a pamphlet, "Is It Dangerous To Consult Psychics?" and took our table to the Fair where we set it in the midst of Tarot Card readers, crystal balls, palmists, others. The tract contained quotations of Scripture warning about witchcraft in all its forms. Our chief complaint was that the psychics were selling self-hypnosis cassette-tapes to children.

Very quickly the Director for the Fair confronted us, and commanded us to leave. We refused, and she called the Police. The Officer who came was very gracious. The Director was not, and she angrily said to me, "Tell the Officer your name!" I answered, "You are a psychic! You tell him my name!" She became incensed. By that time, other psychics, shoppers, and workmen had gathered around us with newspaper photographers taking pictures. Because of the danger to children, we were able to keep the Fair shut down until noon. Finally, the policeman told us we had to remove our table but that we were free to distribute our literature. I never knew for certain but believed he appreciated our efforts. Not only did we distribute our tracts, but moving from booth to booth, we silently took authority in the Name of Jesus over every spirit contrary to the Holy Spirit.

In the mid-afternoon, the Director's husband approached me cautiously, wanting to talk. At first, I distrusted him, but when I saw his sincerity, we walked to the end of a hallway where glass doors opened onto the parking lot. "I've got to talk to you!" He said, nervously, "I've got to talk to you!" I listened, and he continued, "I've worked with these psychics for eighteen years, and I know that much of what they say comes to pass." I nodded in agreement. "Suppose," he went on, pointing to a line of parked cars, "A psychic tells you at this same time tomorrow—1:15 p.m.—There will be a green car there, a blue car there, a black truck comes speeding by, a child runs in front of it and is killed …" I continued listening. "Tomorrow, you come; each car is in place as the psychic said. The child runs out, the truck hits it, and the child is killed! How can you explain that? They accurately predicted it!"

"No! No!," I stopped him, "You don't understand! The psychics are not predicting such events; they are causing them! They merely prepare the way for the devil's actions! If the person believes it, the devil is free to do it!" The man's jaws dropped, his eyes widened, he stood breathless, staring at me. I will never forget his next words: "How do I get out of this?" He said, "How do I get out of this?!" "You need to be saved!" I answered, "How? What does that mean?"

By the exit, I shared Paul's salvation-explanation in Romans 10, then led him in a prayer of repentance and reception of Christ (John 1:12). I have no doubt he was genuinely saved. Afterward, he said with near-panic in his face, "My wife must not know this," he whispered, "She must not know this!" I understood his fear. I remembered my earlier encounter with her. I gave the man—now a brother in Christ—a loving hug and left him standing alone.

Chapter 24

MY BELOVED CHURCH CANCELS MY ORDINATION

Strangely, I still regarded myself as a faithful Primitive Baptist and assumed I would be that forever. In fact, for years, my loyalty to the denomination had me so isolated from the rest of the Christian world that I did not know an international "charismatic renewal" was underway. It never occurred to me that other pastors were experiencing the same Holy Spirit events that were happening to me.

One of our young Primitive Baptist pastors approached me privately, explaining that he believed in the gift of tongues and did not challenge me on the issue. I trusted him and later prayed with him, part of the time in tongues. We parted, and soon afterward I was confronted by a large group of pastors who asked me angrily, "Have you ever prayed in tongues with one of our pastors?!" I did not answer. The pastor was among them. Again, they demanded that I confess to having done so. To protect him, I did not reply. For myself, I would gladly have witnessed about the Scriptural truth of tongues and my love for the gift. But, had I given an explanation to their question, he might have been as jeopardized as I. In good conscience, I would not expose him. The confrontation that day ended in a stalemate. Later, I realized he was a ploy, whose purpose in coming to me was a deception, to solidify their case against me.

In spite of all the chaos and accusation, I was not prepared for what happened: The Miami Church canceled my Ordination. The pastor did not notify me personally; instead, I read about it in a denominational publication. Soon afterward, I received a notice from the church to return my Certificate of Ordination. From that day, many of my pastor-friends never spoke to me again. It was one of the most painful eras of my life, but in obedience, I sent the document to them, including the following note. It explained my position:

"I routinely–sometimes daily–see drug addicts, alcoholics, suicidal, depressed, and sexually-disturbed people, be delivered and permanently

set free by the power of the Holy Spirit. Lives are changed, bodies healed, homes saved, children rescued. What better reason do I need to continue my present work? For their sake alone, if not my own, I could never go back to my former ministry in which I was powerless to help these people. You want me to renounce the baptism in the Holy Spirit though it is the greatest blessing my life and ministry ever experienced."

My plea had no effect, and my Ordination remained nullified. The most shocking aspect was this: One of the men who signed the Revocation Order urgently needed my help. His son had spent years in prison for sexually molesting children. He was now released, but unchanged. I was genuinely puzzled how the father could read my explanation of helping others with problems exactly like his son and still oppose my ministry. It did not make sense. Even so, the father approved my disbarment. The purpose of the denominational action was twofold: 1) They wanted to invalidate my ministry with them and 2) silence my future preaching to others. That did not happen. Numerous friends and churches who had witnessed the Holy Spirit's anointing on me were shocked by the revocation. Even so, the denomination would not acknowledge that "heroin addicts, alcoholics, suicidal-people, and others with massive problems, were being delivered through the power of the Holy Spirit."

In my defense, a Baptist Church in Georgia responded with this declaration:

**Having witnessed the approval of the Holy Spirit
Upon the ministry of Charles Carrin,
Greater Hope Church
Acknowledges and endorses
His original Ordination of
December 25, 1949.**

The position of Greater Hope Church was that the Holy Spirit was still validating my ministry in very obvious ways. The Miami Church could endorse, or not endorse it, but my Call to the Ministry and Ordination was sanctioned by God Himself and witnessed by innumerable people. That was a fact over which no local church had control. It was not the loss of a document that grieved me; it was the loss of old friends whom I loved and believed to be true lovers of Scripture. Now I was forced to see them from a different perspective. They chose church tradition over the plain, straight-forward message of Scripture.

One day when I was feeling rejected and alone, I read a passage in Genesis that encouraged me. It said: "The blessings of thy father ... shall be on the head of Joseph, and on the crown of the head of him, that was separate from his brethren" (Genesis 49:26). I immediately claimed that hope.

I was hungry for fellowship with other pastors. When I learned of a Pastors' Prayer Meeting in West Palm Beach, I hurried to it. The men were all delightful, and they welcomed me into their fellowship with open arms. They understood the pain I was encountering. Some of them had experienced the same rejection from their denominations.

In addition to the cancellation of my Ordination, coupled with the trauma of that event, there was an onslaught of attacks against the church and me. One evening, Laurie and I were having a quiet dinner when the phone rang. The caller yelled in my ear, "Pastor, Do you know your church is on fire?" "No!" I shouted. I ran out the door and looked toward the church building two blocks away. All I could see was billowing black smoke with Fire-Engine lights flashing through it. The road was blocked by half a dozen police cars detouring traffic. Our building was hidden behind a dark, swirling fog. Crowds of people were standing on the sidelines, and everything around the area was in chaos. I started running, reaching the scene out of breath and choking from fumes. When I ran through the security-line, a police officer shoved me back. "I'm the pastor! I'm the pastor!" I yelled, trying to explain but was unheard.

One of the firemen who was a member of the church ran in my direction shouting, "It's OK! Pastor, It's OK" He saw the terror on my face and kept yelling his assurance, "We have it under control!" He knew the building's interior and had been the first to go inside. Smoke was so dense he could only feel his way, praying as he went. Had he gone to the second floor he would have crashed through the stairwell into an inferno below him. Thankfully, the fire was contained to a back hallway, and except for smoke, the sanctuary was unharmed. Weeks passed before the building was free from the acrid smell of burnt lumber and chemicals.

Not long after that, Laurie and I took a trip out of town. We were enjoying a quiet morning when I received a telephone call from a newspaper reporter. "Pastor," he explained, "The Delray Beach News Journal is doing a story about your church crisis—how you have ousted the founding family and taken control of the property—We would like a comment from you." I was shocked by his statement. At first, I declined; he insisted, and then, I said, "I will be in your office by one o'clock …" He interrupted and snapped angrily, "Pastor! This story goes to press at noon!" My answer, unfortunately, as angered as his was, "Then print it!" I hung up the phone. The next day, on the front page of our local paper, was a photo of two of our white-haired, elderly couples—both well-known pillars in the community, standing in front of the church. They had bought the land and built the sanctuary, but it had been stolen from them. I was named as the thief. Our "Absalom-elder" had gone to the paper and arranged the attack.

The truth was that both couples were still present at every service and sat in the same pew where they had sat for years. They were still loved and wanted by the congregation. The public did not know that, nor did it know that the real controversy centered not on their loss of church property but on their loss of church-control. The congregation's growth out-weighed their influence. These two couples were people I had known and loved for many years, and in spite of the conflict, I knew they still loved me. The real problem was the Absalom among us (2 Samuel 13:28).

The newspaper story was a disaster. Until that day, I had worked in many local projects and had been highly esteemed in the community. I had been President of the Kiwanis Club, Chairman of the Ministerial Association, worked with the Landscape Committee that widened Atlantic Avenue, assisted in the annual Garden Club Show, the High School, the Hospital, and other activities. The community appreciated my contributions and presence. That changed instantly: Former friends crossed the street to avoid speaking to me. I wanted to leave. God said "No!" I felt trapped and alone. For me, there was no solution. The pain and humiliation were unbearable. People in the congregation were embarrassed by the publicity, and some left the congregation; a few of the Elders took their home-groups and disappeared. Other crises shook us like earthquakes. If I could have left the earth, I would have done so.

I was in my office one morning when the Elders began filing in. When the last one arrived, one of them made the announcement, "Charles," he said, "we are moving out! We are giving the building back to the family …" "Where will we go?" I asked. "We will have to find a place, perhaps the High School, but one thing is certain: We are not staying here!" I understood their feelings, although I disagreed with their actions. Rising slowly from my desk, I turned toward the wall, grieving over the damage that had already been done to the church's reputation and ministry.

Now, with the move, I knew that more crises were to come; but I was not staring at the wall. I was looking at lives—alcoholic-minds and suicidal people, who had been rescued in that building. The Jewish Cantor came to mind, the Catholic Priest, the Lutheran Pastor, Jennifer with a gun in her lap, the young Norwegian whom we baptized in the ocean, and the crazed youth who was delivered. These and others raced before me.

I agreed to move out of the building. The Elders left, and that night I drove to the Boynton Inlet—the site where the ocean and bay meet. Alone, I walked out on the jetty in the dark, grabbed a metal post and began to sob. Like the tide disappearing into the sea, I felt as if all the good the Holy Spirit had accomplished had been swept away. The loss of my four old friends was a huge part of my grief. While our church had been growing, the Primitive Baptist denomination was dying. Hundreds of churches were closing their doors, and whole states were now emptied of them. I remembered the 3,000 I had written in my early ministry. For our local congregation to deny Scripture and the Holy Spirit's current work was to invoke that same senseless death upon ourselves.

Everything flashed in front of me: The television and prison-ministry, youth and camping-ministry, the Police Captain, the late-night baptisms in the ocean—all of it—had been mutilated and left to die. Everything was gone. We soon made the announcement we were leaving, painted the interior of the building, put a thousand dollars in the church's account (a big amount in that day), gave the family the keys, and filed out of the building singing:

> *"We shall go out with joy, and be led forth with peace,*
> *The mountains and hills will break forth before us,*
> *There'll be shouts of joy and all the trees of the field*
> *Will clap, will clap their hands ... " (Isaiah 55:12)*

The following Sunday we arrived at the High School to discover the janitors had not cleaned the building. The floor was dirty; the chairs were in disarray, and the room was unfit for worship. Children who arrived clean and well-dressed in a few minutes looked like they had never had a bath. I will never forget one little girl in a badly-soiled pink-crinoline dress whose mother snatched her up and stalked angrily to the car. We never saw them again, but we stayed. At that point, we had nowhere else to go.

In spite of that, one of the greatest blessings that came to us at the High School was the arrival of Herb Young, an amazing young man whom God sent to be my helper. Even his introduction was miraculous. One Sunday morning I left my Bible on a chair in the congregation, went forward to make announcements, welcomed others who were entering, then returned to my seat. As I sat down, I clearly heard the Lord say, "The young man beside you is one I have sent to be your helper." I was shocked. The message was as clear as if another person had spoken it in my ear. I said nothing but turned and looked at him. He was a complete stranger, totally unknown to me, and I did not speak to him. Later, while I was preaching, I looked at his chair, and he was gone. Strange! I thought, considering God's word about him, but I continued with the message.

When I walked toward the side of the room, I saw him lying face-down on the floor praying. It was apparent he was in deep intercession (Romans 8:26, 27). This time I heard no spoken words, only an assurance, "This man is real. You can trust him. He will bless you!" Never has a message been more truth and accurate about anyone. Herb proved to be an incredible help. He was an excellent musician, became my personal-encourager, and held us together in the years that followed. Whatever task needed to be done, he would do it.

Eventually, we had to leave the High School and began a pilgrim-journey, worshiping in the Funeral Home, Holiday Inn, Jewish Synagogue, Hotel Ballroom, Lutheran Church, other sites, until Herb found us a more permanent spot at the Delray Beach Lions Club. We welcomed it, even though every Sunday morning we had to clear-away beer cans and party-trash from the night before. Herb accepted this as his personal challenge and always had the building clean and orderly for us. He decorated the Meeting Room with flowers, potted plants, and a carpet for the pulpit area.

A new crisis came on Easter Sunday, 1979, and we had to find another meeting place. This time we rented the Ball Room at an ocean-front hotel and made big plans. My ministry had officially begun on Easter Sunday, 1949. This would be my Thirtieth Anniversary, and we wanted to celebrate. Instead, the event crashed in disaster. People arrived at the hotel, but there were no parking places, and only a few attended the service. When Laurie and I left the building that day, I turned to her and said, "There is no point in trying any longer. I am ready to quit!" For the first time, I had no strength to go on. All the pain came back at once. My Ordination had been canceled; my home church in Miami accused me of heresy, and denominational pastors who had been my long-term friends refused to speak to me.

My best denominational pastor-friend died, and I was not told until he was buried. The newspaper had smeared us; friends abandoned me, and our congregation was a group of homeless nomads. A few miles away, our former church-building was almost empty and unused. A few people sat possessively in it. I was both confused and angry. Worse still, through manipulation and lying, the "Absalom" was the new pastor. Pulling the car onto a side street, I stopped, put my face against the steering wheel and wept. That night I went back to the Boynton Inlet, stood in the dark, spray in my face, and cried, "Lord! Where are You?!"

Cecile knew the grief Laurie, and I were undergoing, and she insisted we join her for a vacation to Wyoming. We went and stayed at the Jackson Lake Lodge, south of Yellowstone National Park. The lobby in this building has an enormous picture window facing the Grand Teton Mountains—one of the most scenic spots in America. An expansive plain lies between the hotel and the Tetons, and the Snake River winds through it. Wild moose, elk, buffalo, grizzly bears, and a host of other great animals inhabit the area. Many of these come close to the hotel—Moose even wandered frequently through the parking lot. In spite of my pain, the view was breathtaking.

One evening I left the lobby and climbed a hill on the north side to be alone. Although the plain was no longer visible in the dusk, I could still see the outline of mountains in the distance. It was a beautiful moment, but my heart was in pain. I had just reached the top, when the Lord suddenly spoke, stopping me in my tracks. In a loving, compassionate voice, He said, "I want you to give up your right to be angry." I was stunned—and stood unmoving. The message was unmistakable: He had not asked me to give up my anger but to give up my "right to be angry."

That surprised me; even God admitted I had a right to be angry. As I struggled with the message, I began to realize that my anger was in direct competition with His desire to be in control. If I wanted Him to take command of the ugly situation in Florida, I would have to turn loose of it, and the only way I could do that was to "give up my right to be angry." Although I did not know it, that was one of the most historic moments of my life. Finally, I said, "Alright, Lord, I'll do it—I give up my right to be angry. I turn loose and trust You to take over." It was that simple.

When I walked back to the hotel, I told Cecile and Laurie nothing of what had occurred—I did not tell anyone. The next day we went to Yellowstone, watched Old Faithful, saw moose, elk, bears, and had lunch in the Lodge's historic dining room. Returning to Florida, I was more relaxed, less tense; and my attitude toward church problems amazingly changed. I said nothing about my God-encounter on the hill, but I didn't have to. People immediately recognized a change in me. I also recognized a difference in them and realized I had underestimated their fortitude and determination. For most, the inconvenience of being without a building of our own was a challenge—not a deterrent. For the next months, the authentic ones were faithful and we survived. Somehow, we "fought the good fight of faith" and were joined by new faces who hungered for the presence of God (2 Timothy 4:7).

As soon as I was back home, I placed a picture of the Grand Tetons and the Snake River on my office wall. It was there as a daily reminder of what happened in my life in that beautiful part of the world. It was there for another reason: I frequently showed it to people who came for counseling and told them the story. And then I talked with them about their need to "give up their right to be angry." Wives who were battling frustration because of derelict husbands, husbands who were angry because of failure in their wives, and scores of other painful situations, found their answer in front of that picture.

Chapter 25

THE HOLY SPIRIT INSTRUCTS A MIRACULOUS PRAYER

Prophesying a Husband for My Daughter

In December 1982, Cecile was living in Atlanta and called to tell us she would be having surgery. It was major and she would be hospitalized for five nights. When the time came, Laurie and I drove to Atlanta and took her to Northside Hospital. Surgery was scheduled for early morning, and the night before, I was standing at her bedside silently praying. Specifically, I told the Father, "Lord, I'm glad to be here. I want to be here, but she doesn't need her father here. She needs her husband here!"

Instantly, the Holy Spirit spoke the "Rhema-word" to me, telling me what I should do to bring that husband to her. It was shocking—but I knew the message was from God. Strangely, He quoted the command Jesus gave to the young man's corpse at the village of Nain: Stopping the funeral procession, Jesus said, "Young man, I say to you, Arise!" (Luke 7:14) That command, "Arise," was my instruction. I was to say to Cecile's unknown, future husband: "Young man! I say to you, Arise!" Without explaining to Laurie or Cecile, I instantly obeyed. Standing at her bedside, I silently addressed the whole of humanity with a spiritual-command for this unknown young man to arise. I did not know who he was or where he was, but the Holy Spirit did.

Surgery the next day was uncomplicated and Cecile returned to her room where Laurie and I waited. At mealtime that night, Neal (Buddy) McGuire, a friend she knew at First Baptist Church, Atlanta, sat at her bedside and fed her. He knew nothing about my instruction from the Holy Spirit the night before, and I knew nothing about his. When he sat at her bedside and fed her, he prophetically fulfilled the husbandly-role.

Buddy and Cecile had previously met at First Baptist Church Atlanta in 1978. They had dated for a short time but had communicated only a few times during the next several years. Buddy felt all along that Cecile was the one he was to marry. Although Cecile admired him in many ways, she dismissed the idea, thinking he was too shy. Then Buddy graduated in

1980 from Georgia Tech, with a Civil Engineering Degree. He was sent to Charlotte, N.C. on a field assignment for six months. While there, he received the Baptism in the Holy Spirit and became involved with ministry at a Four-Square Gospel Church, including the ministry of Deliverance. When he returned to Atlanta, he became actively engaged in street ministry in downtown Atlanta for over three years.

When Cecile was in the hospital, her nurse happened to be Buddy's sister Suzanne. She told Buddy that Cecile was there. Buddy told me several months after they married that the Lord had specifically instructed him to go and visit Cecile. He argued with the Lord. Needless to say, God won the argument and Buddy obeyed. In October, 1983, they were engaged, and the following January, 1984, Laurie and I returned to Atlanta for their wedding.

Do I believe in the spiritual gifts outlined in First Corinthians 12,13, and 14? Absolutely! They are the power in my life and ministry. Also, I think my speaking that night at the hospital and Neal's responding is the principle disclosed in Revelation 22:17, that says, "The Spirit and the Bride say come ...." As a believer, I compose part of the Bride of Christ and when, in obedience to the Spirit's command, I said to that unknown young man "Arise! Come." The Holy Spirit simultaneously spoke to him saying "Come!" The Holy Spirit knew who and where he was; I did not. Thankfully, he came. I am aware that the basic message of the Scripture in Revelation is far greater than the way I applied it—but I obeyed the Holy Spirit's directive, and He responded. Had I been a cessationist, I would never have experienced that wonderful message or had the motivation to obey it. I could never had asked for a more suitable husband for my daughter than Neal. Today, they are both serving the Lord and assisting me in ministry.

Jesus said, "The words that I speak to you they are spirit and they are life" (John 6:63). As Christian, we miss great opportunities by failing to recognize the spiritual-power and life inherent in the Scripture. It is still there. Remember what Jesus said of His teachings: "They are spirit, and they are life." This principle is reinforced in Matthew 18:19, when He said, "If two of you shall agree on earth as touching anything that they shall ask, it shall be done for them of my Father who is in heaven." The key is agreement between two authentic believers and the Holy Spirit. This is the "threefold cord" that is not quickly broken (Mathew 18:19). Without the

Holy Spirit's approval, we can do nothing. Over the years I have witnessed much religious-talk among Christians that is void of the Spirit's approval, His presence, and His power.

Cecile and Buddy's Wedding

Cecile and Buddy were married in January 1984, and the wedding was a beautiful event. Laurie made Cecile's wedding dress, sewing hundreds of seed pearls onto the lace by hand. I conducted the ceremony, and the Reception was grand. Laurie baked the four-layer cake and brought it from South Florida.

Six years later, in 1990, Cecile and Buddy's son, Benjamin, was born. He and I have always shared a very close relationship. He's multi-talented, an Eagle Scout and loves the out doors. He's also very spiritually perceptive and has a successful career in the computer industry. He and his wife, Kendra, have two precious children—Evangeline Hope and Declan Charles, who is named for me. Part of his amazing testimony is included in the Appendix Section of this book.

Chapter 26

A WORD OF KNOWLEDGE MIRACULOUSLY DELIVERS ME AND A CONGREGATION

While I have witnessed most of the Spiritual Gifts in operation, in my own ministry, I have functioned more frequently in the "word of knowledge" than any other. These have been significant messages for me personally. It was a "word of knowledge" that told me in 1949—a month in advance—that I would preach my first sermon on Easter Sunday. At that time, I had never mentioned my call to the ministry to my pastor, family, friends—anyone. No one knew that secret but God and me; however, the word of knowledge was fulfilled exactly as it was told me. My pastor had the same word of knowledge and knew God had called me to the ministry.

I had another word of knowledge when Laurie, Cecile, and I were living at the Lockhart estate in Gulfstream, Florida. I was standing in the doorway one evening, facing the ocean, when the phone rang. Before I turned toward it, the Holy Spirit told me every detail of the call before I answered. Throughout my years of ministry, this "Word" functioned in me periodically, but the gift increased immeasurably after the prisoner laid-hands on me. This miraculous word has not only blessed me but saved my life. For example, I was at our local hospital in Boynton Beach when one of the doctors grabbed me by the elbow and with a push toward the doorway said, "Let me take you to lunch! I need to get away!" Unknown to either of us, a word-of-knowledge was soon to rescue me.

As we drove out of the parking lot he explained, "I must stop at my house for a moment and then we will eat!" He lived close by. We hurried into the house, and I waited inside, standing near the front door. He disappeared. Without explanation, I suddenly knew I must be seated. A "word of knowledge," like a strong shove, pushed me down into a chair behind me. No one else was present. In the next instant two Doberman dogs bounded into the room from a side patio, stopped, and stared ominously at me. These were guard-dogs, trained to attack. I was a stranger, alone in their house. Thankfully, my sitting position was passive and non-threatening. Had I been standing they would have attacked me. The "shove" saved me. I smiled and signaled the dogs to come to me.

A second later they trotted my way, put their faces in my lap, and I was rubbing their heads when the doctor returned. Seeing them, he froze in the doorway—color drained from his face. He thought the dogs were locked in the patio. These Dobermans were trained to protect the house from intruders, I was a total stranger, and had they attacked, even the doctor could not have saved me. He also gained a greater lesson than seeing the dogs nuzzling me. He saw that "The angel of the Lord encamps round about those who fear Him and delivers them" (Psalm 34:7). How does God deliver us? Frequently, it is done by our believing and obeying His words of knowledge. Christians often ignore the "word" assuming it is their own imagination.

But the question arises, why aren't we delivered every time from disaster? I don't have an answer. An angel could have saved me at age three from the tragic fall in Miami. I only know we are engaged in spiritual warfare which we personally must fight. The Gifts of the Spirit listed in First Corinthians twelve equip us for battle—without them, we go naked into the fray. When I hear preachers scorning these awesome gifts, I weep for their congregations. They are victimized by their pastors' ignorance.

In our church in Delray, Bob Stogdill was a man who was mature in the Spirit's work and became a trusted friend. He operated a landscape business. During the day he moved from one location to another. There were no cell phones, and I depended wholly on prayer and words of knowledge to find him. At least five times when I needed Bob and had no way to get in contact—except prayer—I got in my car, placed my hands on the steering wheel, and said, "Lord, you know where Bob is, take me to him."

One instance, I backed out of my drive and heard the Holy Spirit, say "Turn right." I obeyed, drove one mile, passed under a traffic light, approached another, and heard the Spirit say, "Turn left." Again, I obeyed, drove half-a-mile, was stopped at a traffic light when Bob's truck passed in front of me. I blew the horn, he waved and pulled to the curb. Our meeting was the absolute result of the "word of knowledge." That spiritual gift began benefiting my life in incredible ways.

Speaking To The Storm In Jesus's Name

When Doc Shell was pastor at Christ Chapel, in Florence, Alabama, he invited me several times to preach at a series of nightly services. One afternoon I was in my hotel room looking at the Tennessee River in the distance. It was a beautiful moment; the sky was blue and the atmosphere serene. Without any explanation, the Holy Spirit said, "Take authority over the weather." I was puzzled about the message. Still admiring the tranquility around me, I obeyed; and in the Name of Jesus I took authority over the "Prince of the power of the air." I forbade his touching that area of Alabama with a violent storm (Psalm 149:5-9, Matthew 12:29, Luke 10:17-20). There was no emotion in my voice–but I did speak with authority. To most Christians—especially pastors—such action is absurd and ridiculous. I agree. To the natural-person, it sounds that way. But Jesus taught it. He did not ask us to understand but to obey. Nothing obvious happened in the hotel room, and a short time later a driver arrived who took me to the church.

Christ Chapel had a large congregation and was meeting in its gymnasium, and each night the building was filled to capacity. The Holy Spirit's wonderful presence over-lay the meetings. People were healed, baptized in the Spirit, and "signs and wonders" accompanied every service. Many nights the entire floor-area around the building was filled with people fallen under the power of God. Before the worship, that evening, Doc Shell, the pastor, hurriedly spoke to the congregation, "I don't want to alarm anyone, but the safest place in this building is through those large, double doors." He pointed toward the main entrance and a corridor leading into the school's interior. He explained, "You have all heard the warning from the Weather Bureau that a severe storm-front is coming toward us ..."

When he said that, I understood the Holy Spirit's message to me earlier that afternoon. Going quickly to the microphone, I waited until he finished the announcement and then told the congregation about my instruction to "take authority over the weather." I explained: "We are going to obey Jesus and 'speak to the mountain'—in this case, the storm—and forbid it harming us." Briefly, I explained the difference in praying to Jesus about a problem and taking authority over the problem in His name. He taught both principles. Everyone stood. Together we rebuked the storm, telling it specifically not to touch our homes, our property, or our lives.

That was all we did. The service continued without any interruption. There was no disturbance that night from lightning, thunder, or violent wind. I preached and forgot all about the weather warning.

The next evening, when Pastor Shell greeted the congregation, he held up a cassette tape, and said, "This is a copy of the U.S. Weather Bureau's official radio-report about the storm that went through Alabama last night." By that time, everyone knew of the devastation that had swept across the state and into Georgia. Many areas had been severely damaged. Our area had been completely spared. Pastor Shell continued, "The Weather Bureau explained that the front divided just before it reached Florence. Half went to the north, half to the south, missed the city, and came back together on the other side."

We had been surrounded by violent winds but protected in a doughnut-shaped hole. While we thanked the Lord we had been spared; we felt deep grief for those who were not. Many Christians are appalled that others believe they have power to speak to storms, crisis, other disasters, and make a difference. It is precisely what Jesus taught. Please hear this: Speaking to a storm is not a mental activity; it is wholly spiritual. One must get beyond the "mental" concept before he can understand what is taking place. Faith is not a mind-game. Authentic Christianity is not a religious identity; it is an empowerment. Nor was Jesus being ludicrous when He rebuked the disciples after the storm on Galilee by saying, "Where is your faith?" They could have spoken to the wind as He did (Luke 8:25).

Belmont Church

Jim and Anne Bevis invited me to speak at Belmont Church's "Conference On Spiritual Renewal" in Nashville. They had read my book, *Sunrise of David, Sunset of Saul*, and urged me to join Paul Cain and Mike Bickel as a team member. Don Finto was Pastor, Jim was Associate, and denominationally, Belmont was a Church of Christ. The congregation had encountered the Holy Spirit and was hungry for a greater relationship with Him.

Laurie and I were leaving for Nashville, when the Holy Spirit said: "You will soon have your own building." I stopped in my tracks. That was welcome news! As a "word of knowledge," the message was spoken unmistakably clear.

Laurie and I drove to Belmont where God moved in astonishing ways. My assigned topic at the Conference was "Signs and Wonders." The people experienced such powerful encounters with the Holy Spirit that there was standing room only. The next day the Staff moved us to a larger room. We overflowed it and were moved again—this time, to the main auditorium. There was an intense hunger among Church of Christ people to experience the power of the Holy Spirit. They were tired of religion and wanted authentic demonstrations of God. During "hands-on" ministry, dozens of them dropped to the floor in life-changing encounters with Him. History was made at that meeting, and forty years later I still have contact with people I met on that trip. That Conference began a series of visits to Belmont that covered a period of many years. Sandy Patty and Michael W. Smith led worship at some of those early events. Pat Boone grew up in this congregation, and his parents were frequently present.

One young man who was laid-out for a long time was delivered from a tormenting spirit. Realizing he was genuinely free, he brought his parents the next night. The father was a deacon in a local Baptist Church who appreciated my message but became annoyed when I began laying hands on the people. He was complaining to his wife about this when I crossed the auditorium and stopped in front of them. Signaling her to step out, I touched her lightly, and she dropped to the floor. He was shocked but a moment later was sprawled-out on the carpet beside her. That night they experienced a Holy Spirit-baptism that changed their lives.

At that time, I did not know that Belmont Church would play a vital role in my involvement with the Charismatic Renewal Movement worldwide. I was asked to be part of the Intercessory Prayer Team for the World Congress of Evangelization at Brighton, England, in 1990. Jim Bevis, the Associate Pastor at Belmont, made that assignment for me and provided me with a front row seat. At this event, the Archbishop of Canterbury gave his endorsement for the charismatic renewal which was occurring among the 70,000,000 members in the Church of England.

Sitting there I was astonished. God had brought renewal to the Anglican Church worldwide, not by starting at the top with the Archbishop but starting at the bottom with an unknown Episcopal Priest. In 1960, Dennis Bennett, Rector at St. Mark's Church in Van Nuys, California, told the congregation he had been baptized in the Spirit and spoken in tongues. His announcement was met with fierce opposition, and some members leaped onto church pews shouting "Throw the damned tongue-talker out!"

In a less violent way, Don Finto, pastor at Belmont, broke away from the stringent legalism of the Church of Christ denomination and sought a fresh move of God. Their Conference On Spiritual Renewal was a big step in that direction. It was at that time Jim Bevis, Assistant Pastor, invited me to speak at the Conference. I preached several times, and during hands-on ministry, scores of people dropped to the floor under the power of God. It was a revelatory experience for them, and numerous Churches of Christ were brought into renewal by the Holy Spirit.

I was alone in the building one afternoon, walking up an aisle praying, when the Holy Spirit stopped me, pointed to a specific seat and said, "She will be here." The message was precise, and I understood someone in that seat was to receive special ministry. That night, however, the woman was not present. Nor did she attend the next service. Each time, someone else was in that seat, and the "sign" was not on them. The whole experience was puzzling. To my amazement (and disappointment) the meeting closed, and I went home, without ever ministering to this special person.

One year later I returned to Belmont and was concluding the sermon, when I looked across the congregation, and to my absolute joy, there she was! I was amazed. It was a little white-haired lady whom I had never seen but the "sign" was on her. Distinctly, I heard the Holy Spirit say, "This is the one." He not only had told me about her, where she would be sitting but had known it a year in advance. Still preaching, I quickly left the pulpit, walked back to her row, called her out, and laid hands on her. She instantly dropped under the blessing of God. That experience was a turning point in my ministry. But He had made me wait a whole year to learn my lesson. In it, I discovered how to better hear the Holy Spirit and avoid "religious" routines in ministering. More than ever, I realized God's method is always fresh, alive, vibrant. He never follows religious tradition. Our methods frequently become methodical and stiff. That stiffness usually turns into performance.

Chapter 27

GRACE FELLOWSHIP'S NEW BUILDING, NEW LIFE, NEW MINISTRY

Grace Fellowship Church and Conference Center

When the meeting at Belmont Church closed, Laurie and I returned to Florida where I happily learned that our Elders found a small Shopping Center for sale in Boynton Beach. It was well-located on Federal Highway, contained five rented shops and had space for two auditoriums. One could serve as a chapel, seating about eighty people, and the larger one would accommodate more than five hundred. The purchase was a faith-act for our little flock, but several of our families were willing to help with financing. We bought it and immediately began the renovations.

The building had a large tower on one end, and we immediately placed a huge Cross on it. Another sign told the world the property had become Grace Fellowship, Church and Conference Center. In two years, we grew from 60 members to more than 300. Best of all, the Holy Spirit invaded the services, and on Sunday nights people came from numerous other churches in the area. Many were healed, delivered, and filled with the Holy Spirit. Their lives were radically changed.

During that time, I arrived one morning and found workers installing cement-lettering near the main entrance which I had not approved. It read: Charles Carrin Ministries. When I objected, the Elders explained, "We know you will be traveling as an evangelist someday and will no longer be pastor here, but we want it understood from the beginning that you will be the Church Evangelist, and your office will always be in this building— regardless of who is pastor." Our plan, from the beginning, had been to establish Grace Fellowship with the Five-Fold Ministry of Ephesians 4:11-13. With this reminder, I agreed, and the lettering remained.

Within a year of purchasing the Boynton Beach property, we moved into the main sanctuary, with new faces appearing weekly in the crowd. After the sermon one morning, I left the pulpit area and did "Hands-On" ministry in the aisles. People were falling into God's embrace and when I approached new-comers, Tony and Barbara Morrongiello, she quickly came to me. A second later she was resting on the carpet. When I turned back, Tony had disappeared. I was shocked—he was gone—and then I saw him on the floor, hiding under the chairs. In spite of the seriousness of the moment, I was inwardly laughing. Here was the retired First Vice President of the American Express Bank, Wall Street, New York, trying to hide from God. But it didn't work. I called him to the aisle, and in a second's time, he was laid-out beside his wife. It was a life-changing moment for both of them. They became faithful members, and soon afterward Tony sat up abruptly in bed, late one night and said to Barbara, "Charles is going to ask me to become a Board Member and Treasurer for his Corporation!" That happened exactly as he said: After resigning as pastor and beginning my traveling ministry, Tony became the only Corporation-Treasurer I ever had.

Craig and Karen McMichael appeared in our service one Sunday morning in 1992 and for several visits sat on the back row. Craig was a former Marine, served in a special combat-unit in Viet Nam, and was Fire-Arms Instructor for the West Palm Beach Police Department. Watching from the rear, they knew I ministered to individuals at the close of every service. But, because the congregation was standing, they were unaware people were falling to the floor. They had been active in one of the largest Presbyterian Churches in Florida but had not witnessed public manifestations of the Holy Spirit. Karen came forward for ministry one morning and later told me that when I laid hands on her, she saw a ball of "white Light" swirling toward her, knocking her to the floor. That was her introduction to the charismatic-experience. A few days later she reluctantly came to my office saying, "I feel like I am supposed to offer my service to you." I accepted immediately, and she became my personal secretary. Neither of us imagined that she, like Tony, would still be serving in her post twenty years later.

Murry and Barbara Fishman, a Jewish couple who joined when we were at the Lion's Club in Delray Beach, were also God's future-assignments to work with me. Like Tony and Karen, Murry would become part of my ministry Board. Barbara had been baptized, but he had not. We made plans for an ocean-baptism on Sunday afternoon for a large group at three o'clock, and everyone was eager to attend. Though the morning was beautiful, by one o'clock, a severe storm spread over the area. Strong wind, lightning, and heavy rain hit us and by 2:30 everyone had canceled their plans—except Murry. He was eager to be baptized, and I assured him I would be at the ocean, regardless of the weather. When I arrived at the beach, only a few cars were present, waiting in pounding rain. None of us were aware, but everyone was saying the same prayer: "Lord, open a hole in the cloud and let the sun shine through!"

At exactly one minute before three, Beverly Sandidge stepped out of her car into the rain, slapped the hood of my vehicle and yelled, "Aren't you getting out?!" Reluctantly, I agreed, and the second my foot touched the pavement the rain stopped, the wind quit; and a hole opened in the cloud. In the same moment, the sun shone through brightly. Even the birds began singing. Everyone jumped out of their cars, and we went to the ocean. We found it smooth as glass, and Murry was "buried with Christ in baptism" (Romans 6:4). Like the eunuch baptized by Philip, this Jewish believer "went on his way rejoicing" (Acts 8:39).

SALUTE TO ISRAEL

Annually, our church hosted a "Salute To Israel" in which we invited all the local Jewish Synagogues to a Sunday night service, had a Rabbi or member of the Israeli Consulate to speak, and showed the Jewish community that we genuinely loved them. One year our speaker was Gadi Baltiansky, Counselor at the Israeli Embassy in Washington DC. While these were not evangelistic meetings, the Holy Spirit still moved sovereignly among the Jews. I will never forget one elderly Jewish woman who left the service patting her heart and saying in broken English, "I never felt so goood! Vunderful! I never felt so goood!"

On Monday morning after one of these events the secretary called me and said, "Pastor, the Cantor who was here last night wants to speak to you …." Before I could reply there was a loud knock on my door and when I opened it, he rushed in. Without sitting down, he said, "I must ask you something! I must ask you something!" I offered him a seat, but refusing it; he continued, "Last night you asked us to join hands and lift them to the Lord …," He paused a moment, as if hesitant to continue. Then, staring me eye to eye, said, "When I raised my hand with the young woman next to me—something like electricity came down my arm!" His stare became intense. "I want to know! What was that?"

I was gentle as I replied, "That was the Holy Spirit." With that, he dropped into a chair and after a moment said, "That is what I thought you would say!" The stare became more intense. "What does it mean?!" There was almost panic in his voice. He wanted to hear my answer but was also afraid of it. I paused, then drew closer to him, "That is the Holy Spirit's way of telling you that Jesus is the Messiah …." He grabbed his face and began shouting. "I can't deal with that! I can't deal with that!" Leaping to his feet he rushed out of the building and across the lawn yelling, "I can't deal with that!" In a moment he was gone; regrettably, I never saw him again. As he drove away, I prayed, "Lord, complete the good work You have begun in him! Though he fled my office, he cannot outrun You. Challenge his unbelief with another 'sign and wonder!' At least let him become a 'disciple in secret'" (John 19:38). An important question is this: Would that "electricity" have happened with anyone else next to him? Possibly. But I also know the young woman whose hand he held was a high-voltage believer. Her relationship with God was powerful and intense. Scripture says, "Jews require a sign …" (Luke 11:29). To the Cantor, this was definitely a "sign and wonder." He got it.

The Spiritual Significance of the Rainbow

It was near this time, on a flight out of West Palm Beach, Florida, we had just become airborne over the ocean when a boy sitting next to the window grabbed my arm. "Look out there!" he said urgently. "Look!" What I saw was one of the most magnificent sights of my life. Reaching down to the surface of the ocean and rising overhead as far as I could see was the full, unbroken circle of a rainbow. The color was indescribably brilliant with the lower part of the ring seeming to float on the surface of the water. There was no gap in it-just the breathtaking color of God's beautiful sign of covenant (Genesis 9:13).

I had learned a short time before that the complete rainbow, like the wedding band, is a continuous ring. It is much, much more than the half-circle we see from ground level. To behold the bow's full circumference, it is necessary to be above the earth looking down. The spiritual application of this truth is obvious. In this present life, we see only a fragment of the wisdom and strategy of God. Not until we are in Heaven looking back at history will we be able to understand the full scope of His plan and purpose in our lives. But there on the plane, in an astonishing way, I realized the rainbow's message also involves the operation of spiritual gifts (1 Corinthians 12). The bow, which is the sign of Covenant, is circular, like an engagement or wedding ring (Genesis 24:22, 30, 37). Spiritual-gifts are engagement-gifts, which, like an engagement ring, we receive before the wedding: The "Marriage Supper" in Heaven (Revelation 19:9). When you grasp this holy truth, seeing yourself wearing an engagement ring from Christ and seated with Him "in heavenly places," it will release faith powerfully within you (Ephesians 1:3, 20).

Wonderfully, the Holy Spirit showed me the relationship between the rainbow and another biblical, covenant sign: Circumcision. It too is circular. Circumcision means "circular cutting." Beginning with Abraham, every Hebrew male bore in his body this physical sign of God's covenant. Suddenly I realized that the miles-wide rainbow and the few inches of circumcision were identical. Each contained all the glory, beauty, majesty of the other. With that realization, came an important question: "Why did God place the covenant sign on the male reproductive organ?" The answer I received was this: God willed that the conception of every Hebrew child take place in the presence of his father's covenant-sign. Not only so, but the father's genes for every future generation passed through his covenant ring. The creative act of conception, in which those made in God's image and in His likeness, takes place within the "Circle of the Covenant" (Genesis 1:26; Acts 2:39).

The "shedding of blood" in scripture has powerful significance (Hebrews 9:22). The male, representing Christ, sheds his blood in circumcision while His Bride, in the breaking of the hymen, offers her blood back to him. It is the scar of the male's Covenant that breaks and sheds the blood of her hymen. This is not coincidental. Its truth is revelatory.

Trip to Sierra Leone, West Africa, 1991

Youth With A Mission (YWAM) and their Hospital ship, the Anastasis, invited Jim Bevis, Doc Shell, and me, to speak at three Spiritual Renewal Conferences in Sierra Leone, West Africa. These conferences were held in the cities of Freetown, Magburaka, and Bo, in hopes of evangelizing the people and calming the Civil War then raging. Fighting began in 1991 and lasted until 2002. We were there at its mid-way point. YWAM is one of the finest missionary organizations in the world. Their hospital-ship, the Anastasis, contains three state-of-the-art operating rooms, a 40-bed hospital ward, dental clinic, laboratory, X-ray unit, three cargo holds, plus accommodations for the crew and missionary teams. It was an honor to serve with them.

Sierra Leone was a British Colony from 1808 until 1961, when it gained self-governing independence. This was a tragic mistake. The nation went into an irretrievable decline. All maintenance of roadways, buildings, public works, ceased. Telephone poles were cut down and the copper wire sold. This is one of the few places on earth that has an abundance of alluvial diamonds. These are not buried in shafts underground but lie scattered in the topsoil. This factor has been the source of fighting for centuries.

While Jim, Doc, and I were traveling across the nation preaching, the doctors were doing major surgery. They replaced a man's damaged jawbone with a piece of his hip, removed numerous tumors from others, corrected hair-lips in children, and performed scores of other operations. The service was free and natives lined up by the hundreds, hoping to get treatment. While doctors and nurses were treating patients, carpentry teams built latrines and other facilities throughout the area. The ship brought the lumber, tools, constructors, and all the equipment needed.

Jim, Doc, and I were close enough to the war zone to see truckloads of bodies being hauled away from the battlefields. While we were stopped at one Military Checkpoint and were praying for the young Lieutenant in charge, a convoy of trucks loaded with bodies drove by. Later, a pick-up a truck passed us with a man's legs dangling out of the tailgate. It was a sobering realization that these victims were on their way home to families who did not yet know they were dead. In Magburaka, we stayed with young American missionaries, a brother and sister, and it was here an enemy soldier was captured and dragged alive through the city behind a speeding truck. People cheered and clapped as he went by. Later decapitated, his head and body were put on display in separate places. The rebel group was responsible for brutally killing 7,000 victims and burning many alive in their own houses. Other victims had their hands, feet, other parts chopped off by machetes and left to die. Inhumane violence surrounded us. Before its end, the war killed more than 50,000 people.

One village we visited was mourning the death of a baby that had been eaten by a python during the night. The snake came into the hut while the parents slept nearby. Here, we saw monkey-bodies hanging in the trees and being butchered for food. In Bo, a number of Muslim men were saved, and one came to me with a problem: He had four wives, and Christianity permitted only one. I listened prayerfully, knowing that divorced wives in that part of the world frequently starved to death. This was something he could not allow. My advice, right or wrong, was that he divorce none, marry no others, and not serve in any leadership-capacity in the church. Ultimately, the choice was not left to me but to the congregation he joined.

Our closing Conference was held at the Miatta Center in Freetown, and I was the final speaker. At the end of the message, the congregation stood, was singing, when the Holy Spirit began sweeping through the auditorium in an astonishing way. The people spoke Creole-English and fifteen other tribal-languages—but, suddenly, the words rising from us were none of these. Instead, we were caught up in the glory of singing in the "tongues of angels" (I Corinthians 13:1, 14:15). This mixed group instantly became the "Body of Christ" as our separate identities disappeared into an ocean of God's love. Such an experience is impossible to adequately describe but, I "saw" the worship as if it had been a gigantic column of fire. I will go to my grave remembering the awesomeness of that day when we were "singing in the Spirit!" (I Corinthians 14:5, Colossians 3:16)

The next day our departure plans were suddenly changed, and we were taken by boat to Conakry, Guinea, and began our flight home from there. I have never known for certain but assume the sudden change was because of the fighting. Later, we learned that our missionary-host, the young American male in Magburaka, was killed when his car plunged into a crater in the road. He was a victim of highway neglect. The road, like other public facilities, had been abandoned and craters, such as the one that killed him, were the direct result of neglect.

Chapter 28

DEREK PRINCE CHANGES MY LIFE FOREVER

God began sending internationally known Bible teachers to Grace Fellowship, and Derek Prince was one of the first to come. He was followed by Charles and Frances Hunter, Norvel Hayes, Charles Capps, and numerous others. A Palm Breach society-photographer, Paul Natali, was a member of the congregation and made numerous photos during their visits. His cameras and film were some of the best available, but when the pictures were developed of Norvel's hands-on ministry, we were startled to see spots of "light" scattered across the photos. These had not been visible to our eyes, but the camera detected as many as a dozen in each picture. Norvel's ministry was characterized by an unusual presence of the Holy Spirit, and we regarded this "sign and wonder" as part of it. The camera and film were not faulty.

Of all the guest-preachers who came, Derek Prince made the greatest impact on my life, Laurie's life, and my ministry. He was a legendary man I regarded as one of God's great gifts of modern times. Before we met in the 1980s, Laurie and I received his teaching tapes through the mail, and we would sometimes take them to a lonely beach location and listen carefully to every word. It was not unusual for us to hear a tape twenty times. Laurie also made a habit of listening to Derek's teaching tapes or Scripture tapes every day until the week she passed away in 2012. Through the power of the Word and the Holy Spirit—with Laurie's full cooperation—she experienced a miraculous healing from Depression around 1990, and she NEVER relapsed into that dark abyss again. Even my travel schedule, which sometimes left her home alone, didn't mar her joy and gratitude. She fully supported my being in ministry, hosting intercessory prayer meetings daily when I was away from home.

Theologically, no one else impacted us as Derek did, and I will carry his influence to my grave. Why Derek responded to me personally was a mystery. He was a scholar. I was not. He was an international figure. I was not. Even so, he respected me in a way that was both humbling and honoring. After preaching at Grace Fellowship, he and his wife, Ruth, became our committed friends.

Once when we were in a restaurant in Florida, I shared with him about ministering Deliverance to a young man with a sexual-identity problem. As I told how the demon bellowed like an angered bull—the noise too loud to have been human–Derek said, "Charles, please write that testimony for me! I want to include it in my new book, They Shall Expel Demons." I obeyed, and years afterward, I would sometimes go in a bookstore or pastors' office, see that wonderful paperback on the shelf, re-read the testimony, and have a flash-back to those wonderful days with Derek.

Although he was British to the core, Derek had been born in Bangalore, India, in 1915 to Military parents. His grandfather was an Army General, and his father was a Colonel. At age five, he spoke Hindustani so fluently that his parents became fearful India's influence would be damaging. So they sent him to a boarding school in England. Academically, he was superior, and at age ten began a serious study of Greek and Latin. He later added Hebrew, Swahili, and several European languages to his vocabulary. By age 13, Derek's scholarship gained him admission to England's distinguished Eton College, and at 18 he became Cambridge's Senior Scholar of the Year. To this was added the honor of "Kings Scholar." Eventually, Derek taught at Eton College and Cambridge University. He specialized in Platonian Philosophy using the ancient Greek text in which it was written. The Church of England offered him no real answers, so he pushed deeper into secular philosophy—hoping to discover "the meaning of life."

When World War II began, Derek left Cambridge and joined the Royal Army Medical Corps. Having to travel light, he took a single "philosophical" work with him, a book he had never read: The Bible. Ignoring the jeers of fellow soldiers who ridiculed his getting "religious," he propped against pillows in his bed each night and studied the Scriptures. To his shock, it had the answers he sought: What philosophy could not provide was here in this ancient volume. God was guiding, and soon afterward, Derek was saved in a back-street Pentecostal Church in England. Two weeks later, in his army barracks, he was radically filled with the Holy Spirit and laughed uncontrollably for more than an hour. The power of that encounter with God reinforced the all-important issue of his career: Scripture—not philosophy—had the answers he sought. When the war ended, he gave up the opportunity to return to Cambridge and plunged himself into ministry. Derek was married twice, first to Lydia, a Danish woman who ran an orphanage in Israel and was a forging-influence in his life. Several years after her death, he married Ruth, his only wife I knew personally.

230

In time, Derek became the author of more than 45 books, some of which have been translated into 60 languages. His radio broadcasts, "Keys To Successful Living," and "Today With Derek Prince" have been heard in more than a dozen languages around the globe. These include translations into all major Chinese dialects: Amoy, Cantonese, Mandarin, and Swatow. Other broadcasts went out in Mongolian, Arabic, Malagasy, Russian, Samoan, Tongan, Spanish, and English. Millions of Chinese who knew Derek as Ye Guang-Ming (Clear Light) assumed him to be Oriental. More than 100 Spanish-language radio stations in Spain and Latin America dispatched his messages locally and to 15 other nations. In the U.S., his broadcast is still carried by some 115 stations. Millions of Derek's teaching cassettes, books, and videos have been given away free of charge to spiritually-hungry people around the world.

The Call to Be a "Jephunneh"

Near the time of Derek's visit to Grace Fellowship, I was at home, sleeping soundly, when about 4:00 a.m, a shout in my ear, "Jephunneh!" startled me awake. I was physically shaken. God had called me by that name, and I did not know what it meant. Stumbling out of bed, I grabbed my Bible Concordance and found the name in Numbers 14:6. Immediately, I turned there and recognized the story: Moses sent 12 spies into the Promised Land, and on their return, only two of them, Caleb and Joshua, believed they could subdue the enemies. Jephunneh was not one of the faithful men. Realizing that, I began weeping—believing I had failed the test. God had rejected me.

Then, composing myself, I read the passage and discovered Jephunneh was not a spy; he was the father of Caleb—one of Israel's greatest leaders. Instead of my being a failure, God wanted me to father His modern Caleb's. That was one of the great moments of my life. Almost overnight, younger men began seeking me and bonding in a beautiful father-son relationship. "Sons in Ministry" meetings resulted, in which these men gathered for days for fellowship, teaching, and fathering. While I never had an organizational structure for them, at its highest, the number was about forty. Many times during "hands-on" ministry, they were laid out on the floor, vibrating in the power of the Holy Spirit.

The "Jephunneh-Caleb" relationship is an enlargement of what I had with the prisoner in the Atlanta Federal Penitentiary: After he and I parted, the Holy Spirit used me to impart the gifting to thousands of others. I remember once sitting on a front-row church pew when a lady rushed to me, but we never spoke or touched. Instead, she was knocked backward to the floor under the power of God. It was not unusual for people leaving the worship service to embrace me and drop to the floor. This later happened in parking lots, hotel lobbies, malls, and other public places. God seemed to be no respecter of places or situations.

Grace Fellowship became well known in Boynton Beach, and word spread through the community that we did Deliverance Ministry. Almost immediately, we were busy helping people who battled drug addiction, alcoholism, sexual disorders, rage, depression, and other problems. I shared my testimony of Deliverance from depression with many, and pastors came from out-of-state to receive help. One told us afterward that he brought his gun: "If this ministry had failed," he said, "I was not going home alive!" But, thankfully, he went back to his family and church as a man renewed in the power of God. Jesus promised our generation, "These signs will follow those who believe. In my name, they will cast out demons ..." (Mark 16:17). He had a demon of depression, and it was cast out in the authority of Jesus's Name. Derek knew of our success in Deliverance Ministry and invited me to be part of his Pastors Conference in Moscow. I was thrilled to go.

After arriving in Russia, our Ministry Team met Derek for breakfast, went to the auditorium, and sat in rapt attention as he taught. One thousand pastors from Russia and Central Asia listened intently, taking notes. Every seat in the auditorium was filled, and I stood with other team members against the back wall. What amazed me most was that I heard and learned more than Derek said. His humility was like a magnifying lens that enlarged the message he spoke. One afternoon, with an interpreter beside him, he was delivering a two-hour message when suddenly, he stopped. For the moment he seemed distracted, then, took command over the spirit of epilepsy in the congregation.

Everyone was puzzled, but, instantly, three epileptic seizures erupted in the audience. Victims slammed to the floor in various parts of the auditorium. Everyone was astonished, but Derek never left the platform. Instead, in his staid British-style, he said, "You who are close by know what to do. Minister deliverance to them, and I shall carry-on." And that is exactly what he did. He resumed at the same sentence where he left off, while little groups in the audience gathered around the fallen and successfully cast out spirits of infirmity.

In the evenings we attended the Russian Ballet and Moscow Circus. Never have I been more terrified, as I watched Russian trapeze stars at the circus. Their balancing acts seemed to defy gravity—with no safety-nets to protect them. I sat much of the time with my eyes clenched shut. We also attended a stage play where the auditorium was packed with a very somber, unresponsive audience. I came to realize this was typical of Russian behavior. Years of oppression had made them apathetic. This attitude dominated the spiritual climate, until later when the amazing fragrance of lilacs covered the city. The sweet smell of the lilacs lifted my spirit. Later, I stood in Red Square in front of Lenin's tomb, preaching the gospel and giving Bibles to a large gathering of Russian soldiers, office workers, tourists, and other passers-by.

I cannot speak for anyone, except a group of the young soldiers. These listened intently and followed me back to the bus, where they stood outside my window staring at me. They wanted one more handshake and Word of Gospel hope. Although they did not understand what was happening, the Holy Spirit touched them with the "Jephunneh-bond." Decades later, the memory of their faces is still vivid in my mind.

Although our group was in the Ukraine Hotel, one of Moscow's best, American jovialness was easily misunderstood. Even so, I would not submit to despair. One day I rushed across the lobby, approaching a group of Americans and Russians who were seated in a four-sofa-square, facing each other. The sofa nearest me was empty, and the same height as my belt line. I acted as if I did not see it, ran into its backside, did a complete somersault with my feet flying over my head and landed, sitting on the floor. The lobby exploded with laughter. A group of men watching from the balcony burst into hilarity. Silly as it was, that action broke the ice, and from then on, the "officialness" in the Staff relaxed. We Americans were accepted as friends.

On that trip, I was approached by several Russian pastors who asked if I would return to Moscow the following winter and teach in their Pastors School. I agreed, and plans were made for my visit. When Derek's meeting ended, we said tearful goodbyes, and two days later I was back home. Grace Fellowship was thriving and new faces appeared weekly. Office appointments filled the calendar, but I felt called to evangelism and encouraged the Elders to search for an assistant. We interviewed a number of good men but none who we felt was God's choice. So we kept looking, seeking, praying.

Months later, I returned to Russia and I have never been with students more eager to learn. The old Elbros Auditorium where we met was huge but unheated, and I wore a heavy coat and a layer of scarves around my neck. It was so frigid that students could see my breath as I spoke. In Russia, it was not the temperature that determined when buildings were heated—but the date. That was the government rule. Hospitals were heated first, but even they stayed cold until their official time on the calendar. Offices, apartments, homes, remained unheated until a later day of the month. Even with that discomfort, I loved being there, felt a strong devotion for the Russian Christians and admired their undaunted commitment to Christ.

At the end of the Moscow school, I took the train to Smolensk, preached at several churches and ministered privately to people in the area. This was a delightful experience, and all but one of the personal-ministries had been successful. In this case, the demons in the woman howled so loudly that neighbors in the building began banging on the wall, threatening to call the police. With that danger, the woman's daughter, Anka, insisted I go. A few days later, I returned to Moscow by train, and to my surprise, Anka was in the same car with me. She was returning to her home in Moscow. During that long ride, she explained that her mother had undergone "Deliverance" many times in the past, but none had been successful. She would soon relapse into the old problem of extreme moodiness and bipolar symptoms.

When I quizzed her about her mother's personal history, she told me about her harrowing escape from the Nazis during World War II. In August 1943, the Germans invaded Smolensk, killing thousands, and her mother, as a five-year-old barely, escaped. Moments after fleeing with her parents over a bridge, it was bombed, and everyone else was trapped in the city. These were machine-gunned to death, including her grandparents, friends, other children, pregnant mothers, and weeping fathers. The Nazis, like beasts, spared no one. I sat there, grieved, listening to the horror story.

Chapter 29

A PSYCHOTHERAPIST SEEKS HELP FOR HER PATIENTS

One of the appointments awaiting my return was with a local psychotherapist who asked if I would minister to eight of her worst patients. These represented a wide spectrum of mental disorders—all very different from what I had worked with in the past. I agreed to help, and we scheduled the appointments. After hanging up the phone, I became angered at myself for accepting the request. I had no experience with patients suffering from psychiatric disorders. All mine were demonic cases. Also, I knew that certain individuals under my care received freedom but had been unable to keep it. I feared this would be repeated with the psychotherapy patients.

Finally, the day came for the first patient, and as I waited, God strangely brought the Smolensk story back to mind. Somehow, I felt there was a connection between the Russian woman and the patients I would be seeing. What that was, I did not know—but, I became convinced the Russian woman's failure to receive lasting deliverance was related to her childhood trauma. As I waited, praying, I became convinced she was an example of what the Apostle James called "double-minded," being "unstable in all her ways" (James 1:8. 4:8). In trying to escape the memory of the Nazi bloodbath, her mind had fragmented, and part was still hiding from the recollection. In the Greek text, "double-minded" is translated from *dipsuchos*, literally, "two souls" or "two psyches" (*sucho/psycho*). Until recently, this condition was identified as a split-personality, schizophrenia, bipolar disorder, dissociative identity disorder, or fragmentation (James 1:8, 4:8). Since I had no training in this field, I was totally dependent on the Lord's revelation.

When the first patient arrived, a young woman in her 30's, the Holy Spirit confirmed the connection between her and the woman in Russia. In a flashing-vision, I actually "saw" the patient as a four-year-old child, hiding under an old-fashioned wicker sofa. The sofa, which was against a wall, was white, had no cushions, and the child's arms and legs were tightly gripping its under-structure. She refused to come out, and it would have been impossible to force her without injury. The Lord explained, "What you see is that part of her mind that is still in hiding." The woman who was sitting in my office—in part—was still a four-year-old behind the sofa.

In her case, two "souls" (*dipsuchos*) were living competitively in the same brain, refusing to acknowledge the other. In effect, the part under the sofa was protecting itself from a tormenting fear which no longer existed. The other part of her mind had become amnesic to the injury and no longer remembered it. The woman's need at this point was not deliverance, even though demons were present. What she needed was for that hidden part of her mind to be coaxed out of hiding. That was key. Her non-communicating part needed to be reconnected and reconciled with the other. Normalcy depended on the two merging cooperatively.

Deliverance ministry might have appeared successful at this point, but she would have quickly returned to her tormented state. I remember praying desperately saying, "Lord, what do we do?!" The instruction I received was to speak very lovingly, very gently, to that part under the sofa. I was to tell it the danger was gone; it no longer needed to hide, and Jesus was now its protector. I was not to command it as I would have a demon but to appeal to that tiny, frightened little girl to turn loose of the sofa and come home. The word "home" particularly impressed me. I was to say to it, "I know you can hear me—there is no more danger, it is safe now. You can come home."

Further, I was to remind the traumatized part that no one else could fit into that empty place but it. That was its true home. It could fit nowhere else. It wanted to come home. It was tired of hiding, tired of separation, tired of loneliness. All those would end when it slipped back into place. I would then wait, repeating the appeal, and coax it by saying, "Jesus will come with you. He knows you cannot come alone. So, follow Him and come home ... you want to ... we will wait ... you don't have to hurry ... but you do want to come home. There is no need for fear. The danger is now gone. God has promised to protect you. He has not given you the 'spirit of fear but of power, of love, and a sound mind'" (2 Timothy 1:7). This process was gently repeated a full hour to all the patients for the next two weeks. In the end, we ministered "Deliverance," commanding every unclean spirit to go.

Soon afterward I received an excited phone call from the psychotherapist. Speaking of that first patient, she said, "I had her for two years and achieved nothing. You had her for two weeks, and she is normal! I want to do what you are doing! Will you teach me?" The good news is that all of the patients were completely restored or dramatically helped. One even sent a generous donation as an expression of gratitude. For the next six weeks, the therapist brought her husband to my office weekly. We had lunch together, read the Scripture, and I went through two processes of teaching: Reunion of the divided mind and the exorcism of unclean spirits.

I emphasize this point: We ministered Deliverance successfully to these patients only after the fragmented condition of their minds had been corrected. I believe now that the Russian woman could have been healed—at least dramatically helped—had she received this type of ministry. Can I explain what happened inside these patients' brains? No. Nor am I suggesting I have the remedy for other mental needs. I do not. Nor do I think all mental illness is spiritual in origin. There are many factors, and I still experience failure, but what I did worked in these cases. I am not a medical person. I am a believing disciple of Jesus. In addressing the question as to why Deliverance Ministry is not successful in unhealed bipolar patients, it seems that the offending spirit uses the person's double-mindedness as its place to hide. For successful ministry, this gap must first be closed.

In the first century before Christ, Cicero, Rome's leading political-philosopher, described this condition as "a second self." This is an aberrant personality which is distinct from the person's normal or original one. Such an individual may lead a double life. The term describes dissociative identity disorder—as it is called today. When the book, *Dr. Jekyll and Mr. Hyde*, appeared in 1886, by Scottish author, Robert Louis Stevenson, it revealed to many readers for the first time the reality of a double personality.

Deliverance Ministry is not a one-time experience. While it may bring immediate results, there must also be renewal of the mind. This is a process. One without the other is not only futile but dangerous. Jesus taught that demons return to unprotected houses (Matthew 12:44). Everyone undergoing this type of restoration must defend themselves from spiritual re-infestation. To do so, they need to be filled with the Holy Spirit, become active in a full-gospel church, stay in fellowship with other believers, daily nurture themselves in the Scripture, and maintain a loving relationship with the Lord. This is mandatory.

Two other psychotherapists offer their opinions about combining Deliverance Ministry with mind-renewal. I am aware that over the years the psychotherapy-community has changed many terms and definitions in classifying mental disorders. Even so, the message of these Christian-psychotherapists is very valuable:

"As a licensed psychologist for many years and now teaching at a university, I have had experiences with patients with high recidivism rate (Pedophilia and Axis II disorders, etc.), for whom psychology seems to offer little hope. Years ago, I came across Brother Carrin's newsletter and gleaned from its pages helpful principles of kingdom living. His teachings on 're-gathering the mind,' 'homecoming,' and 're-infestation' appear to be God-given keys of kingdom living. Jesus talks about the keys of the kingdom. What are these keys? These are the keys that would open the doors that hitherto have been closed to difficult cases in psychology; if only we could appropriate them. Psychology does not have access to these keys—simply because they are available only to the children of the kingdom. Until now, the doors to the kingdom have pretty much been closed to these individuals. However, with these keys, they will finally be re-gathered home to stay" (Matthew 16:19)
—Abiola Dipeolu, Ph.D.

"When Brother Carrin came to the aid of the Christian psychotherapist, he was probably unaware that many experienced and skilled psychotherapists perform as mirrors for their patients. I am a certified clinical psychotherapist practicing for a number of years. When reflecting the patient's verbal and nonverbal behavior, some improve dramatically in therapy. However, when one considers severe mental disorders such as Schizophrenia, Multiple Personality (now called Dissociative Identity Disorder), and others, facilitating positive change can be quite elusive. What brother Carrin describes with concepts such as "re-gathering the mind," preventing "re-infestation, and "homecoming," goes a step farther. During his work with the therapist's patients, he was able to mirror the Holy Spirit. Essentially, Brother Carrin found a way for the Holy Spirit to confront the person's mental-emotional demons which resulted in them not only being healed, but delivered, and eventually freed."

—Dr. Joseph Donaldson, Ph.D.

The most extreme case to which I ministered was a young female-victim of childhood Satanic Ritual Abuse. She had been deliberately made schizophrenic by her parents and controlled through her alter-ego—Latin for "other self." This dividing of this young woman's mind had been done deliberately in early childhood by her parents forcing her to torture her pets to death. In the most gruesome ways imaginable, she slowly killed kittens she loved, watching them suffer and die agonizingly by her own hands. To escape that reality and guilt, part of her mind "went into hiding" and severe denial. It wasn't true. She never did that! The mental-part that was guilty assumed a different personality with a different name and became a cooperative Satanist. At the same time, her innocent part was an educated, medical technician and believing Christian. Impossible, you say. Not so! She would sometimes read her Bible, pray, go to bed at night bathed and clean but wake up in the morning, soiled, with blood and dirt under her fingernails, and a hundred-plus miles on her car—all of which she had no conscious memory.

The Satanic-control operated in this way: She would receive a telephone call in the night, and be addressed by her alter-ego name. That personality would respond and obey the caller. In such a state she participated in rituals that were very alien to her true self. In part, this is what Scripture calls the "depths of Satan" (Revelation 2:24). I have personally known babies born in public hospitals who were put through Satanic-ritual abuse within hours of their delivery. Such victims may show symptoms immediately or function normally for years before suddenly going berserk and committing horrific crimes.

Parents need to be aware of that abuse-possibility and protect their newborn. Thankfully, the current trend in infant-care is to leave babies with their mothers. This is why "renewal of the mind" is essential (Romans 12:1,2). As to those who abuse infants, Scripture forewarns: "The devil, who deceived them, was cast into the lake of fire and brimstone where the beast and the false prophet are. And they will be tormented day and night forever and ever" (Revelation 20:10). To that, we say, Thank God!

Christians and "Captivity Of The Mind"

While visiting a South Florida home, I unexpectedly witnessed a graphic illustration of demonic-infestation and "captivity of the mind." A young man had captured a fully-grown, wild hawk and converted it into an obedient Falcon. At the sound of a whistle, the bird would fly from its perch, light on his captor's arm, take food offered it, and on command return to its roost. Outdoors, where it was free to escape, the hawk made no attempt to return to its natural state. Instead, it would catch its prey and obediently give it to the one who had captured it.

I was amazed that this wild creature could be made to abandon its instinct, normal behavior, ancestry, and submit to the command of a stranger who had deprived it of conventional life. More so, I was astonished to learn the hawk's complete transformation had been accomplished within a few days of its removal from the wild. In that brief-time it had become a submissive prisoner, voluntarily doing the will of its captor and adapting to a strange and unnatural environment. As a further sign of mental-regression, some falcons even revert to baby-bird chirping. But as I watched, I saw much more than a falconer and his captive bird. I saw spiritual truths enacted before my eyes. With that realization, a theological question came to me: Can human beings be spiritually-captured, removed from their natural state, subdued, and forced into a lifestyle that is alien to them? Let me illustrate what I mean:

In 1973, four bank employees in Stockholm, Sweden, were captured during a robbery and kept inside a vault. Within six days they became so attached to their captors they not only resisted rescue but afterward refused to testify against the criminals. This psychological phenomenon of a person's submission to his captor became known as the "Stockholm Syndrome" and is equivalent to what happened to the hawk. That day, watching the captive bird willingly yield to its abductor, I recalled the 1974 kidnapping of Patty Hearst, the 19-year-old billionaire-heiress of the William Randolph Hearst family. This innocent young woman was kidnapped, kept in a dark closet, blindfolded, unfed, raped, abused for weeks, but then strangely renamed herself "Tanya," and joined her gangster-captors. She even took part in robbing a bank which she and her parents owned.

After serving her captors more than 19 months, Patty was captured by the FBI, tried in court, and tragically sentenced to 35 years in prison.

Many across America protested her sentence, I among them. Thankfully, three years later President Jimmy Carter commuted her prison term. As Christians, we see a parallel of people, like Patty, becoming captive to Satan and refusing to escape when they have opportunity to do so. In a similar way, I think this is what happened to my parents who did not flee the house in Miami when they realized we were endangered by it. Why did we stay? The answer is found in the "Stockholm Syndrome," to which my parents had remotely become victims.

The nation was again shocked by the kidnapping of Elizabeth Smart, a 14-year-old Utah girl who was taken from her bed at night and kept by her abductors nine months. Later, when she had opportunity to escape, she made no attempt to do so. That happened in 2002. In another case, an airline hostage became so emotionally attached to her captor that she married him. In some cases, former hostages have visited their captors in jail, recommended defense counsel, and even started security-funds to protect them. Similarly, we see this in the behavior of battered-wives who voluntarily stay with an abusive and dangerous husband.

According to psychologists, the victimized person submits to the abuser as a means of enduring the violence. A psychotherapist explained, "When someone threatens your life, deliberates, and doesn't kill you, the relief resulting from the removal of the threat of death generates intense feelings of gratitude. The victims' need to survive is stronger than the impulse to hate the captor." The victim sees the captor as a savior—this is Satan's ultimate deception. Be warned; this is the exact pattern used by religious cults. The tactic is usually isolation, dependence, then fear.

A short time after mine and Laurie's return to Florida, the world was shaken by the 1978 mass-murder and suicide of more than 900 members of a religious cult in Jonestown, Guyana. Most were Americans, as was their leader, Jim Jones, who seduced them to his agricultural commune in the jungle of South America. Here, cut off from families and friends, he first poisoned their minds, then, their bodies. Entire families were wiped out; this included some 300 children and young people under 17 years of age. A fruit drink, laced with cyanide, tranquilizers, and sedatives, was squirted into the mouths of babies and children, then drunk by adults. Jones died of a self-inflicted gunshot wound. How did the disaster happen? First of all, Jones was a severely demonized man whose hypnotic-presence forced the people into submission. This climaxed with their suicide. On a small scale, his mind-control achieved what Adolph Hitler accomplished on Germany's national scale: Absolute obedience.

Had the people in Jones' organization operated in the Holy Spirit's gifting, specifically, "discerning of spirits," all of them might have survived (1 Corinthians 12:10). Additionally, believers are encouraged to have their "senses exercised to discern both good and evil" (Hebrews 5:14). This is a reference to our five physical abilities of hearing, seeing, tasting, touching, and smelling. In His desire to protect us, the Holy Spirit will use these human abilities to bring revelation to us. For example, scripture warns: "Know those who labor among you" (1 Thessalonians 5:12). While we do that through spiritual gifts, we also enhance that through observation, physical and spiritual. Human knowledge which is anointed by the Holy Spirit provides much deeper benefit than superficial acquaintance.

Chapter 30

CRISIS: KINDNESS IS REPAID WITH BETRAYAL

While my traveling ministry continued to build, it had become apparent that I needed a trusted assistant at my home church. I was excited about the potential this opportunity would provide for both of us. The day before I left for Moscow with Derek Prince, a pastor came to visit me, whom I thought might be a possible candidate. I prayed with him and then made arrangements for the Elders to meet with him in my absence.

While I was in Moscow having dinner one evening, I mentioned the name of the Florida pastor who had come to my office the day before I left. Instantly, another American sitting close by spoke up and said, "I met him!" The man went on to give a glowing report about the prospective candidate's successful ministry. (Unfortunately, he did not know of other frightening factors, which we learned after it was too late.) The next day I called Grace Fellowship and spoke with one of our Elders, telling him what I had heard. He was delighted and said, "Wonderful! We have already met with him, and all of us feel like he should come on board. As soon as you are home, we will decide."

Regrettably, I made a grave mistake by not instructing the Elders to do a thorough background check. We acted too quickly, and a key person was brought on staff without properly discerning the situation. My own future as the Church Evangelist was destroyed.

For the first year, all went well, and I began giving him more pastoral responsibility, as my traveling schedule increased. Finally I gave him full responsibility as pastor, and I became the Church Evangelist. At that time, my travel schedule was very busy, and during some periods, I was on as many as 70 flights yearly. I worshiped at Grace when I was home, although I did not attend Elders Meetings, Brotherhood events, or fellowship dinners. Instead, I kept out of sight. I wanted the new pastor to feel free of my presence.

Then everything identified with my ministry was removed from the church calendar. Important features that had attracted much of the membership to us were discontinued. Our annual Salute to Israel, a few months away, was canceled. Although I said nothing, this was a major disappointment to me. Personal Deliverance Ministry stopped totally.

Whenever I was in town, however, my office at the church was an enjoyable and peaceful place. Then one morning, unexpectedly, I was ordered by the Elders to pack up and leave. I was stunned beyond words.

Concerned members of the congregation began demanding explanations from the leadership. When they learned how I had been ordered out, numbers of them left. The church never recovered. Unknown to me, the ugliness intensified: Churches who did not know I was gone, sent contributions to me at that address. Their letters were returned with a scribbled message on the envelope, "Moved. Left no forwarding address." The truth was, I was only a mile away, and whoever returned the letters knew where I lived.

My grief worsened when a young college professor asked to join me at future Conferences never showed. Months passed, and when we accidentally met, I inquired why he failed to attend. At first, he stumbled for words, then finally said, "I called your church office, asked for you but was told you were no longer there. When I asked "Why?" I was led to believe you had been put out of the church for moral reasons." I dropped into a chair, cupped my face in my hands, and began weeping. "Why? Lord," I cried! "I did everything to welcome this man with open arms! Gave him all I had achieved! Why am I lied-about and treated with treachery?" These men had loved me, and we were long-time Christian-brothers until the source of division came aboard.

The pastor remained at Grace a few years, but the "Anointing" was gone. Attendance radically declined, and he was soon followed by another who was not able to restore the church. In time, the Elders were left with a half-million-dollar balloon note, a small congregation, and little income. Finding another group of believers in need of a building, they merged with them. Financially, it was a wise move—except the "signs and wonders" never returned. Today, under new leadership, the building is wonderfully filled, people are being saved and indoctrinated, but the "demonstrations of the Spirit and power" are memories of the past (1 Corinthians 2:4).

Even so, I can truthfully say I have no unforgiveness toward any of those involved. That includes the new staff member, and I have proved that to each of them personally. Jesus said, "If you do not forgive men their trespasses, neither will your Heavenly Father forgive your trespasses"

(Matthew 6:14-15). If I want forgiveness, I must give forgiveness, even when no one asks for it. In sharing this, I am breaking a silence after many years.

Understandably, someone asks, if I have truly forgiven everyone involved in the attack why am I repeating the story now? The reason is this: My first responsibility is to protect the Kingdom of God; secondly, I have a responsibility to other pastors who may needlessly suffer as I have. Before protecting myself or another man, I must protect the Church and the Kingdom. Part of the failure at Grace was my own: A rightly-placed telephone call could have prevented the tragedy. I discovered years later that facts of the man's past ministry were vastly different from what we were told.

Would I suffer this pain again if needed? Absolutely! Seventy years ago on a street corner in Miami, that question was settled forever. I am not my own; my total-self belongs to God (1 Corinthians 6:20). At the cost of my own life, if need be, the Kingdom must be protected! For that reason— only—I am obligated to caution other congregations: "Know those who labor among you!" (Matthew 5:17, 1 Thessalonians 5:12, Joshua 4:9-16). Scripture commands me to "speak the truth in love" (Ephesians 4:15). Today, I pass that beautiful multi-million dollar building in Boynton Beach and bless the current congregation. Hundreds are crowding into its services weekly. For this, I thank God. Also, I remember those awesome days when the Holy Spirit moved in power, delivered the demonized, healed bodies, rescued psychotics, alcoholics, restored depressed minds, and salvaged those in sin. As for my Heavenly future, I believe this:

> "There shall I bathe my weary soul
> In seas of heavenly rest,
> And not a wave of trouble roll
> Across my peaceful breast!"

Warning Of Another Kind—Admonition to Churches

While I am on this topic of church crisis, I am constrained to share a different kind of danger. Again, I do this as a warning to others. The congregation of which I speak is where I was a guest speaker many times and saw some of the greatest "signs and wonders" of my career. The church was blessed with a young pastor and staff who were hungry for the truth and power of God. Their building was big, beautiful, and prominently located in a large city. The church was well known and respected in the community. I was always happy to be with them.

It was here one night, I saw a young couple standing rigidly in the rear, not responding to the offer for personal ministry but whom I felt were in great pain. I did not know the horrific tragedy they experienced the year before or how severely they were wounded. I went to them, signaling them to step to the aisle. I said nothing, laid hands on them; and both crashed to the floor. The Holy Spirit came on them instantly and bathed them in His glory. After returning home, I received this message from the woman. She wrote:

Dear Pastor Carrin,

Your ministry has changed my husband's and my life. We lost our 4-year-old daughter in a boating accident. We were Christians but knew nothing of the deeper workings and the healing power of the Holy Spirit. We were both very depressed and angry at God. When you ministered to us, we were "slain in the spirit" for the first time. The Holy Spirit began a healing work in us that has given us a reason to live and to worship His Holy Name. A hunger for more of God began in us that summer night—and praise God—the hunger has never been satisfied!! Since that time, we have received the baptism of the Holy Spirit, and the fruit of the Spirit operates in our lives. Thank you for giving your life to the ministry of people who are hurting; hopefully, my husband and I will have the opportunity to give to others as you have given of yourself. GOD BLESS YOU!

S.A,, Alabama

The miraculous-grace I saw the Holy Spirit perform in this couple and that beautiful congregation over a period of many years remains unequaled to this day. Later, I was told that the couple who lost their daughter went to Russia, adopted a family of orphaned children, brought them to the U.S. and reared them as their own.

During my ministry there, word quickly spread through the community that the Holy Spirit was restoring lives and rescuing the hopeless. Many visitors came, and unfortunately that included some curiosity-seekers who cared nothing about the Holy Spirit and His work. Their only interest was to be entertained. One evening three such pastors attended, sat on the front row by the aisle, where they could have a better view of the congregation. They listened to my Scripture-saturated message and watched as I laid hands on many in the congregation. Miraculous signs and wonders were obvious.

One elderly man dropped to the floor, his feet, legs, arms rigidly at his side, began vibrating in a way that was humanly impossible to do. His eyes were clenched tightly; spiritually, he was in Heaven's realm. As everyone watched, he vibrated down the aisle, came to the section where the three pastors sat, turned, and passed within inches of their feet. What they witnessed was a physical impossibility, an authentic "sign, and wonder." Strange? Yes. What did it mean? My only answer is that it challenged human logic. Unfortunately, the visitors saw only its novelty—not God's miracle—and apparently left unchanged.

Hear this carefully: If a congregation wants such blessings as came to the couple who lost their child, it must also be willing to accept the strange display that came to the old man vibrating on the floor. We dare not criticize the choice of God. I also know the Holy Spirit will deliberately challenge human logic with "signs" that go beyond our intellect. I also know that people who undergo such physical events also receive a confirmation of God's love that can be gained no other way. I have another reason for mentioning this church: The congregation was not only the site of the Holy Spirit's greatest "signs and wonders" in my ministry but became a target for the devil's concentrated attack.

On my last visit, I met a new member, a man who had purposely endeared himself to the pastor, his family, and made himself indispensable both in their personal lives and to the church. He did this in a calculated way, and they became obligated to him. He was an eager worker and capable in many areas of the church's need, but from the onset, I distrusted him and was uncomfortable in his presence. What I experienced was the "discerning of spirits" gift that warned me about him (I Corinthians 12:10). It came as no surprise when the pastor came to me and said the man was highly critical of the Holy Spirit's "signs and wonders" and wanted to challenge both my theology and practice. And, he wanted to do that in a Board Meeting with all the Staff present.

I said, "No." I was not available for such a meeting. Several days passed, and the pastor approached me again with the same request. Again I said "No." Finally, when he persisted, I agreed, and we assembled in the Board Room. As we were seated, the man opened a large satchel and began stacking piles of magazines, papers, and other publications on the table. I realized he was merely trying to impress us with the amount of his negative material. Our discussion would not be Bible-centered, so I rose to my feet, explained why I was not staying, and prepared to leave the room. The pastor begged me to be seated, and momentarily, I did. Finally, seeing the futility we faced, I took my Bible and walked out. God continued to bless the meetings, and several days later I left the church.

A year passed, and I had no contact with the congregation; but one day a Staff Member called to explain that not long after my visit the pastor rushed into his office, angrily emptied his desk, gathered his books, personal items, and announced he was quitting the ministry. In a few minutes, he was gone. The congregation was shocked, and even his family did not understand what happened. The one who called me, like others in the congregation, was bewildered by his hostile actions. "I can tell you what happened!" I answered angrily, "I can tell you!" Referring to the man who opposed the Holy Spirit's miraculous works, I said, "He is a Warlock! He came to the church specifically to destroy it! He bewitched the pastor and ruined his ministry! That was deliberate!" Am I certain of that? Absolutely! Jesus warned of wolves who would come in sheep's clothing (Mathew 7:15). Paul gave the same precaution (Acts 20:29).

Another Example Of Church Control

One Sunday morning I worshiped in a church that was "border-line" regarding Deliverance Ministry and the Holy Spirit's visible demonstrations. The singing and sermon were excellent, and I enjoyed being there. An elderly woman recognized me, rushed into the aisle and held out her hand. When I touched it, she instantly screamed in a raucous, demonic shriek and pitched to the floor (Mark 1:23-25). No one caught her. The congregation was shocked. They had no teaching in this area and stared at me with bewilderment and surprise. Because of the violence in the shriek, I did not want them assuming the little woman was secretly an evil person.

So I went to the microphone and explained what had happened. In spite of the noise, the incident was very good. She had been delivered from a spirit of infirmity that ultimately would have destroyed her health. Craig and Karen McMichael, my secretary, and her husband, were also present that morning and witnessed the deliverance take place.

My disappointment is this: There were dozens more in the congregation who equally needed ministry but never got it. The suddenness of the woman's Deliverance indicated that this was an "anointed moment" when the Holy Spirit was present to heal and rescue others. The building was crowded with many in need. Why did not the pastor stop everything and provide for more of his members to be set free? Such an opportunity was never given.

The "Word of Knowledge" Gives Us A New House

In 1979 after my Ordination had been canceled, Laurie and I moved out of the church's pastorium. We had no place to live, no money, and searched desperately for an apartment we could afford. Finally, we discovered a one-bedroom efficiency and moved into it. Staying there several years, we then bought a two-bedroom condominium in Boynton Beach. We were grateful for it, but there were nighttime safety-issues which concerned us. We needed a house but had no cash.

In 1999, I was preaching at Grace Chapel, Jacksonville, Florida, and on Sunday evening, I returned to my room and called home. Laurie was excited and said, "Carolyn Folina has friends in the north who have offered to buy us a house! She even took me house hunting today, and we found the most wonderful one in Boynton Beach!" Carolyn, a widow, was one of our dear church friends.

Laurie continued, "You would love the house we found! It is in Leisureville on Lake Constantino with a hundred feet of seawall ..." When she identified the house, I immediately knew which one it was; two years earlier she and I had become lost in that neighborhood, stopped in front of this same house and admired it. I remembered saying, "Lord, whoever lives there is blessed!" I did not covet the house but greatly admired it. As Laurie talked, I felt a strange, inner-witness of its belonging to us. "Unfortunately," she said, "The house is already sold!" She then told me the price. When I hung up the phone, I was confused. Why did she even tell me about the house since it was already sold? Why was it a house with which we were already acquainted and had admired? Why? Nothing made sense. Spiritually, I felt a connection to the house and had taken only a few steps from the phone when the Holy Spirit said, "You can still have it."

For a second, I stood unmoving, awed by what He said. I distinctly heard, "You can still have it." The price—or it's being sold—did not concern Him. We could still have it. I immediately called home. Laurie and repeated what the Lord had said. "Call the Realtor in the morning," I said, "Tell her we know the house is sold but make her take our name and number." The next night I rushed to my room, called Laurie and asked, "Did you call the Realtor?" "No," she replied slowly, "I didn't." I was annoyed and said impatiently, "Call her first thing in the morning! Make her take our name and number!"

Tuesday night, hurrying back to my room, I called, Laurie explained she spoke with the Realtor but was told the sale was guaranteed, and there would be no cancellation. Even so, she insisted the Realtor take our name and number. Laurie hung up the phone, but within five minutes the Realtor called back in a state of shock and said: "Since we spoke a minute ago, that house came back on the market! I will hold it for you!" The timing of the calls was shocking.

I flew home on Thursday. Laurie, Carolyn, the Realtor, and I met at the house. We were discussing the contract when I became nervous. If I put a deposit on it and our donor failed to comply, I would be caught in a serious financial problem. Leaving them in the kitchen, I went to the bathroom: "Lord!" I said, "There is no way we can handle this!" Instantly, He spoke again, saying, "I will pay for it!" With that assurance clearly spoken, I went back to the Realtor, told her we would take the house. It would be cash at closing and gave her my check.

A few days later, Harvey and Vera Patrick, our new friends, arrived from Maryland, and we explored the house together. They admired its two bedrooms, two baths, largest lot in the subdivision, with a magnificent lake-front location. I stood there aghast! I could get in a boat and probably travel 50 miles through South Florida's lakes and canals. The couple said nothing about the purchase. We went to lunch, but two days later the Ministry received their check for $100,000. Laurie and I were stunned. I had never seen that much money in my entire life—but it was there in my hand. At that moment, I realized again, the value of spiritual gifts: It was through a "word of knowledge" that the house was provided (I Corinthians 12:8). If I had not believed the two messages, "You can still have it!" And "I will pay for it!" We would have missed God's great provision. Now, I was holding a $100,000 check in my hand because of my belief in the Scripture and my obedience to it.

There is more to the miracle. The house was $129,000, and we needed another $30,000 to finish the payment. Even so, we never asked anyone to help with the additional cost. God had said He would pay for it and we totally believed Him. A month later, at the Ministry's Board Meeting, when every expense was paid, we had the same amount of money in the treasury we had before purchasing the house. To this day, we do not know how the extra $30,000 came into our bank account. The only explanation was that "a good measure, pressed down, and shaken together," had been delivered to our bosom (Luke 6:38).

Laurie lived in this wonderful place fifteen years before she died March 24, 2012, soon after our 60th Wedding Anniversary. I have lived in it longer than any other house in my entire life. It has been perfect for every need. We were only one mile from the ocean, hospital, stores, doctors, restaurants, and everything we needed. The Mall was a mile-and-a half-away and I-95 only one-quarter mile from the house. Even so, the cul-de-sac gave us privacy from heavy traffic. God chose it specifically for us. Thankfully, that night in Jacksonville, I recognized and obeyed the Spirit's "word of knowledge" when He said "You can still have it" (I Corinthians 12:8). Do I have proof of spiritual gifts today? Absolutely!

Later, we discovered that Carolyn had written the request to her friends on Christmas Day, 1999—the Golden Anniversary of my Ordination in 1949. She was totally unaware of that fact when she sent the appeal. In every detail, the Holy Spirit directed our acquiring the house; each person responded, and God's will was done. I am a bird lover and have a flock of wild Egyptian Geese who come daily for food and take the grain from my mind. Ducks, ibis, herons, storks, roseate spoonbills, numerous others, are in my yard daily.

Today, I have a favorite prayer-spot where I sit many mornings at 5:00 a.m., have a cup of coffee, visit with the Lord, and watch the sunrise on the lake. If my request is granted, it will be in this same spot, someday, that someone finds my empty body. This I know: I will never again deny the awesome spiritual gifts that have blessed my life. Luther saw them and when he composed his Hymn of the Reformation, included the line, "The Spirit and the Gifts are ours." Read it!

> *"The Prince of Darkness grim,*
> *We tremble not for him;*
> *His rage we can endure,*
> *For lo! His doom is sure,*
> *One little word shall fell him.*
> *That word above all earthly powers,*
> *No thanks to them abideth;*
> *The Spirit and the Gifts are ours*
> *Through him who with us sideth!*
>
> *Hallelujah!"*

Chapter 31

A PRINCE OF PREACHERS ENLARGES MY LIFE

Returning home from a week of preaching, a message from Derek awaited me, asking that I join his ministry in Almati, Kazakhstan. This is a former Communist nation that shares the western border of China. The Tian Shan Mountains, a spur of the Himalayas, marks the boundary between these countries. I made the 7,000-mile flight from the U.S., met Derek, Ruth, others, and was delighted to be with them again. This was shortly after the collapse of Communism, and public sentiment was strongly against Marxism and its ruthlessness. The public attitude was now open to new ideas—including Christianity. Arriving in the city, I was amazed to see huge images of Lenin's head that had been toppled from monuments around the area. Some lay in places where they fell, weeds now growing around them. Others had been rolled into alleyways and side-streets. The people's contempt for Communism was very apparent. Our hotel was large, excellent in every way—except for the public restrooms. They were atrocious—shocking—and consisted only of a hole in the floor and designated places to put the feet.

The auditorium where Derek spoke was large, comfortable, and the assembly contained a mix of nationalities. One handsome young Turkish man, a former Muslim, who attended all of Derek's Asiatic-events, traveled more than 1,000 miles, hitch-hiking, riding trucks, buses, whatever conveyance he could find. He and I first met in Moscow, bonded in a beautiful "Jephunneh" relationship, and in spite of the miles between us, he has remained a "Son" to this day. I will never forget him. While in Almati, I had the opportunity to pray with numerous Chinese pastors who smuggled themselves across the border. In every case, I have never seen men hungrier for God's word and fatherly-love.

As in the past, Derek taught several hours at each session, while interpreters translated the messages into half-a-dozen Asiatic languages. Many of those present spoke no English but had no difficulty receiving a Jephunneh-impartation: I discovered the Holy Spirit's power was oftentimes ministered through a fatherly-hug the same as through the laying-on-of-hands. In the beginning, all my "Calebs" had been Americans, but that had changed. Others from China, Middle Asia, Europe, and Latin America, had become part of the family. The spiritual-bonding remained even when we never saw each other again.

The Mission School

During Derek's Conference, a Christian Mission School near Almati was holding its Graduation Ceremony, and Derek arranged for me to deliver the Baccalaureate Message. When I arrived, I was happy to discover that the school met in the old Communist Youth Indoctrination Center. After graduation, some thirty students were taking the gospel to Uzbekistan, Turkmenistan, Afghanistan, Iran—and other Muslim countries. Their courage in facing such danger astounded me. My message of encouragement to them was based on the Queen of Sheba's statement to Solomon when she exclaimed, "Happy are these your servants ..." (1 Kings 10:8). I compared Solomon's earthly kingdom to the Kingdom of God and that the missionaries should have far greater joy than what the servants of Solomon had. Jesus told his followers to "Enter into the joy of your Lord" (Matthew 25:21,23).

At the end of the message I gave the first graduate—a young woman—her diploma and laid my hand on her shoulder. The instant I touched her, she slammed to the floor and burst into riotous laughter. Everyone was astonished—I among them. She did not fall easily but crashed to the floor. The next graduate, a young man, rushed forward, took his diploma, and the same thing happened to him. Others began hurrying to me, and no one was omitted. Finally, the entire class—about 30 students—was laid-out on the floor and anointed with the "joy of the Lord" (Isaiah 61:3 Mathew 25:21, 23). In the language of Scripture, "There was great joy in that city" (Acts 8:8). I was as shocked as they. All I did was present the Scripture, prayerfully lay-hands, and the Holy Spirit came upon them. Unknown to me, the Director of the School was very distraught—angry. He was embarrassed—especially when the noise was heard outside the building, and many non-Christians began crowding in. The visitors wanted to see why such riotous laughter was coming from the Communist Youth Center.

The visitors lining the back wall were staring wide-eyed, realizing the students' happiness was very real. Nothing was faked. When I invited them to come forward for ministry, some did; one woman who was holding a bag of groceries dropped under the power of God and sent her oranges rolling across the floor. The scene was chaotic. One of the Kazakh men— the darkest, most ominous looking person I had ever seen—came running forward, grabbed me under my arms, lifted me from the floor, and swung me around, dancing. His was the happiest embrace I have ever felt—and never have I been in such a joyous situation. The School Director never understood the intense-jubilation God imparted to his graduates. He left without saying goodbye and blamed me for what the Holy Spirit did. A year later I was still hearing reports of his anger. Apparently, he never knew how Derek experienced the same riotous laughter in his army barracks the night he was filled with the Holy Spirit. I have often thought about those courageous young people who dared to take the gospel into Muslim nations. I wonder if they are still alive if they have been imprisoned, tortured, or beheaded. This is the customary treatment in Islamic countries.

At the end of the meeting, hundreds of men and women seemed to vanish into the night. Many had to smuggle themselves across the China border to get back to their families and churches. For some, that meant crossing the mountains at night. Our group left Kazakhstan on different flights. I hugged Derek and Ruth goodbye and returned home by way of Frankfort and New York. That was in the summer of 1995, and I had the privilege of flying over Germany on a very special day: It was the Golden Anniversary of the 1945-end of World War II.

As a teenager, I well-remembered that awesome day: I was in High School when the announcement came over the PA system that Germany had surrendered. Students leaped to their feet, yelled, cried, threw books in the air and celebrated. The news was too good to be true. But it was true! Now, fifty years later, staring out the plane window I looked down on lush fields of German farms, clean villages, and a beautiful landscape. How different the sight when these had been bombed-out towns and a barren wasteland. Adolph Hitler and President Roosevelt both came to mind. Memories of black-outs, torpedoed ships on our beaches, Hitler's screaming rampages, prisoners of war passing our house, and other memories raced through my mind. This was the same land where millions of Jews had been herded into gas chambers and killed. Then, wonderfully, the lines of an old hymn appeared:

"When the war is over, We shall wear a crown,
Yes, we shall wear a crown
In the new Jerusalem!"

With Derek In Turkey

Returning to the U.S., I became very busy traveling and preaching. Laurie maintained a daily prayer meeting in which she and others interceded for me. As a result, the Holy Spirit confirmed the Word with "signs, wonders, and mighty deeds." A stream of testimonies began coming from people whose lives had been radically changed. This included alcoholics, drug users, people who were suicidal, and others who were physically healed. In all the meetings I did "hands-on" ministry, and ninety percent of the people dropped to the floor under the power of God.

A year passed, and I was involved in a two-month long revival near Atlanta. Laurie, Karen McMichael, Tony, and Barbara Morrongiello, flew up to take part. People from all denominations came, were healed, filled with the Holy Spirit, and experienced the power of God. A famous Atlanta athlete appeared one evening, was delivered from serious drug-addiction and his career saved.

Near the end, Derek sent me a fax asking that I join him in Turkey for his Balkan Pastors Conference. When I replied I could not come, he faxed me again saying, "I don't want you to disobey God, but please pray again. I would like for you to be present." The result of that prayer, thankfully, was that I flew to Istanbul and joined him at two locations in Western Turkey. This nation is 99% Islamic, and many of the pastors attending were former Muslims. Such men are always in danger, and everyone felt the tension for them. For security reasons, no photographs were allowed, and as much as possible, our presence was secret.

The first night, a twenty-eight-year-old Turkish man whom I met at Derek's Conference in Moscow, saw me and came rushing across the room, shouting "Papa! Papa!" Hugging me, he lifted me from the floor, kissing me on both cheeks. At our meeting in Moscow, he had experienced a true "Jephunneh-bonding," and I remembered his special need for fathering: When he became a Christian ten years earlier, his Muslim father declared him dead, and the family refused to see him ever again. God filled the void.

Later, that evening I was standing at the rear of the building when Derek called for representatives from the twenty-seven nations represented to come forward for prayer. As they assembled, I suddenly had a "word of knowledge" that there was a young man to the right of the pulpit, whom I could not see but on whom I was to lay-hands. There was no other explanation. Pushing through the crowd, I made my way to the front, and immediately recognized which one God intended: A former Muslim, ministering in a dangerous situation.

He needed an "impartation of spiritual gifts" (Romans 1:11). When I laid my hand on his shoulder, the Holy Spirit struck him as if by lightning. He dropped, and half an hour later was still unconscious, vibrating in the glory. His heels were banging on the floor.

Finally, we carried him to the rear of the auditorium but unknowingly placed him in the walkway where Muslim waiters passed from the kitchen to the dining room. This site was significant. Many of the hotel staff stopped and stared at him in amazement: They knew they were seeing a genuine manifestation of the power of God in our Christian meeting. The man was obviously experiencing rapture, and the waiters were deeply affected. Several of them returned afterward, privately asking questions, and wanting to know more about Jesus. One was genuinely saved and "became a disciple in secret" (John 19:38). Later, Derek had me lay-hands on all the pastors, and the Holy Spirit came in power; each one dropped to the floor and experienced the Glory. This was what Derek wanted when he sent me the fax saying, "I don't want you to disobey God, but please pray again …."

We were near the ruins of ancient Ephesus, and one morning the team piled into a bus and drove to the site. This is an incredible spot on the Mediterranean where archaeologists are restoring parts of this beautiful city. The 25,000-seat amphitheater where Paul stood and the people shouted "Great is Diana of the Ephesians" is in amazingly good condition. The Temple of Diana is now gone. The original structure, built in 550 BC, was destroyed in 356 BC. In time, many of its stones were salvaged for use in other ancient structures. What few realize is the immensity and power of the Diana cult—its demonic-control was incredible. Many of us have been to Athens, Greece, visited the Acropolis and admired the Parthenon, which is still standing. Most others have seen its photographs. The Parthenon is magnificent. What is rarely known is that the Temple of

Diana was four times larger and more awesome than the Parthenon. As a building, the temple at Ephesus was rightly acknowledged as greatest of all "Seven Wonders of the Ancient World"—its grandeur surpassing the Pyramids of Egypt. Artistic renderings of it are available online.

Later, at Derek's request, I preached in the theater at Ephesus, standing very close to the spot where Paul once stood (Acts 19:27, 28, 34, 35). The city, partly rebuilt, has a boulevard lined with stone columns that in the first century were lighted at night by overhead bonfires; this provided city-lights. During daytime hours it was air-conditioned by a system of fountains spraying a mist of water onto the streets. Even the public toilet is still intact, and underneath its long stone-seat is the running-water trench that kept it clean.

Nearby were the remains of an ancient, 3rd-century church building with its baptistry still in excellent preservation. It was a trench, built into the stone floor with steps at either end. A circular area in the middle, provided space for two ministers to stand facing each other. The person being baptized approached from one side, was immersed, and exited at the other end. The baptistry was so well-constructed that with little restoration it could be used today. I stood, staring, for a long time, remembering that in early centuries the newly baptized received "laying-on-of-hands" to be filled with the Holy Spirit. Also, it was somewhere in this city that Paul asked the Ephesian believers the all-revealing question, "Did you receive the Holy Spirit when you believed?" (Acts 19:2-6).

Tragically, in the eleventh century, Muslim armies swarmed over this area of Western Turkey, killing, destroying, and enslaving all Christians. Standing there, I wondered if the spot beneath my feet had been covered with the blood of martyrs. Years before, inside the Hagia Sophia Cathedral in Istanbul, I had experienced the same frightening question. That ancient building, begun by Emperor Justinian in 537 AD, was, at that time, the greatest engineering marvel and largest building in the world. In 1453 it was captured by the Muslims and converted into a Mosque. It too, like other holy sites, was baptized in the blood of martyrs.

When the Conferences in Turkey ended, I returned to the U.S. and was soon called to the hospital. One of the women whose photo had been on the front page of the Delray News Journal years before was dying. This was a woman I had known and loved for years. Recognizing me, she spoke faintly, "Brother Charles, I want you to forgive me for what I did to the church." I listened intently, my heart aching, and took her hand. Holding it, I said, "Esther, there is nothing to forgive! I have never blamed you for anything that happened." Again, she made the request—and again—I assured her of my love. Her daughter and her daughter's husband were two my dearest friends. She said, "Charles, she wants to hear you say it." I did. I said it, but in my heart, I had never quit loving this beautiful person or the other three involved.

She, like them, had been deceived by an Absalom-fraud. A few days later she died, and the church property was sold to another congregation. Her brother, whom I dearly loved, and was also in the newspaper-photograph, told me repeatedly before his death, "Brother Charles, I never heard you preach anything you could not support from Scripture!" Looking back, I think that was his form of apology. He too, realized they had been betrayed.

The man who deceived all of us tragically became a victim of his own evil. His wife left him for another man, and his career ended. In the past, he had been a handsome, well-dressed person with a strong family-bond. That radically changed. The last time I saw him I could hardly believe my eyes. Standing alone in a busy, public building, he wore a dingy undershirt that struck him above the belly. His hair and beard were shaggy, needed cutting, and he had no teeth.

His appearance was that of a derelict. I genuinely grieved for the man, remembering the scripture that warned evildoers, "In the net which they hid, their own foot is caught" (Psalms 9:15). He had delighted in putting us out of our building; God had delighted in putting us into a much better one than we could ever have imagined. Like thousands of others, that Primitive Baptist Church is gone today. The Holy Spirit will not compete with human stubbornness. Scripture is the final authority: Church tradition must bow to it—doctrinally and in practice.

Derek Prince Dies

September 24, 2003, I was at home when Sally Fesperman called, warned me she had bad news, then told me Derek had died. He was at his home in Jerusalem. Her message was soon followed by another from Derek's son-in-law, David Selby. I dropped into a chair weeping, thanking God for the privilege to have known this incredible man. Sitting there, the

Charles Carrin

Scripture that came to mind was the statement King David made when he heard of the death of Saul: "A Prince and a great man has fallen this day in Israel" (2 Samuel 3:38). A few days after his death, Derek was buried in the city he most loved—Jerusalem.

After Sally's call, a torrent of memories began flooding me. One was Derek's telling me how, as a young British soldier, he had been filled with the Holy Spirit. That happened in his army barracks one night, and he laughed until he was exhausted. It was in that way his incredible ministry of teaching, preaching, writing began. At a Conference in Brighton, England, in the early 1990s, I met numerous pastors from Africa, Asia, and the Pacific islands, whose ministry had been birthed and empowered by Derek's teaching. The nation of New Zealand is saturated with his ministry. Today, the DPM International Office, located in Charlotte, North Carolina, still directs his work through a network of foreign branches in Singapore, Australia, New Zealand, South Africa, Canada, England, Holland, and Germany. I was personally acquainted with members of the International Council and say without hesitation that these are the finest, most committed Christian men and women I have ever known. Derek is gone, but "his works follow after him" (Revelation 14:13).

Chapter 32

GOD TOUCHES THE CHURCH WITH NEW POWER

In the mid-1980s, an unknown South African evangelist, Rodney Howard-Browne, came to the U.S. and brought renewal to thousands of churches. Through his "laying-on-hands," he changed American church history. He and I soon met in a small church in Stuart, Florida, where I received personal ministry from him. It was near that same time, 1994, he also ministered to a young Vineyard pastor, and former Baptist, Randy Clark. He, too, began experiencing phenomenal manifestations of power. Simultaneously, John and Carol Arnott, Canadians, were returning from Argentina, where evangelist Claudio Freidzon laid hands on them. Claudio's powerful ministry and the Revival in Argentina were the direct outgrowths of Tommy Hicks' crusade in 1954.

At that time, the Arnotts were serving a Vineyard Fellowship located at the end of the Toronto Airport runway. A wire fence was the only barrier between them and the planes. Back in Canada, they heard about Randy Clark and invited him to Toronto. He came, and on January 29, 1994, the church exploded with Holy Fire. Miraculous signs and wonders touched everyone. People fell, shook, groaned, vibrated as if electrified by high voltage. Some laughed, others cried, and unusual sounds came from many, as demons were exposed and cast out (Acts 2). Most importantly, the Holy Spirit fell as at Pentecost. News of the event traveled worldwide. Thousands began coming, and six months later I was there.

Taking another brother from Grace Fellowship with me, Bill Dymond, we waited in a long line before pushing into the building. During that wait, I visited with a quiet, young Oriental man who, once inside, suddenly roared like an African lion. The building shook. He was shocked, stared wide-eyed, as if to say, "What happened?! Why did I do that?!" Strange? Yes. In part, what we witnessed was the Holy Spirit's public exposure of unclean spirits in some, while others experienced bliss. Scripture tells about demons in the Synagogue in Capernaum who remained secure and undetected until Jesus arrived (Mark 1:22-28). His presence jeopardized their safety and forced them into noisy exposure.

261

Many visitors who came only to be spectators, suddenly found themselves on the floor laughing riotously or growling demonically. Critics delighted in ridiculing the move of God in Toronto, and eventually, this wonderful body of Christians was disfranchised from their parent organization, the Vineyard Fellowship. Cessationist preachers made Toronto the brunt of their jokes and good people failed to see God's presence. It was easy to claim, "these people are full of new wine" (Acts 2:13). In spite of criticism, millions of people kept coming and found themselves radically changed—wonderfully transformed by the power of God. Bill and I met Christians from Madagascar, Indonesia, Japan, New Zealand, Norway, and other remote nations. Nearly every country on earth was registered among its guests. Significantly, we found ourselves sitting in front of two Canadian couples who worshiped with us at Grace Fellowship in Boynton Beach every winter. One husband and wife were from Ontario, the other from Vancouver, British Columbia. In that crowded building, the six of us had unknowingly chosen seats beside each other.

After returning home, I went to a James Robinson meeting at the Dallas Arena, where he and John Wimber were ministering. Thousands packed into the stadium and saw the Holy Spirit's wonderful work. I stood next to John on the Platform within inches of a young woman for whom he prayed. As he held her hand, she began to vibrate, as if electricity were passing through her body. I was astonished and knew it was real, but more importantly, I saw an expression of God-like rapture spread across her face. It was apparent that the Holy Spirit was working through John. Watching in astonishment, I had no hint that in coming years the Holy Spirit would release the same power through me.

Opposition to the Airport Vineyard continued, and John Wimber wrongly gave his endorsement to the action against them. Later, John suffered a fall that caused a brain hemorrhage and death. During that illness, he acknowledged he had misjudged a genuine move of God in Toronto. In 1996 and again in 2010 the Toronto church's name was changed. The title they have maintained is: "Catch The Fire." A London newspaper labeled it the "Toronto Blessing," a name still in use in many places today. In spite of the crisis, grace prevailed, and John and Carol realized they had to keep the movement free from denominational control.

On my first visit to Toronto, Bill and I did not meet John and Carol, but Jack Taylor later introduced us. I returned to Canada and preached for their Saturday and Sunday services. The Holy Spirit moved in power. Thousands were impacted, and like Cane Ridge, hundreds fell in heaps. The Arnott's Personal Assistant, Petra Dmovscek, lay two hours immobile on the floor near the pulpit. She later wrote, "The Lord totally blasted me that day, and I honestly have not been the same woman since. The depths were stirred, and the Holy Spirit did something that still excites me now in my heart."

Multiplied thousands of visitors from around the world began flooding into the Toronto Church and have taken the power with them to remote parts of the planet. The impact from the Revival has been so great that the Canadian Board of Tourism added the church to its list of Canada's major attractions. In the minds of many, the church was a spiritual "Niagara Falls." In a short time, foreign groups came in chartered flights from the Orient, England, other sites; more than 5,500 Anglican Churches were impacted by the revival.

One of them, Holy Trinity Brompton (HTB), a church in London, experienced an invasion after its clergy visited Toronto and returned with the Holy Spirit's anointing on them. The two-hundred-year-old building was suddenly invaded by the power of God, and scores of sophisticated Anglicans found themselves laid out on the church floor in riotous laughter that included men and women of all ages, social stations, educations, and wealth. England's current Archbishop, Justin Welby, was on staff at HTB at the time and received an anointing that has since been carried to thousands of other Anglican Churches worldwide. One of the church's greatest contributions has been its Alpha Course, a discipleship training program which has impacted more than 20,000 Churches across the earth.

An interesting side-note of Holy Trinity Brompton's baptism in the Spirit is that when R.T. Kendall was pastor at Westminster Chapel, London, he heard of HTB's noisy laughter, and he warned his congregation to stay away. It was not of God. Later, he saw the remarkably changed lives and a renewed church. Realizing he was wrong, he had the grace to return to his pulpit and acknowledge his error. Strange as it was, what was happening at HTB was an authentic, God event.

The Holy Spirit was sovereignly awakening the church with His miraculous presence. Steve Hill, an American evangelist, visited Holy Trinity Brompton, received the anointing, went directly to Brownsville

Charles Carrin

Assembly at Pensacola, Florida, preached on Father's Day, June 18, 1995, and the meeting burst into holy flame.

The Revival that followed lasted five years with more than four million attending from around the world. David Rhea and I—separately—were among them. As a result of this revival, it would be hard to find a church in America today that does not have some Spirit-filled believer praying for the church's restoration. Christian leadership may deny the current charismatic renewal, condemn it, and fight it with all their strength; but all such efforts will be in vain (Acts 5:39; 23:9). As determinedly as an incoming tide, the Holy Spirit is reclaiming His church. We are now in the "latter days," and the Church worldwide is being prepared for the Second Coming of Christ. Toronto is part of that preparation.

Chapter 33

DAVID RHEA: GOD'S SPECIFIC GIFT TO ME

In 1999 a group of churches in Murfreesboro, Tennessee, invited me to conduct a city-wide Crusade held in their High School auditorium. The hall was filled every night; the Holy Spirit moved in power, and countless lives were blessed. Scores of people had dynamic encounters with God and dropped to the floor in deep, spiritual peace. Some were filled with the joy of the Lord. Others were immobile and lay quietly, while many vibrated as if electrified. At the close of an evening service, a friend, Don Vinson, and I were talking when I noticed a young man a short distance away, lying on his side, pulsating intensely. Don knew who he was and asked that I go back to him. I went, knelt at his side, and distinctly heard the Holy Spirit say, "Take him 'under your wing.' Speak into his life spiritually, fatherly, educationally." I explained nothing to him but prayed over him, unaware that I was quoting specific requests he had already made of the Lord. Then, offering no explanation, I asked for his name, phone number, and learned he was David Rhea.

He had grown up in the Church of Christ, and the year before we met, April 1998, he went to the Brownsville Revival at Pensacola, Florida. He was baptized one evening, and when the two ministers laid him into the water, the presence of God hit the tank electrically. David was knocked unconscious, left floating, and the two pastors slammed against the wall. Assistants rushed into the tank, carried David to another room and laid him on the floor to recover. Later that year, in August, he and Don returned to the Revival, where they had another power-encounter with the Lord. David described their return home:

"Donald and I started the eight-hour trip back to Tennessee. I was driving, and Donald talked about the sensitivity of the Holy Spirit. When he had finished, we both settled in the seats with our thoughts on the Lord. We were so deep in the Spirit, we can only remember a few places along the way. I put some worship music on and started thinking how awesome the presence of the Lord had been in the church that morning. Suddenly the Holy Spirit started settling on me. The 'Presence' was so strong that it scared me to be driving. At that moment He began to lift, and I said in my heart. 'Don't go! Please don't go!'

Immediately He settled back on me. Again, there was some fear in my mind, and He lifted. This happened a few more times, and the only way I can describe what happened next is that I became childlike with all my heart reaching up to his parent. I said 'Don't go! Please don't go!' The moment my heart felt 100% that it wanted only Him, I was suddenly caught up out of my body. The last thing I remember was shoving back against the seat yelling from the impact of what happened.

An angel must have done the driving because I was out of my body in another realm. Suddenly, I was standing before the Lord. We communicated without using words. Love, Purity, Holiness, and so many more feelings that I have no words to describe were bursting forth from Him. I knew in my natural body it would have killed me. Even being there, I knew I was receiving only a speck of mist coming from an ocean of His Love and Glory. It was like the love of a mother and a father all mixed into one. He made a move toward me with His arms reaching for me yearning for me. These words fall void in trying to explain the message that He revealed to me. He has a fiery, unquenchable, vehement flame of love for His children. We are beyond cherishment in His eyes. This love is going to catapult His Bride into her destiny and eternity will not even begin to exhaust it."

I knew none of David's personal history the evening I knelt beside him in Murfreesboro. Two weeks later I called and asked him to meet me at Central Baptist Church near Chattanooga where I was preaching. On the way, he stopped at a restaurant and saw the same friend, Elizabeth Padgett, an authentic "prophetess," who had invited him to the meeting in Murfreesboro. Coming to his table, she said, "The Lord told me that you will be traveling with Charles Carrin." David explained he was then on his way to meet me in Chattanooga. He arrived a few hours later. We spent the weekend working together. I preached, he assisted me, and David has been my wonderful Assistant ever since. In all those years, traveling from London to Alaska, New England to California, Central, and South America, he has never disappointed me. In every situation, David has proved himself to be faithful and trustworthy. We have never had a difficulty or quarrel, and I am grateful for God assigning him to my ministry.

Soon after our meeting, David arranged for me to speak to his Church of Christ in Tennessee, and the Holy Spirit moved in shocking ways. People were healed, filled with the power of God, delivered from demons, with many "signs and wonders" taking place. David's mother, who suffered a nervous breakdown in his early childhood and remained house-bound for many years, came and sat near the door. This was her first public appearance since David's boyhood. When I gave the opportunity for personal ministry, she did not come forward. I then went to her, called her to the aisle, and laid hands on her. She dropped to the floor and was instantly delivered from demons that had harassed her for decades. In two minutes time, she was normalized. The next week she joined the Women's Aglow organization and began visiting the hospital to pray for the sick.

Another woman who had a fist-sized tumor on her leg stepped forward for ministry, but before getting to me, the growth was gone. She was healed. Others, in true New Testament style, were delivered from demons. Incredible as it seems, several in the church discovered their teeth had turned gold. It was in that logic-defying fashion that the Holy Spirit moved in the Church of Christ. Unfortunately, not everyone was happy, and one night an usher brought me a lengthy, anonymous letter, criticizing my presence and what I claimed was the Holy Spirit's visible demonstrations. One special aggravation was the gold. This "sign" was the most challenging. Many in the congregation were overjoyed, while others were "confused, amazed, and perplexed" (Acts 2:6,7,12).

At lunch one day, I was severely rebuked by the church's senior deacon for having introduced practices unapproved by the Church of Christ. I tried to show him where "signs and wonders" occurred in the New Testament, but he would accept no Biblical explanation—though he did accept his pagan-position as a high-degree Mason. Its symbols were displayed obviously around his house. In spite of tension, the Holy Spirit continued to move in the nightly meetings, and numerous people were healed, delivered, and experienced the power of God. The meeting ended successfully for many individuals, but unsuccessfully for the church.

On Saturday morning a group of men met at the church to tell me goodbye. Others were accompanying me to the airport in Nashville. Suddenly another car raced into the parking lot; the driver jumped out and hurried toward me. Weeping, he said, "I must apologize to you! I must apologize to you!" "No! No!" I replied. "You have not offended me! Apologies are unnecessary!" "You don't understand!" He answered, "I am the one who wrote that ugly letter." Again, I tried to stop him, but he continued, "When I got home from church last night I looked in the mirror—and this is what I saw!" Opening his mouth wide in the sunlight, his entire lower jaw was brilliant gold. Every tooth blazed in the sunlight, and a dozen men witnessed it. I was shocked. One by one, everyone in the parking lot took turns looking at the gold—most making several examinations. Everyone was astonished. God had done in the skeptic the very thing he denied was real in others.

There was an era in which "gold displays" occurred in many congregations worldwide. The cessationists had a holiday, screaming about charismatic absurdities. Were some of the claims fraudulent? Probably. There are always charlatans and false prophets, secular and religious, who fake their way into the people's pockets. But, remember, people only counterfeit what is real—never something phony. When gold first began appearing in Christian meetings, I too thought it was another silly hoax and warned others to avoid it. Only later did I learn that, anciently, the last thing a young Jewish groom did before claiming his bride was to send her a gift of gold. If that is the meaning for us, we gladly say, "Even so, come quickly Lord Jesus!" (Revelation 22:20).

David Meets Marelise

In the summer of 2004, Laurie and I were planning a Bahamas weekend cruise with Buddy, Cecile, and Benjamin, when she suggested that David join us. The morning before we were to board the ship, he flew to South Florida. When he dressed, he put his passport in the shirt pocket, finished packing his bag, and was heading out the door, when he decided to change shirts. Tossing the first one onto the bed, he re-dressed and drove to the Nashville airport, an hour away. Just before boarding the flight he discovered the mistake—he had no passport—and no time to go back for it. Without it, he could not get on the ship. He called me, and we prayed. He then called his mother and asked her to overnight the Passport to my address. I was between flights in another airport on my way home. Calling Laurie, I asked her to pray. As I hurried down the concourse, I passed a black man whom I suddenly knew was a believer. Going to him, I explained the dilemma and said, "Will you please pray with me?" Grabbing my hand, he said, "Now don't you worry! God's gonna' get that Passport to you! You trust Him! He's gonna do it!" He then began thanking God for answering our prayer, and a moment later I went to my plane rejoicing. David and I arrived at the Palm Beach Airport simultaneously and went home. We spent a nervous night. The next morning all of us were standing in the yard waiting for our transportation to the ship, everyone praying desperately that the passport would arrive first. Seeing a vehicle approach, we held our breath and then started yelling. It was the Passport's delivery truck! The Passport had arrived!

All went well. Our ship was the Majesty of the Seas, Royal Caribbean Line. One morning at breakfast, Cecile told David that a Christian girl, Marelise Petzer, from Cape Town, South Africa, was the ship's gym instructor. She thought he should meet her. David left immediately, and as soon as I finished eating, I followed him. Stepping into the gymnasium, I saw the two of them seated together on an ottoman, facing the ocean. No one else was there. They did not see me, and as I started in, the Lord spoke commandingly, "Get out of here!" I left immediately. Wonderfully, in that first meeting, a powerful bonding took place between them. David spent most of his time in the gym, and we saw him mostly at meals. By the end of the cruise, a serious relationship had developed. Several times David said to me, "Charles, I have never felt like this for a girl before!"

The following week when Marelise's ship docked in Key West, David was there to meet her—as he was every time she had a Florida port of call. Some of his Tennessee to Florida trips provided them with a visit only a few hours long, but he made them faithfully. In October, the following year, they were married in Cape Town, South Africa, and returned to McMinnville, Tennessee, where their new house was under construction. Their son David was born on October 28, 2007. Later, God brought them to Florida, and they lived with me for two wonderful years. From my house, they moved to Boca Raton. This had been God's destination for them from the beginning. Their son David needed to be in South Florida.

Charles Carrin

When he was eight years old, David began ministering prophetically, experiencing accurate words of knowledge and participating in Deliverance Ministries with his father and me. Adults sometimes came to me, shaken by the accuracy of what he told them. At some of my local meetings he played the piano, sang, and led worship. When he was ten, he excelled in piano and was being taught by world-renown pianist professors at Florida Atlantic University.

Chapter 34

JACK TAYLOR AND R.T. KENDALL BLESS MY LIFE

Jack Taylor and I met in the late 1980s when we were speakers at a Conference in Atlanta. An immediate bonding took place, and we have remained brother-friends ever since. He is a west-Texan, born in 1933, and graduated from Hardin-Simmons University and Southwestern Baptist Theological Seminary. Jack rose quickly in the ranks and became Vice President of the Southern Baptist Convention. In this role, he visited more than 53 countries worldwide and was one of the Convention's best-selling authors. He and his first wife, Barbara, had two children, Tim and Tammy, and several grandchildren.

In 1970, while pastor at Castle Hills First Baptist Church in San Antonio, Texas, Jack invited Bertha Smith, the Baptist Missionary, who had been part of the 1933 charismatic-outbreak in Shantung, China. That year the Holy Spirit fell and converted thousands of Buddhists and others to Christ. Presbyterian, Methodist, Baptist missionaries, and others were impacted and radically anointed. During Bertha's visit to Castle Hills, the Spirit came with astonishing signs, and in six months, more than 3,000 people were brought to the Lord.

That event launched Jack into a greater ministry of worldwide preaching and becoming the author of 14 widely-circulated books, CDs, and video series. In recognition, he was given an Honorary Doctorate from Saint Thomas Christian College in Jacksonville, Florida. During a visit to Toronto in August 1994, Jack's ministry experienced another dramatic increase in the power of the Holy Spirit. Today, he "fathers" scores of men and women worldwide with a major preaching focus on the Kingdom of God and its universal reign.

Soon after our meeting, Jack invited me to a Baptist pastors' event at the Atlanta Airport Hilton Hotel, co-hosted by Ron Phillips, pastor at First Baptist Church, Hixson, Tennessee. The purpose of the meeting was to discuss spiritual renewal among Baptists. I was only a visitor, but they asked me to share my testimony. As I returned to my seat, the Holy Spirit pointed to a young man sitting by the wall and said, "Lay hands on him!" I obeyed, and he was instantly jolted by the power of God. I started to sit down, when another pastor and his wife sprang into the aisle, saying, "Lay hands on us!" When I did, the Holy Spirit slammed them to the floor, and holy-chaos hit the room. In a matter of minutes, people were laid-out in riotous laughter, while others stared in frightened unbelief. Many were delighted, but a full row of men leaped to their feet and fled out the door. Many others rushed forward, wanting to receive an impartation from the Lord.

I will never forget one pastor and wife, both well-dressed, dignified, who could not stop laughing—hilariously. Both were "full of new wine" (Acts 2:13). Finally, they left the mezzanine, with the woman bending over the escalator-rail in the lobby, laughing at the top of her lungs. With their Baptist name-tags prominently displayed, they found themselves surrounded by a large cocktail party below. It was obvious to everyone that the "joy of the Lord" was far better than a dozen martinis. The couple left the hotel through an underpass that went to the parking lot, but I was told later that the wife fell out in the tunnel. Someone says, "Isn't that embarrassing?!" The answer is an emphatic Yes! And that is exactly why God does it. The best way to humble the heart is to humiliate it. But for those experiencing it, such a God-encounter is life-changing, freeing, and empowering. The Book of Acts, chapter two, explains why the disciples were accused of being full of "new wine."

In 2000, Jack and I were preaching in Hixson, Tennessee, when his wife Barbara called to tell him she had been diagnosed with melanoma-cancer. He packed immediately, and I drove him to the airport for his flight home. The cancer was unstoppable, and Barbara died the following year. This was soon after their 47th wedding anniversary. Jack later became engaged to Jerri Bollinger, a lovely woman who, before the wedding, was diagnosed with cancer. Even so, they married in 2001, but within a year she died.

I MEET R.T. KENDALL

Two years after meeting David, he and I were back at Central Baptist, when R.T. Kendall and I shared the platform. Dr. Kendall was pastor at Westminster Chapel, London, and had recently gone public in his endorsement of all the charismatic gifts. At that time, Westminster was the "Flagship" for the Reformed Theological Movement worldwide, and thousands of churches had relied on its leadership for the previous century. Drs. G. Campbell Morgan, John Henry Jowett, Martin Lloyd-Jones, and R.T. Kendall, provided the Chapel with a century of world-renown ministry. That day at Central Baptist (now known as "Abbas House"), Dr. Kendall preached his signature-message on "Total Forgiveness." When he finished, ninety percent of the congregation responded to his challenge and came forward in an act of commitment. I followed, speaking on the subject of prayer in the capacity of the Holy Spirit's "groaning-intercession" (Romans 8:23).

When I finished, I asked the congregation, "Please do not fake anything, but offer yourself to the Holy Spirit and allow His Intercession to speak through you." I then started down the steps, but before reaching the floor, the Spirit fell on the congregation. Scores of them were gripped in "groaning intercession." Many dropped to the floor; others stood wailing; it was a break-through for many to experience authentic intercessory-prayer. Though radical, R.T. knew it was very real and followed behind me, as I laid hands on the people. He and I did not meet immediately, but later as David and I were leaving the building, I turned to him and said prophetically, "You and I are going to London!" In the afternoon, R.T. and I visited at his hotel and immediately bonded in a beautiful way. He was interested in my unusual mix of "Reformed Theology" and Holy Spirit-empowering. Unknown to me, this was a combination he wanted at Westminster Chapel in London.

During our hotel visit, I learned that he was born in Ashland, Kentucky in 1936, into the Church of the Nazarene, a holiness group with which I was well acquainted. Louise, his wife, was from Sterling, Illinois. They married in 1958 and had a son and a daughter, TR, and Melissa. Although he believed in the gifts of the Holy Spirit, R.T. was also a committed Calvinist and held a Ph.D. from Oxford University in England. I was overwhelmed when I learned that he had degrees from Trevecca Nazarene University in Nashville, Tennessee, as well as the Southern Baptist Theological Seminary in Louisville, Kentucky, and the University of Louisville. Later, a Doctor of Divinity from Trevecca Nazarene University was added to the list. I was overwhelmed with his humility and awesome education. R.T. was a prodigious writer and had blessed the Christian world with scores of books.

We bonded during that first visit, and the following August when he and Louise returned to the U.S., they visited Laurie and me in Florida. It was then that he invited me to preach at Westminster Chapel. I had only one date available, and he had only one. To our joy, they were the same.

Six months later, David and I flew from Atlanta to London, but all did not go well on the flight. We were eight hours late arriving in England. Rushing to the Chapel, we arrived at the first meeting on time.

Westminster has two pulpits, one above the other, and two levels of balconies, both encircling the building. It seats about 1,500 people. R.T. was in the lower pulpit, and all went well until his opening prayer remorsefully reminded God about our long flight and how tired I was. I said nothing, although I did not want to begin the service with such negativity. When he commented the second time about my being weary, I spoke out and said, "No! I am not tired!!" He kept his eyes closed but turned toward me, and in a very sanctimonious voice—scolded me, saying, "I'm praying!" At that moment I knew he and I were well-teamed.

My topic that evening was The Covenant, as it regarded the New Testament's inalterability—no part being defunct. Even First Corinthians 12,13,14, was still "the inspired Word of God" and "profitable … for doctrine, for reproof, for correction, for instruction in righteousness" (2 Timothy 3:16,17). That wonderful Friday night, the Holy Spirit fell in astonishing ways; the people happily accepted it, and the Chapel became "charismatic." Momentarily, it also became chaotic. Still preaching, I signaled two ladies sitting near the front to come forward. As they approached the pulpit, they were suddenly slammed upward and backward with a crash. I never touched them. No one caught them. Many in the congregation leaped to their feet. Others gasped. That began the Holy Spirit's public invasion of Westminster Chapel with "signs and wonders." I continued preaching for a short time and then began hands-on ministry. People instantly dropped to the carpet; some experienced noisy Deliverance and others were healed. Many were filled with the Spirit, and someone fell into the orchestra-pit—clamorously into the cymbals.

A German woman—muscular and tall—came forward. As I laid hands on her, she lunged at me, eyes glaring, and began growling like an angry Doberman. Everyone in the Chapel saw her and was aghast. I tried restraining her, but she was very strong, and her snarling became vicious. David ran to me. Catching Louise Kendall's eye, I signaled her to come, but she shook her head with an empathetic "No!" A moment later, however, she came running, hurrying David and the woman to the vestry.

274

I continued hands-on ministry to the congregation, and an hour later, David and the other two returned. When I looked at the German woman, I knew she was free. David later explained her background: In the Second World War, her parents operated Concentration Camps and participated in killing Jews. After the war, she had continued the murdering-spree by having eighteen abortions.

The Kendall's daughter who had left the Chapel, because of abuse by another female member, was peeking through a small window in the foyer. Seeing what was happening, she slipped in and was restored. Numerous other Deliverances took place that night. Many were filled with the Holy Spirit, and that first service was a "break-through" experience for the Chapel.

Saturday morning was very different. The service was held in the Lloyd-Jones Hall and restricted to Chapel members only. My sermon failed miserably. It was dead—lifeless. I had no anointing to preach, and I was terrified. The Queen Mother's personal physician was on the second row, and a group of Ph.D.s from local Universities were present. Other dignitaries were there, as were ordinary Londoners. Everyone was polite—pretending to listen, but nothing I said was worth hearing. Finally, in a sense of desperation, I stopped preaching, went to David and half-shouted in his ear, "Pray!"

With that, I stepped to a man on the second row. When I laid hands on him, the Holy Spirit hit the room like an electoral-storm. The man yelled, hit the floor, chattering in tongues. One of the Ph.D. professors leaped to her feet shouting, "He's here! He's here! Get in the river! He's here!" People around the Hall began falling out of their chairs, waving their arms, some laughing as if in glory. In all seventy of my years in ministry, I never saw anything like it—before or since. People were laid-out like the aftermath of a battle. That Saturday morning was a radical turning point in the history of the Chapel. But why the embarrassing sermon-failure? I had assumed I should preach. If I had I prayed and listened, I am certain the Holy Spirit would have instructed me to go immediately into personal hands-on ministry; but I followed a religious routine in assuming I should preach first.

More importantly: Why does the Holy Spirit cause such strange physical symptoms? In my opinion, the human body is not designed for the surge of power that suddenly invades it. Twice, in my bed at night, I was electrified by the Holy Spirit with what I thought was a killing bolt of lightning. Why that demonstration? I don't know. I only know it happened. Jonathan Edwards did not answer the question in 1742 but simply reported this fact: "If there be a very powerful influence of the Spirit of God in a mixed multitude, it will cause in some way or other a great visible commotion." The Dean of Yale University, Samuel Johnson, described those scenes like this: " ... Even their bodies are frequently in a moment affected with the strangest convulsions and involuntary agitations ..." Is that what happened at Westminster Chapel? Yes. Did the Holy Spirit cause it? Yes. Later, R.T. reported in the Chapel's News:

"We have just had one of the greatest weekends in my nearly 24 years at Westminster Chapel. Someone told me that having Charles Carrin was the greatest risk I have ever taken, but all I know is— we thank God that he came. He is such a gentle, humble man but has power that flows from his lips and hands, unlike many people I know It was just so wonderful—almost impossible to describe unless you were there ...."

Philip Evans, Editor of The Chapel News, reported the Holy Spirit's invasion this way:

"... The traditional service ... was lost ... halted as abruptly as it had been by an air-raid warning on the day the Second World War was declared. Charles called forward people who felt the call to intercession—and perhaps as many as one-third of the congregation responded. As he prayed for people some fell, some groaned ... Writing this, it occurred to me to turn to Jonathan Edwards narratives of the revivals in his church in 1735 and 1740-42 for help in describing what I saw. He wrote this: "There were some instances of persons lying in a sort of trance, remaining for perhaps a whole twenty-four hours motionless, and with their senses locked up but in the meantime under strong imaginations, as though they went to heaven, and had there a vision of glorious and delightful objects.""

What R.T. had seen at First Baptist, Hixson, Tennessee and wanted to happen at Westminster Chapel, had come to pass. In many ways, it was more significant. Being a scholar and church-historian, R.T. was not shocked by it. He also knew that Jonathan's wife, Sarah, lay "slain," immobile under the Spirit's power, for seventeen days. In the 1600s, the Puritans in England, and their congregations in the Colonies labeled the incident as "swooning." Pastor James Glindening, a British Puritan, had the deacons remove the fallen from the meeting house and lay them under the trees until they recovered. Although Hixson, Tennessee, and London, England, are an ocean apart, that same "commotion" had taken place in both places.

A sidenote to that first preaching-trip to Westminster Chapel is that I told R.T: "I am not leaving London, until someone at Holy Trinity-Brompton, lays-hands on me—even if it is the church janitor." My reason was this: Holy Trinity had received the anointing from Toronto, and one Sunday morning the Holy Spirit suddenly invaded the building, putting the entire congregation on the floor in explosive laughter. England's best educated, most dignified, and wealthiest were laid-out and unable to get up. This was significant: The church was one of England's most sophisticated and cultured congregations. God was showing them what He could do to their religious formality. At the same time, He was ministering to their deepest needs. I have seen people who suffered from severe depression be hit with the power of God, be laid-out on the floor in laughter, and then rise totally delivered!

On the way to the airport for our flight back to the US, we stopped at Holy Trinity Church, and I explained my need to the secretary. She apologized, saying that all the Church Staff was away, none was available. "The only ones here are the janitor and me…" I interrupted. "Get him!" A few minutes later a workman stood before me with a puzzled look on his face. I explained my mission. He obeyed, laid hands on me, and I was electrified by the power of God. Like the eunuch—after Philip baptized him—I "went on my way rejoicing" (Acts 8:39). Weeks after getting home, a member at Westminster, wrote:

"Dear Charles, I still think of your visit to us at Westminster Chapel. Never before had I met someone who had been entrusted with God's power like you! We continue to receive the Holy Spirit and are just so more open and free (2 Corinthians 3.17) … The week prior to your visit I prayed, and the Lord showed me two long lines of people at Westminster Chapel waiting to be ministered to ... May God richly bless your ministry, 'Waking up the Church,' not with buckets of cold water but full of the Holy Spirit!"

Yours in Christ, Ingrid Macmillan, London

This I know: Westminster Chapel, you, nor I, can expect the Holy Spirit's full endowment of power if we reject any portion of the New Testament. First Corinthians 12,13,14, must be accepted, endorsed, and preached equally with all other New Testament passages. We dare not refuse any Bible teaching because of denominational prejudice. The gift of tongues is always the big offender. However, Paul is very emphatic about the value of praying in tongues. He explained, "For if I pray in an unknown tongue, my spirit prays, but my understanding is unfruitful." (My humanity cannot comprehend the language of my spirit.) "What is it then? I will pray with the spirit, and I will pray with the understanding also" (I Corinthians 14:14,15).

Paul declares that he will use both mind and spirit as essential means of prayer. He explains why: "Likewise the Spirit also helps in our weaknesses. For we do not know what we should pray for as we ought, but the Spirit Himself makes intercession for us with groanings which cannot be uttered" (Romans 8:26). Our concern is this: If the greatest writer of the New Testament needed the gift of tongues for effective praying, can you and I get by with less? In 1 Corinthians 14:4-5, Paul said, "He who speaks in a tongue edifies himself, but he who prophesies edifies the church. I wish you all spoke with tongues, but even more that you prophesied; for he who prophesies is greater than he who speaks with tongues, unless indeed he interprets, that the church may receive edification." Why does the modern church go into screaming opposition to the gift of tongues? It attacks a man's religious ego and pride. Pride is the direct opponent to true spirituality. The other gifts are not safe without this protection of tongues. All spiritual gifts work together as one composite; we cannot remove tongues without disrupting the system of the whole.

When R.T. retired from Westminster Chapel and returned to the US, he built a waterfront home on Key Largo, and I enjoyed visiting him and Louise there. In July 2002, David Rhea, Don Vinson, and I met him at a nearby restaurant and were having a delightful visit, when Don asked where he was traveling next. His answer, despondently, was "Israel!" He then explained why he did not want to go. Conditions were very hostile, and Arab-Israeli conflict might quickly become violent. Unfortunately, he had agreed to escort a group of Englishmen there. The moment R.T. answered, the Holy Spirit came visibly upon Don and David. I was sitting across the table from them and saw David gripping his chair—trying not to slide under the table. Finally, Don spoke and said, "R.T, you are not going to Israel for the reason you think! God has His own plans for your being there!"

A few days later, R.T. flew to Tel Aviv, got a cab at the airport and started to Jerusalem. In a short distance, the driver made it known that Yasser Arafat was his cousin. R.T. then explained to the driver that he prayed for Yasser daily and had done so for a number of years. The driver was shocked. As a leader of the Palestinian Liberation Organization, Yasser was much feared by people everywhere. At that time the State of Israel had Yasser so confined that even CCN and other international television networks could not reach him. The driver asked, "Would you like to meet him?" Astonished at the possibility, R.T. answered that he would.

They continued their trip to Jerusalem, and a few days later R.T. received a phone call from Andrew White, the Archbishop of Canterbury's personal Envoy to the Middle East, confirming the visit. R.T. and Yasser were soon together in the first of five visits; each time R.T. shared the gospel with this powerful Muslim and gave him gifts. On one of the visits, they watched the "Jesus" film together. R.T. even told Yasser that if he would accept Jesus Christ, he would gladly die with him. Yasser then invited Louise to come with R.T. on her birthday and visit him. When the time came, they went but plans for this visit ended in tragic disappointment. Yasser was strangely taken ill that day and soon died. Was there a connection between Yasser's death and R.T's visits? Did Yasser's guards become fearful of his becoming a Christian? Who knows? R.T. does not comment on that possibility.

Chapter 35

WORD, SPIRIT, POWER, CONFERENCES REACH THOUSANDS

Jack Taylor, R.T. Kendall, and I had preached with each other but never as a three-partner team. When the two of them were in Oklahoma, Jack suggested to R.T. that they travel together, doing Word and Spirit Conferences. R.T., who had just returned to the U.S. from his twenty-five-year pastorate in London, was immediately interested, with the request that I be included. Jack was happy with that arrangement, I accepted, and we called our meetings Word, Spirit, Power, Conferences. The consensus was that R.T. would preach first, emphasizing the importance of the Word. Jack would follow, stressing the work of the Holy Spirit, and I would conclude, underscoring the need for the Spirit's Power.

We planned that each would speak fifteen minutes and provide 45 minutes of instruction. Afterward, we would offer personal hands-on ministry to the congregation. When our plan was made public, many pastors were eager to host the Conference, and our first event was held at Columbus, Georgia, in the year 2000. Pastor Al Young was the director. It was very successful. A number of churches participated, and many people were blessed. Here is a testimony from a couple who attended the Conference. It was sent to Pastor Young afterward:

"Dear Al, Just a word to let you know how much we enjoyed and benefited from this Conference. We brought a couple from our church in McDonough, Georgia, who were truly in alien territory. They had never been in anything like this. The wonderful worship put them at ease, and they were able to listen with open hearts. The lady with us had an extremely bad case of tendinitis in her shoulder. During the service, the pain was so severe she had to rest the arm carefully on her coat. She was the first person Charles Carrin laid hands on Thursday night. And the Holy Spirit's wonderful power put her on the floor, wouldn't let her get up, and healed her arm. Needless to say, our friends' view of the Holy Spirit has been radically changed. God also healed my wife of a difficult problem with her inner ear, so extreme that she would become nauseated. Friends had to bring her home from work on several occasions. She too was healed. Thanks for a wonderful event!"

—Jeff and Margaret Robinson, McDonough, Georgia.

During my message that evening, I had a "word of knowledge" about the woman in pain and went to her immediately when the sermon ended. Signaling her to step to the aisle, I laid hands on her. She crashed under the power of God and was restored. I went back to the front of the auditorium. Little did Jack, R.T., or I know that in the next twenty years we would conduct nearly 100 of these Conferences from London to Alaska, Canada, across the U.S. and see numerous others be healed. That woman was the first of many. Later, when Jack, R.T., and I were preaching at Christ Chapel in Florence, Alabama, Jack met Friede McDonald, a lovely German widow. They married and have since traveled the world, carrying the gospel. These two men, Jack Taylor and R.T. Kendall, have impacted my life as have no others. Traveling together, we have heard each other preach hundreds of times—always to our blessing and delight.

Word, Spirit, Power, Conference In Toronto

In January 2002 we were invited to hold our Word, Spirit, Power event at the Toronto Airport Christian Fellowship, simultaneously with the church's annual four-day Pastors' Conference. The meeting that year commemorated the Holy Spirit's historic fall eight years before. R.T., Jack, and I preached to more than 2,000 pastors and church leaders from 63 different nations worldwide. One afternoon as I finished preaching, John Arnott, the Church's founding pastor, called out from the audience, "Charles, Go down the aisle! Go down the aisle!" When I did, David Rhea with me, people raced to the walkway where a wave of power knocked hundreds to the floor. Some were heaped on top of others.

A thousand more ran to the rear and sides of the building to stand in line. Probably more than 2,000 were visibly touched by the Holy Spirit that afternoon. Radical "signs and wonders" took place before us. Lives were changed. Bodies were healed. Ministries were empowered (Acts 1:8). In short, the Kingdom came, and people were overwhelmed with the Glory of God. There is no way to describe the power that went through the building. Dave Calyn, cameraman at station #2 that afternoon, was on a platform nearly two feet above the floor. He tells about his encounter:

> "I came to the Toronto Airport Christian Fellowship in mid-1999–have had many Christian experiences–but none changed me like the day Charles impacted my life with something so chaotically beautiful that it literally blew me away ... I was so engrossed in staying on my camera. I never heard much of his sermon. But I do remember something about his visiting a prison—and then, suddenly, God hit me like a bolt of lightning. It felt like someone stuck a cattle prod into my belly and I literally flew off my platform backward. I saw both my legs and feet in the air in front of me as I crashed to the floor. I lay there for a second before I audibly said, 'What happened!?' I was in total shock. Wherever Charles moved—and he moved all over—people were being blasted by the power of God. Every time I would shoot I saw crew members and others getting knocked down by the Holy Spirit. I grabbed my water bottle and splashed it on my eyes and forehead ... Then I fell off my stand again, this time stumbling back and grabbing the pole behind me … By this time the Director thought that I was a lost cause and as I replaced my headset, I heard him say, 'Camera # 5, go help Dave!' … When cameraman # 5 got close to me, he touched my elbow, and we both fell to the floor. The Ministry Team member tried to catch him as I crashed down again with no one to help. There was a big bang, and another wave of Heavenly Glory hit the audience … By this time our hand-held cameraman had fallen down again, and camera # 5 was not working. The Director was pleading with us to stay alert even though all of Heaven was breaking loose … I don't understand. I just conclude that 'God uses the foolish things to confound the wise' and I was his fool that day. But, I love Him for it and give Jesus all the Glory."
> —Dave Calyn, Toronto Airport Christian Fellowship

Here is another who wrote about her God-encounter in Toronto:

"Dear Charles ... You came to the row where I was sitting at TACF with folks from my church and when you touched my forehead the power of the Holy Spirit hit me like lightning striking a tree. A little while later you came back through our whole row. Once again, the power of the Holy Spirit hit me ... I felt if you had not stopped I would have died! I can't thank you enough for your ministry in Toronto! I needed a power encounter with the Living God!"

—Betty, Washington Crossing, Pennsylvania.

A Methodist pastor wrote:

"Charles, I heard you speak in Toronto for the first time and again at Pat Robertson's headquarters in Virginia Beach. In Toronto, I had my first great encounter with the Holy Spirit. You preached, and then we're going to lay hands on everyone. To get things started, you called all the 'Bobs' and 'Marys' up front. That is when I said to God, 'Why didn't he call any Johns?' Next thing I know the wind of the Lord knocked me out. And I got up from the floor two and a half hours later. The woman who was sitting in the chair in front of me said she felt the wind come from you, go around her and hit me. I was floored, and I've never been the same! I can't get enough of our Father...."

—John Cowen, East Randolph United Methodist Church, New York.

Jack, R.T., and I were asked to write a book about our ministry with the same title as our Conferences: Word, Spirit, Power. We did so and won the coveted Best Book of the Year Award in 2013. We have now conducted more than 90 Word, Spirit, Power Conferences all over the U.S. In each of our Conferences, we experience "signs and wonders," some of which are identical to those occurring in America's "Great Awakening" in the 1700s and the Cane Ridge revival of the 1800s. While these unusual "signs" may be new to the current church, they are not new to Christianity and were very common in the ministry of George Whitefield, John Wesley, Jonathan Edwards, James Glindening, William McCullouch, and numerous others.

Toronto: God's Power Plant and the Breaker Anointing

Jack, R.T., and I are great admirers of Heidi Baker, whom we regard as the Holy Spirit's modern missionary miracle. Without question, Heidi is one of the most astonishing evangelicals of modern times. A petite, Ph.D., from King's College, London, she is more attractive than most Hollywood Stars, yet her whole devotion centers on the Kingdom of God and her role in it. At a time when she was nearing physical and mental collapse, fighting to maintain a small orphanage in Mozambique and assisting a few struggling churches, she went to Toronto where Randy Clark laid hands on her. Her anointing with the Holy Spirit that night was one of raw power that shook her visibly and astonished everyone present. Not only was she personally revived, but her ministry was anointed for shocking success.

Today, Heidi's organization, Iris Ministries, maintains missions in 36 countries where she feeds, houses, and educates more than 10,000 children daily. Her workforce has trained and equipped more than 30,000 Christian laborers in developing countries. In Mozambique, part of this growth occurred while the nation was in civil war. It is for reasons like this (the Holy Spirit's anointing) that 85% of all Christian conversions taking place worldwide are achieved by those who have experienced the Holy Spirit's baptism and gifts. Cessationists have missed the "boat" in this arena.

Heidi and I met when we were speakers at Cornerstone Church, in Davie, Florida. Later, while visiting in the pastor's office, she rose to leave, stopped suddenly, and said of me, "This man has a breaker anointing!"(II Samuel 5:19-20). I was ignorant of what she meant. Others later explained that some individuals and churches do not willingly yield but change only because of a "breaking" experience. I was one who would administer that breaking.

As an example: When Loren Wilson was pastor of Grace Chapel in Jacksonville, Florida, the church invited me to hold a three-day meeting with them. One of the visitors who came was an atheist College Professor, Ph.D., a middle-aged bachelor, who taught philosophy at the local University. Before the service, he boasted to me that he had studied everything Carl Marx wrote. Marx, an atheist philosopher, was co-author of the Communist Manifesto, one of the most inflammatory political documents of all time. Knowing that, I did not argue with the professor but trusted God to correct his life.

The Holy Spirit moved in power that evening, and during "hands-on" ministry most of the congregation dropped to the floor. The professor personally knew some of the people were educated, mentally responsible individuals. He also knew that something real had happened to them, but he had no philosophical explanation for it. Finally, I went to him, "As a philosopher," I said, "You are one who 'loves wisdom' and wants to know the truth" (*philo*=love, *sophia*=wisdom). "Yes!" He answered, "That is true—I love wisdom!" I went on, "If God is real you want to know it."

He thought for a moment then answered sarcastically, "Yes. If God is real, I want to know it." "Can you say, 'God, if you are real, show me?'" I asked. He hesitated a moment then slowly responded "Yes," and said, "God, If, you are real, show me." I left him briefly, laid hands on a few others and came back. This time, I never spoke but touched him lightly on the cheek. The touch knocked him to the floor. Nor did he fall gently—he went down with a crash—grabbing the air; no one caught him. For some twenty minutes he lay immobile on the carpet, weeping. After he was helped to his feet, still crying softly, I handed him the mike and said: "Tell us what happened." With no hesitation, he shouted, "I found God! I found God!" I touched him again, and once more he dropped like a stone.

There were numerous people present that evening who witnessed his fall and heard his acknowledgment of God. When he finally left the church, he was too inebriated to drive home and spent the night sleeping on a friend's sofa (Acts 2:13). More interestingly, the next day he returned to the University, resigned his post, left town, and years later his close friends had not heard from him. Perhaps like Paul who went into Arabia after his encounter with Jesus, the professor needed great seclusion to adjust to his new Christian life (Galatians 1:17). Through the "Holy Spirit's anointing," he encountered God. This is an important fact: The professor was not converted by my intellectual argument. He was converted by a personal encounter with God. His atheism was broken through the Holy Spirit's anointing; the "laying on of hands" (Acts 8:18). Any ministry today that does not include "signs and wonders" through the laying on of hands is an insufficient ministry. I heard Derek Prince say that any pastor who did not provide signs and wonders for his congregation should apologize to them.

In Scripture, there is nothing said about the "breaker" anointing, but we see it happening in a variety of ways. While I was speaking at Central Baptist in Hixson, Tennessee, and came into the lobby of the Hampton Inn early one morning, two couples hurried toward me. One of the women was suddenly slammed to the floor. Her husband, only seconds behind her, also fell. Almost instantly, the other husband and wife dropped—all of them under the power of the Holy Spirit. None of us had touched. I will never forget the expression on the face of the desk clerk, a tall, young Hindu from India, who stood on his tiptoes, peering wide-eyed over the counter at the people who appeared to be dead on his floor. I quickly explained, "Don't worry! This is God's work!"

Later that day David Rhea and I were leaving a restaurant when a vehicle screeched to a stop beside us. Two women jumped out, left the doors open, engine running, hurried to me and said, "Please pray for us!" I started to pray, and the power of God knocked both of them to the pavement. It was a sunny afternoon, the parking lot was blistering hot, but the Holy Spirit seemed not to care. The women wanted a God encounter, and He happily obliged. That same day, we went to the Mall where a young woman recognized me, rushed up, gave me a hug and immediately dropped to the marble floor. Shoppers looked on in amazement and hurried away.

We then went to Applebee's Restaurant where a large, circular table of young people saw us, waved, calling us to join them. As we neared, the Spirit began knocking them to the floor. Some fell into the aisle; others slid under the table. Later, as we entered Central Baptist, a pastor from Kentucky shook my hand and dropped to the cement step. He was electrified, kicking and laughing in the "joy of the Lord." That is God's work? Yes. Strange? Yes. It was a "sign and wonder."

Late that night I returned to my room, was preparing for bed when there was a loud knock on my door. It was the young Hindu man and his wife. "We want to know Jesus!" He spoke abruptly, almost pushing his way in, "We want to know Jesus!" I welcomed them, read Paul's salvation explanation in Romans 10:8-13, led them in that confession, laid hands on them and they dropped to the carpet—filled with the Holy Spirit. God will minister to people wherever they are. And He comes in parking lots, malls, motels, office buildings, any place He finds the hungry and hurting. He does not wait for Sunday service. To the scoffers whose dignity and pride ridicule such moves of God, I say, "Just wait. Your time is coming!"

Charles Carrin

Here I was, an old-school, Calvinist Baptist pastor who once scorned such "stupid people," now seeing the Holy Spirit break all my religious rules. In a more gentle way, the writer of the following testimony was also changed, and is now changing others:

"Dear 'Daddy' Charles, A few years ago you were in Fairbanks, Alaska, for the Word, Spirit, Power Conference. At one session you called me out from my seat and prayed over me. That night I had an electrical current running through my hands, and you told me, 'God has put healing in your hands. Go lay them on people!' I work in the hospital recovery room where surgeons and nurses come to me when they are in pain. They find relief in my touch. I explained about the Conference and told them that it came from the Lord. Charles, I wanted to thank you for your continued faithfulness to our Lord. You are touching people in Jesus' name, and He is using you. I'm so blessed and excited about what I'm doing."

Lovingly,

Maria Crites, Fairbanks Alaska

Chapter 36

GOD SENDS ME TO SOUTH AND CENTRAL AMERICA

Omar Cabrerra and Carlos Anacondia in Argentina

For several years I spoke at Conferences in Argentina, Honduras, Ecuador, and Peru. In Argentina, I met people who witnessed the Holy Spirit's outpouring in Tommy Hick's revival. They assured me, it was real. In the city of Resistencia, I preached to part of Pastor Omar Cabrerra's 300,000-member church—an outgrowth of Tommy's ministry. Only a portion of the church was present, as no stadium in Argentina was large enough to accommodate the entire membership. This church, plus numerous others of the 30,000+ member size where I also visited, are results of the Tommy Hicks Crusade. Before Tommy's arrival, Protestants claimed less than one percent of the Latin American population. Today it is growing at an unprecedented way. Many Baptist, Presbyterian and other mainline denominations in Latin America accept all the spiritual gifts and experience their power.

When I learned that Carlos Anacondia was preaching in my area of Argentina, I went, wanting him to lay hands on me. His meeting was held in an outdoor stadium that served part-time as a ball-field and cow pasture. Carlos' ministry was anointed in an incredible way, and when he gave opportunity for everyone to receive personal ministry, I ran forward and stood in the line. As he laid hands on the people, the Holy Spirit slammed everyone to the ground; some were growling, others laughing, and many were vibrating in the power of God. I too crashed, in an area with sand spurs and cow-patties close to my face. That did not matter. I wanted all God would give, regardless of the surroundings. Strangely, at that moment, I had a flash-back to the torture-chamber I saw in Havana's Morrow Castle years before. Lying there in Argentinian dirt, I was experiencing the religious freedom earlier believers had been denied. More importantly, their shrieking prayers were being answered by Latin America's unstoppable revival.

Before leaving Argentina, friends and I went to the National Congress Building in Buenos Aires and had lunch in the Senate's private dining room with the Secretary of Commerce and his wife, Dr. and Mrs. Arturo

289

Hotton. These were Spirit-baptized believers, who like many others, hold high-ranking positions in governmental leadership. I then walked to the Presidential Palace, Casa Rosada, across the way. With my heart racing, I stood on the steps near where Tommy Hicks and the guard must have talked that momentous day in 1954. At that moment, I did not think about politicians and Presidents, soldiers and citizens. I thought only of the amazing grace of God—— Grace that loves dictators, as well as peasants, uses unknown preachers as well as celebrated evangelists. With tears, I thanked the Lord for letting me get that close to the Burning Bush in Argentina, close to the power that turned an entire nation around and awoke a slumbering Continent. More than that, I prayed, "Lord, do in North America what You did in the South."

Tegucigalpa, Honduras

David Rhea and I ran the full length of the huge Intercontinental Airport in Houston, Texas, to catch a flight to Tegucigalpa, Honduras. Our arriving-plane was late, and we reached the departing gate just as they were closing the doors. Dropping into our seats, out of breath, we thanked God we were on board. I was to speak at a Conference in Tegucigalpa that evening. Flying over the Gulf of Mexico was restful, passed quickly, and we were soon looking down on the mountains of Central America.

The church in Tegucigalpa was in the countryside and met in a large tin-roofed Tabernacle that seated more than one thousand. Several English-speaking pastors preached, I among them, with interpreters translating the messages. People crowded closely, stood patiently listening for hours, hungry for every word of Gospel that was spoken. All were former Catholics to whom the gospel offered great hope. Burning candles, praying to statues and saints, was gone from their lives forever. They were now born-again and baptized in the Holy Spirit. Jesus lived in them and had become their closest friend. When the meeting finally closed that first night, many of them walked miles to get home, sometimes carrying children and bags of food.

After my preaching, David and I prayed endlessly with the people. We did not understand their Spanish, nor they our English, but the Holy Spirit still ministered in power. These meetings were attended by thousands, and God honored each event with "signs and wonders."

Lima, Peru

Lima, Peru, on South America's Pacific Coast, was established by the Spanish in 1535. It was fiercely devoted to the Catholic Church, and until recent times continued the terror of the Inquisition. Knowing the history of Latin America, I was awed that we Evangelicals could be there, freely preaching the gospel in a Catholic nation. In the lifetime of missionaries I knew, Evangelicals had been dragged through the streets of Peru by the air of their heads and killed by mobs. Priests could have stopped the violence but did not. Two of the horrific sites we visited in Lima were the Court of the Inquisition where heretics were tried and sentenced to death.

In Lima, one of the churches where we preached, Iglesia Biblica Emmanuel, is located in the downtown part of the city and overshadowed by Lima's tallest buildings. This congregation, served by Pastor Humberto Lay and a team of others, conducted six services each Sunday to standing-room-only crowds and two packed-out services on Wednesday night. The auditorium seats over 1,000, but in all our services the aisles and walls were jammed with people standing. When I arrived on Sunday morning to preach at the 11:00 service, it was almost impossible to get into the building because of the crowd.

The nine o'clock congregation was still leaving, as our American Team struggled to get through. As we had hoped and prayed, the Holy Spirit fell on the congregation in astonishing ways. People were healed, delivered from demons, and many were filled with the Holy Spirit, and The American Baptists with us stood back in amazement. They realized what they were seeing was real, but it proved their Baptist cessationist-theology was terribly wrong. David Rhea and Don Vinson experienced the greatest anointing I have ever seen on them. People for whom David prayed were knocked to the floor with such force that he was sometimes slammed down with them. There were blasts of Holy Spirit-power. At times, Don could wave his hand, and people dropped under the presence of God. David's brother, Tom, a former Baptist, was thrilled, realizing the Holy Spirit was using him.

Quito, Ecuador

Quito, Ecuador, is one of South America's loveliest Colonial Spanish-cities. Snow-capped volcanoes rise above the city, and it lies in an Andes-valley nearing 10,000 feet elevation. Here, at this high elevation, the city enjoys a spring-like climate year-round, even though the equator passes through the nation. Quito, the Capital City, is thirty-three miles long and three miles wide. The town is so compressed between mountains and the airport so narrow, that when our plane touched down on the runway, we could see the food on people's tables. Inaquito Church, who hosted our Conference in Quito, had 2,500 in attendance for each of three Sunday services. The church's compound spreads over a large, enclosed acreage containing several auditoriums, a gymnasium, and office buildings. Our American sponsor for the Conference was First Baptist Church, Shelbyville, Tennessee. The pastor, Drew Hayes, was a wonderful man who wanted to go forward with God and not be restrained by Baptist tradition. His congregation was also home to the largest Spirit-Filled Spanish Church in Tennessee, and it was this pastor, David Carrera, a native Ecuadorian, who made our South American arrangements. David Rhea, Don Vinson, Craig, and Karen McMichael, went with me.

Strangely, Inaquito Church had never experienced a visible demonstration of the Holy Spirit. On Sunday morning after I concluded the sermon and called the U.S. ministry-team forward, the Holy Spirit came in such power that hundreds of people fell before Him. Elderly Spanish men, women, children, people of all ages, and Inca women in their beautiful, traditional dress, were among those laid-out in the power of God. Numerous physical healings, baptisms in the Spirit, deliverances, and other works of the Spirit took place. The pastor, Fernando Lay, was ecstatic and told us with tears that he had prayed for ten years for this to happen. I had a very personal thrill when this congregation began singing "Mighty One Of Israel," a song which had been written by Ginger Hendricks, one of my members in Delray Beach. I sang in English, they sang in Spanish, and together, we praised the Lord.

Every service was anointed by the Holy Spirit; seemingly no one was missed, and after getting outside the building, we were mobbed. At our final service, I gave the opportunity for anyone needing deliverance from drug addiction to come forward. One of the church ushers, a handsome, well-dressed young man, ran to the front and leaped onto the platform. The instant I laid hands on him, the demon in him roared like a madman, and he lunged at me. Instantly, the power of God slammed him to the floor, where he began writhing and growling (Mark 16:17).

Craig raced down the aisle, leaped onto the platform and held him, while David, Tom, and others, rushed to help. It took five men to restrain him, but within a short time, he was completely delivered. He stood up laughing, weeping, leaping, clapping his hands, and worshiping Jesus, Who set him free (Mark 5:2; 9:20). The next morning at 3:30 a.m., when we arrived at the airport for our early departure to the U.S., he was at the Terminal waiting. Reaching through the barricade, he hugged me weeping, kissed me repeatedly on each cheek, and spoke the only English word he knew. "Papa! Papa!" Without realizing it, he had experienced the Juphunneh "Call" and was responding to it.

Drew Hayes, the Baptist pastor from Tennessee who sponsored the Conference, was experiencing a struggle: He wanted me to preach in his church but was fearful of how the church would respond to people falling to the floor, experiencing noisy deliverance, and the things he saw happening in South America. Finally, he asked if I would return with him to Tennessee and preach on Sunday morning—with this difference: I would do no "hands-on" ministry. I wanted to go straight to Miami, but yielded and agreed to go to Tennessee. But plans did not go well: At the Quito Airport, we learned our pilot was sick; there was no replacement for him, and we could not fly until he recovered. The airport was mobbed; there were not enough seats, and even the outside steps and staircases were filled. Hours later we left, but because of the delay, we were re-routed through New York. Late that night, exhausted and tired, we stood in the dark outside JFK terminal waiting for a taxi to take us to the hotel. I was angry at myself. If I had not accepted the request, I could have been at home asleep.

First Baptist, Shelbyville, Tennessee

Sunday morning, at First Baptist, Shelbyville, Tennessee, God honored us with a message that was anointed, penetrating but non-threatening to Baptists. My text was II Corinthians 2:15, that explains how God made

Christians to be the "fragrance of Christ to those who are perishing and those who are saved." To illustrate the power of this fragrance, I told how certain tribes of bees regard their own relatives as enemies and will sometimes fight to the death inside the flower. Other insects, moths, butterflies, and ants do not bother them. According to entomologists, they don't like their own smell in another bee. Once they have become dusted with pollen and their body odor perfumed by the blossom, they no longer find each other offensive. My point was, that, like Zechariah the priest who burned incense in the Temple and carried the fragrance of worship to everyone around him, we too should carry the perfume of Christ (Luke 1:9-11).

The message was simple—totally acceptable to Baptists but anointed. I applied it to our personal Christian lives. When I finished the sermon, I asked the pastor to take charge and sat down. He quickly came to the front, commented briefly about the message and then to my shock, said, "If any of you would like Charles to pray and lay hands on you, please come forward." I was surprised that he had changed his mind. He looked back at me, signaled me forward where some twenty-five people had immediately gathered. When I started to pray and lay hands on them, we had a repeat of the South American scene: There was a holy-explosion. People were blasted to the floor, many were electrified, vibrating, others were groaning, and some laughing.

I was too involved to see the deacons rush to the opposite end of the building for an emergency meeting. Nor did I know some angry members were hurrying out the door. I only knew one thing: God had come in power to First Baptist Church, Shelbyville, Tennessee. People were filled with the Spirit, delivered from demons, and anointed for new life in Christ. It wasn't until later I learned the deacons' emergency meeting was to fire the Pastor. In every instance, I had simply obeyed God and the Pastor; even so, I was branded as a "church-splitter." The "breaker-anointing" was at work.

A few days later, the church had an emergency Conference, and many shared their testimonies of how the ministry that morning had changed their lives. These were thrilled, happy, and one of the men begged the deacons to listen: "I came alive that morning!" He pleaded, "For the first time I have experienced the power of God!" His cry went unheard. The deacons refused, and the pastor remained fired: The 700-member church split. The community was jarred, and the Spanish congregation relocated. In time, four new charismatic congregations formed out of the wreckage.

One was led by the pastor. Tragically, the South American Conference they had planned for the next year never took place.

The outlook for such Baptist Churches, nationwide, is frightening. Recently, the President of the Southern Baptist Convention announced that half of their American churches will permanently close their doors by the year 2030. The overwhelming membership is "Senior Citizen" and will be dead by that time. By contrast, Centro Misionero Bethesda (Bethesda Missionary Center) in Bogota, Colombia, an outgrowth of Tommy Hick's 1954 ministry, recently built an outdoor amphitheater that seats 1,000,000 people. The church has services in their downtown facility around the clock, seven days a week. It never closes. There is constant prayer, worship, preaching, ministering to the sick, deliverance for the demonized and lost, every day, all day and night. The pastor is a young man, Enrique Gomez, who is baptized in the Spirit, experiences His power, and is taking it to the nation. How is his church different from the Baptists? His charismatic church believes and practices First Corinthians 12,13,14. Baptists do not believe it and will not allow its practice. It is that simple. Cessationism has killed thousands of such churches and robbed the people of their Biblical inheritance. I grieve for them: In many of the cities where I preach there are big, beautiful, Baptist Church buildings, that will soon be empty. Instead of closing their doors, Baptist Churches need to open their hearts and minds to the Holy Spirit, receive His anointing, accept the full gospel, and watch the Kingdom come in power!

My friends, Baptist Pastor Todd Mozingo and his wife Jan, of Stuart, Florida, went to South America, visited a full-gospel meeting, received "hands-on" ministry and were baptized in the Spirit. When they got home, they were immediately fired by their church leadership. Today Todd and Jan serve Revive Church and are flourishing in the power of God. I have preached for them numerous times and always experienced the Holy Spirit's presence.

Chapter 37

SONS IN MINISTRY SHARE THEIR TESTIMONIES

Honorary Doctorate

In 2009, Dr. David Donally, the President of the Evangelical Bible College and Seminary in West Palm Beach, Florida attended a Pastors Luncheon where I spoke. My topic was about changes I would make in my ministry if I could do it over. It was a precaution to the men not to make the same mistakes. Everyone listened with rapt attention, and afterward, Dr. Donally approached me privately to explain that the Seminary would like to award me with an Honorary Doctor of Divinity Degree. I agreed to pray about his offer, and then a week later called and accepted the honor, which was presented during the School's next Graduation Ceremony. Several more years passed, and then Dr. Donally approached me again, asking if I would serve as Chancellor for the school. I felt both actions were a privilege and was humbled by their choice. This College and Seminary is primarily a missionary-organization, providing education for many foreign-born Christian students. In 2018, in recognition of my 70 years of ministry, they also honored me again with a "Legacy Lifetime Achievement Award."

Sons In Ministry

Many of my sons-in-ministry have written their testimonies, and I share three examples: Mario Bramnick, born in Cuba, Shane O'Connor, U.S.-born, and Leif Hetland, born in Norway. Mario is now an American attorney, an Ordained Pastor, strong political leader in South Florida's Spanish community, and a guest of President Trump in the White House. Shane is an American businessman and Elder in the Church of Christ. Leif was born in Norway and is an evangelist with an astonishing International Ministry. Meet these three sons:

Mario Bramnick came to the U.S. as a Cuban refugee. He earned his degree in Law and was admitted to the Florida Bar. Later, he was saved, called to the ministry, ordained as a pastor, and became active in South Florida politics in behalf of the Latin community. When Donald Trump announced his candidacy for President, Mario supported him. Since the election, Mario was appointed to the White House Faith-Initiative and was received numerous times into the Oval Office. At President Trump's request, he is in frequent contact with other Latin American Presidents and been a guest at White House banquets. Today, Mario assists local Jewish causes and maintains highly-significant contact with the nation of Israel and its President. I am proud to call him my son.

Shane O'Connor is an Elder in the Church of Christ and an executive with the FedEx Corporation in Memphis, Tennessee, where he supervises their multi-million-dollar gifts to charitable needs. The Company has 170,000 vehicles on the road globally and is very concerned about pedestrian safety around the world—especially that of children. Shane travels internationally for FedEx and directs millions of dollars to various charities, chiefly in the cause of public safety. I will let him tell the story of how we met. He wrote:

"Charles, In March of 1994 you lead a three-day Conference on the Holy Spirit at the Holiday Inn Medical Center in Midtown Memphis. I had never been to a meeting like that in my life. I listened to your message Wednesday night, running it through my Church of Christ Seminary Degree book, chapter, and verse, mental filters. I found nothing suspicious in your message; on the contrary, it was quite faith-building. When you were through, you pointed to my wife and me and said: 'That couple right there!' I surmised you wanted to pray for us, which was fine with me, so we went forward.

In front of two hundred people, you first gently prayed for my wife, then moved onto me. I don't remember your touching me, but I do remember that the next thing I was lying flat on my back on the floor of the Holiday Inn Ballroom looking up at the fluorescent lights in the ceiling. My thought was, 'What in the world just happened?! What am I doing on the floor —I don't believe in this stuff!' ... The third night, around 10:00 pm as I saw you across the ballroom you lifted your hands in my direction and from about 20 feet away I was down on my face again in the Holiday Inn Ballroom. No sooner had I hit the floor when a flood of belly-laughter began pouring out of the depths of my being. I lay there for about 45 minutes in non-stop laughter—being 'filled with an inexpressible and glorious joy' (1 Peter 1:8). I experienced first-hand Psalm 126:2, 'Our mouths were filled with laughter ....'

That evening opened a glorious new dimension in my walk with our Lord. The blinders were taken off, and I learned about the Kingdom of God that Jesus brought. I experienced new life and power in my personal walk and in my ministry to others. I cherish my personal friendship with you, Charles, that we developed through the years; your influence in my life and the pattern you set for me in your unquenchable desire for more of Him has given me an everlasting example. I Love you!"

Shane

The following testimony is from my Norwegian son Leif Hetland, an amazing evangelist who ministers to multiplied thousands around the world. We met years ago when I was preaching in a Baptist Church in Columbus, Georgia. He wrote:

"Dear Papa Charles, I want you to know how much I love you and appreciate the way you touched my life. During the darkest time in my ministry, you came with love and life; you brought an orphan-heart into sonship. My marriage and family are living in genuine revival. My ministry is growing and changing. Its organization came to full fruition a few months after our first meeting. Just last year, we began more than 1,400 home-churches in foreign countries. Nations are being changed, and next year we believe more nations will be visited by the Father's love. Since my first meeting you, over 500,000 people have been saved, tens of thousands of pastors have been trained. Being one of your sons has released the inheritance of the nations in me (Psalm 2:8)."

Love, Your son,
Leif

The statistics in Leif's letter are not exaggerated. In fact, they are insufficient—now out-of-date. I have seen videos of his work in Asia, where countless thousands of people, under hazardous conditions, have crowded into his meetings. Scores of healings have occurred. Lives have been filled with hope and happiness, and people have been baptized in the Father's Love. Many-times Leif has been shielded from view to protect him from sniper-fire. One nighttime, when his vehicle was stopped at a military checkpoint, a soldier held a pistol to his head half an hour threatening to kill him, while the driver pleaded for his life. How powerful is the Jephunneh-love for my sons? Leif is an example: In a hotel parking lot in California when we met, hugged, we were both knocked to the pavement by the power of God. In a public parking lot? Yes! Was there "Impartation?" Yes! What did strangers think? It didn't matter. God cares nothing about our social-image—only for the empowering of our lives. "Signs and wonders" cannot be limited to well-disciplined church services. Miracles far more astonishing than ours were common-place in early Christianity; such "signs" forced the pagan-world to acknowledge the power of Jesus Christ. Nor has God changed His will to accommodate our sophistication.

Chapter 38

WHAT I WOULD CHANGE IN RE-LIVING MY MINISTRY

Many of my sons have asked an important question: If I had my ministry to do over, what would I change? What would I do differently? The seriousness of the question drove me to my knees, and I could not give an immediate answer. After serious prayer, here is how I responded:

1. First of all, I would do nothing until I had been filled with the Holy Spirit. I would lock myself in with God and not come out until I was absolutely certain that His anointing and empowering were upon me. As a young pastor, I knew nothing about the baptism and gifts of the Holy Spirit. That loss was tragic to my congregations and me. As with most pastors, I had momentary anointings on my preaching when the Dove of the Spirit would temporarily alight, bless the ministry of the Word but not remain. Without the baptismal-anointing, our preaching may be accurate, interesting, informative—but remain spiritually powerless(Acts 1:4-9; 19:1-7; I Corinthians 12-14).

2. I would develop a lifestyle of prayer that was unrelenting. My closet would become more important than my pulpit; my private devotion more prized than my public preaching; my meditation more valued than my ministry. My continuous conversion to Christ and death-of-self would become my greatest pursuit. I would focus on genuine spirituality and not on a counterfeit religious performance.

3. I would zealously commit more Scripture to memory and seek its deepest meaning. I would let the Bible speak for itself rather than let others control me by their opinions about it.

4. I would seek to love everyone more eagerly, more generously, more obviously.

5. At the same time, I would waste no effort on insincere Christians and "false brethren." While I would cultivate a merciful spirit, I would confront and expose senseless tradition, falsehood, scriptural abuse, without hesitation. I did not always do that. Everyone suffered because of my failure.

6. I would focus on a Kingdom Ministry and nothing on denominationalism. In my later years, I came to see the hypocrisy of denominational-division. It is a delusion for which truth and integrity are needlessly sacrificed. Good men reject each other for the sake of a false, sectarian identity and obey denominational rules in deference to Scripture. Being orthodox for the sake of protecting myself or others would never again be a consideration. I would become radical for God, rather than remain a decoy for the devil.

7. I would more boldly preach against pride, self-centeredness, false piety, and egotism in my church and leaders; instead, I would expect genuine humility, godliness, sincerity, in all who worked with me. I would absolutely stop the "elitist" spirit in deacons, elders, etc. Everyone holding church authority would periodically submit to deliverance-ministry and discerning of spirits or not function.

8. I would fight church politics as a deadly disease.

9. I would never again allow church leaders to usurp a God-given vision for the sake of protecting their own opinions and self-esteem.

10. In many ways, I was naive, too trusting. I would never do that again. Instead, I would base my trust on people's verified integrity, and not on my assumptions about them. If I were to repeat my ministry, I would seek to be "wise as a serpent, harmless as a dove." I would definitely be wiser.

11. I would seize every opportunity to learn from older ministers, to explore their hearts and minds, and learn from their successes and failures. I would devour as much information as possible from every stream of church history and intensify my education in those areas that directly benefited the Kingdom of God.

12. I would devotedly pour my best contents into every young pastor possible, lovingly help him avoid my mistakes, capitalize on my successes, causing him to see that my highest achievement should be the level where he begins.

13. In my personal life, I would more carefully expose everything to the investigation of the Holy Spirit, to Scripture, godly advisors, and my heart-conviction. I would never be without a team of accountability-partners to whom I could expose myself and benefit by their correction. A God-given ministry is too valuable to be wasted on self-deception, religious hobby-horses, or the previous generation's prejudices. I would want to hear what "the Spirit is saying to the churches" currently and move forward with that alone.

14. Theologically, I had to escape my Calvinism long enough to quit blaming God for all the negative circumstances in my life. I had to exercise the gifts and spiritual authority Jesus gave me, and take full responsibility for my part of ministerial success or failure. Where my first ministry blessed a few hundred people, my second ministry blessed tens of thousands. Would I go back to the first? Never! The first was Denominational. The second was Kingdom.

Chapter 39

MY WIFE, LAURIE, AND MY BROTHER VAN GO TO GOD

Laurie's health declined over a period of several years. We especially wanted to reach our 60th Wedding Anniversary together. That was September 1, 2011. When that wonderful day came, we celebrated, but the following months were increasingly difficult for her. In March, 2012, she was seized with terrible pain at home. I called 911, and the paramedics came quickly and took her to Bethesda Hospital. Almost immediately, she began losing touch with her surroundings, and I stayed with her, leaving her bedside only briefly. Two days later when I came into the room, she said, "Did I die?" "No, darling," I replied, "You are still with us." She was disappointed and said, "I thought I died ...." A moment passed, and then she said, "Is this Heaven?" Again, I answered, explaining she was still on earth. A day later, her last words, "I am so happy I am finally going!"

Saturday night I was in the hospital lobby when I received a phone call telling me that my brother Van had just died. I dropped my head and leaned against the wall. Van was gone! With Laurie in a dying condition, there was no way I could attend his funeral. If she died soon, there was no way his family could be present for hers. For years, when others faced situations like this, I had quoted Paul's exhortation when he said, "I have learned, in whatsoever state I am, therewith to be content" (Philippians 4:11). It was good advice for me, and I heeded it. Sitting there in the lobby, a flood of memories rushed through me: It was Van who paid me ten cents to read my Bible. He was present the day we tried to bury the dead horse. That stormy morning in 1935, it was my cousins and Van who ran in the house yelling that a hurricane was bearing down on us. Now he was gone. Thankfully, I knew Heaven awaited both of us. There, we would be welcomed by James, Ellis, Mamma, Daddy, and a host of others who had already gone before us

A few minutes later I whispered to Laurie that Van was gone. She did not respond. Sunday morning, I came in her room, kissed her, and bending closely, and reminded her that Cecile and Benjamin were arriving that afternoon. "Don't leave Darling until they get here. They want to see you." There was no response, but I am convinced that she heard me because she continued to hold onto life.

Cecile and Benjamin's flight had mechanical difficulties, and they finally arrived at 5:00 pm that afternoon. They hurried to her bedside, kissed her, and spoke lovingly to her. Cecile remained at her bedside praying. At 5:20 Cecile told her mom again how much she loved her. Then she felt very impressed to tell Laurie, "Mom, I sense the presence of angels. I believe the Lord has sent them here to take you Home." With those words, Laurie took one final breath and was gone. Cecile had such an intense awareness of the actual presence of angels that she could only cry in the joy that the Lord had made Laurie's last moments such a Holy and peaceful time.

A nurse came with a stethoscope, listened to her heart, and confirmed that she was gone. She had passed as gently as she lived. A few minutes later, I stood at her bedside, held her hand, and quoted the poem I had written to her years before:

To Laurie, From Charles

I love thee like the moonlight loves the sea,
Touching every wave and ripple tenderly;
Like the morning loves the mist,
Flower and grass-blade gently kissed,
Not a leaf or petal missed,
All this is how I love thee.

I love thee like the twilight loves the night,
When cares and burdens vanish out of sight,
And we who through the day have lived apart,
At nightfall join in rhythm as one heart,
When love joins hands, anew to start,
All this is how I love thee.

I love thee with a love that knows no end,
Sweeter than lilacs in the wind,
More gentle than the willows downy touch,

Purer than the Spring flower's early blush,
Love thee like the swallows in their nest,
Will love in life, and after death,
Love thee with every yearning breath,
All this is love.

And this is how I love thee, best.

Ralph Beisner and his wife, Inger, became our special friends, and he graciously conducted Laurie's funeral service. Ralph is a retired Supreme Court Justice from the State of New York and works closely with "Catch The Fire" Ministry in Toronto. We met many years ago and have remained friends. Laurie would have been delighted to know her funeral was in his care.

Buddy, our son-in-law, also shared some things for which he fondly remembered Laurie:

> "Laurie was a life long learner who believed in education and encouraged others to embrace that as well. She was well versed on a variety of subjects. She was always reading and studying. Her Bible was at the top of the list.
>
> We used to say that Laurie was into nutrition before the 'Hippies' were, in the 1950s and 1960s. She believed we should all take care of our temples.
>
> Laurie modeled a life of frugality and generosity. She never made a large salary, but she was a saver and paid for our family to go on five Caribbean cruises, which made many special memories we will never forget. Cecile and I often say to each other that Laurie and Charles have done the most with the least of anyone we know.
>
> Laurie and Charles believe that tipping waiters and waitresses that "serve" us in the restaurants is "alms" to the poor. It is part of our giving to the Lord, and we should tip generously. I have personally witnessed their giving a $50 or $100 gift to a waiter on a cruise ship, and then that waiter would come back and tell how a family member was in desperate need of medical care, and that was the exact amount they needed."

Laurie would also have been overjoyed that her friend, Rosina Zimmer, sang two of our Wedding songs: "O Promise Me," and "Through The

Years." As I listened to the funeral service at Grace Church that morning, it wasn't Ralph who stood before us or Rosina's voice I heard: It was Durand Smith, my wonderful Father-Minister who helped me in the early days as a pastor. It was he who performed our 1951 wedding service. The voice I heard was not Rosina's but the beautiful tenor voice of Laurie's brother-in-law, Jim Pettigrew. For a moment I was in two worlds—the "now" and the "long ago."

When Ralph concluded, and the congregation filed out, Rosina sang, "I'll Be Seeing You." It is impossible to explain the impact of that moment. The line, "… All the old familiar places/That this heart of mine embraces …." froze me in my chair. It was a 1930's song I knew well. People, events, memories suddenly flooded me. My age-three fall from the balcony, the 1935 hurricane, High School debate trips, my orchid-hunting in the Everglades, swimming at Biscayne Key, the visit to Cuba, and a thousand other scenes flashed in front of me. Most prominent of all was that 1948 morning in Miami when I looked up and saw the Vision of myself preaching: God has made all things "work together" for my good (Romans 8:28).

The Sage-Fields Of Heaven
Charles Carrin

I see them running to me
Across the fields of Heaven
Mama with her arms outstretched,
Papa shouting anxious welcomes!
"You're home! You're home!" They greet me,
Amazement floods my soul.
All that was lost is recovered
All that was broken is whole.

"I'm home! I'm home!" I answer,
Aglow with the brightness of dawn,
Their arms fall like light about me
To the strange excitement of song.
The full restoration has happened,
Eternity has swallowed time,
For home in the sage-fields of Heaven
Is as much before as behind.

Chapter 40

HOORAY AND HALLELUJAH:
I CAN SEE THE OTHER SIDE!

Looking back, I thank God for ignoring my panic that morning in Miami when the Vision appeared above me. His choice was much better than mine. In the years since, I have wept as much as others, known sorrow, grief, and tragedy; but I have also laughed and played. I never believed God intended the Christian life to be dull and boring. I climbed the Pyramids of Egypt and in the Mayan-Yucatan. In South America, I hiked the Andes above 10,000 feet, the Alps in Switzerland, the Thien Chan range between Kazakhstan and the China border, the Rockies in Alaska, Canada, and the U.S. I flew over the Atlas Mountains in North Africa, the Pyrenees between France and Spain, Mount Olympus in Greece, Mont Blanc in France, and Mount Sinai, where God gave the Ten Commandments.

I watched the volcano Stromboli spewing fumes into the Mediterranean air. Various times I crossed the Lebanon Mountains into Syria, the Tarsus range in Turkey, hiked Mt. Rainier, Diamond Head, the Appalachians, and a dozen mountainous islands in the Caribbean. In Mexico, I saw the volcano Popcatepell erupting clouds of smoke into a beautiful, blue sky. It was awesome. I've watched the sunrise over the jungles of Africa and seen it go down across the Pacific. In Moscow, I attended the Operetta, the Kremlin Ballet, and held my breath watching the trapeze act at the Russian Circus. Here at home, I have been part of a prayer-team in the White House. My life has been exciting and blessed!

I've been in the presence of two Kings, a President, the Pope, and crossed the Atlantic countless times. I've preached in Red Square at Lenin's Tomb, Westminster Chapel in London, as well as to pastors from 63 nations at Toronto's "Catch-the-Fire" Conferences, historic Anglican Churches in England, and war zones in Africa. God let me travel with Derek Prince, R.T. Kendall, Jack Taylor, and a host of others. John and Carol Arnott became dear friends. A huge part of that memory is Mrs. Abernathy, her hearing-aid, and the panic she caused with the young people.

I've wept to see truck-loads of bodies hauled away from battlefields and rejoiced to see other bodies be miraculously healed by the Holy Spirit. In Haiti, during the revolution, I escaped after midnight. Ten times I visited Israel and the Middle East and hid during fighting there. I remember our crippled plane's emergency landing at Beirut Airport with an escort of fire trucks and ambulances. In the Aegean during storms at sea, I fought seasickness and had emergency inoculation for cholera and other diseases. One ship I was on was later bombed and sunk by terrorists. I wandered through Bible-land deserts, where God hammered faith into some of His greatest saints, retraced the missionary journeys of Paul, and visited all seven sites of the churches in the Book of Revelation. In Ephesus, I preached in the same amphitheater where Paul caused a riot two millenniums ago (Acts 19:23-34). In the Coliseum in Rome, I stood where Christians were torn apart by lions.

In more recent years, I have been writing more and traveling less. In 2017 I completed writing an exhaustive project, a catechism book. It is entitled Spirit Empowered Theology and contains 300 questions and answers that cover all aspects of Christian living. Since then, I have continued to write my memoirs and conduct Word, Spirit, Power Conferences. This past year we conducted three major conferences in Stuart, Florida, Columbia, SC, and Abilene, TX. In September 2019 we will conduct our 90th WSP Conference! It's astonishing to me!

Today, the lines of life and love are blurred, and I am in three worlds: The one that was—the one that is—and the one that soon will be. They have strangely run together, and

> *"I know I'm near the holy ranks*
> *Of friends and kindred dear,*
> *I brush the dew on Jordan's banks,*
> *The crossing must be near ...."*

Now, the most thrilling moment of my life has come. It is the last! My ministry is almost complete. That day, 70 years ago when I looked up and saw the Vision of myself preaching—seems like yesterday. It is gone in the blink of an eye. and ...

"I have fought a good fight, I have finished my course, I have kept the faith: Henceforth there is laid up for me a crown of righteousness, which the Lord, the righteous judge, shall give me at that day."

2 Timothy 4:7

Now, I am back at Biscayne Bay; the atmosphere is electric, strangely fragrant, and I am here alone. It is early morning; the water is still, clear as glass. Birds are singing in the palms; but this time, it is transparent, and I can see through it to the other side. But, I am not on the Bay, I am on the Jordan, alone. Everyone else is gone; they have crossed over before me. Mama, daddy, my brothers, uncles, aunts, my grandparents, old friends, are already on the other side. Strangely, I can hear their singing and desperately want to join them and …

> *"On Jordan's Holy Banks I stand,*
> *And cast a wishful eye*
> *To Heaven's fair and happy land,*
> *Where my possessions lie.*
> *Oh, the transporting, rapturous scene,*
> *That rises to my sight!*
> *Sweet fields arrayed in living green,*
> *And rivers of delight!*
> *I am bound for the Promised Land!*
> *I am bound for the Promised Land!*
> *Oh, who will come and go with me?*
> *I am bound for the Promised Land ...."*

―――――――――

Hooray and Hallelujah!

APPENDIX

Testimony of Our Grandson Ben

When our grandson Benjamin was born, he brought special delight to Laurie and me. She became "MeMa," and I became "Poppy." Ben was very alert and cooed peacefully on Cecile's chest within minutes after being born. Then he was whisked away "to be checked out by the doctor." Strangely, Ben was not returned to the room for twelve hours. When Cecile asked about him, the nurse gave excuses—claiming the doctor had not yet seen him. She and Buddy were concerned but trusted the explanations and exhortations for Cecile to get some rest.

Finally, when the nurse brought Benjamin back to the room, he had a glassy look in his eyes and appeared to be very traumatized. He refused to have any bonding connection with Cecile. For months he made deliberate head turns away from any eye contact with her, although he responded to other people.

When Ben was two-and-a-half years old, Cecile learned that children could frequently remember their birth experience until age three. She asked Benjamin if he remembered being born. He replied, "Yes." Then she followed with several more questions, to which he replied, "No." Then he interrupted her and said emphatically, "Mommie! Mean people stealed me away from you!" Cecile was shocked because she had never shared anything with Ben regarding his birth trauma. She and Buddy had a growing concern that Ben had experienced some type of abuse during the hours after his birth, but they were powerless to prove any foul play.

From early childhood, Benjamin was tormented by demonic dreams and unnatural spirit-visitations. Later, through interviews with survivors of satanic ritualistic abuse, we learned that witch covens strategically place nurse-witches into hospital nurseries to prey on unsuspecting families. We also discovered that there were several witch covens located in the mountains, just a few miles from the hospital, and that there was a full moon the weekend Ben was born.

The manifestations increased dramatically when Ben was six years old when he donned a voodoo mask, which he found at a neighborhood yard sale. We all became involved in Ben's recovery. Buddy and Cecile provided Christian Counseling, and I ministered Deliverance. Other times I took Ben with me to week-long ministry sessions.

A major breakthrough came at a "Catch the Fire Conference" in Toronto in 2011, where I was preaching. John and Carol Arnott, Jack Taylor, and others ministered to him. Then a life-changing event took place when Carol prayed for Ben. He said he had never felt the tangible Love of God, but the Love of God was coming through her so powerfully, that the demonic stronghold in him could not resist it. (Mark 1:26; 9:26, Luke 4:41). Benjamin received helpful ministry at other events, as well. His recovery was a process.

The happy word is this: Today Benjamin is a totally free man! Old things have passed away. All things have become new! (2Cor. 5:17). In 2016, I had the privilege to conduct the wedding ceremony for Benjamin and his beautiful wife, Kendra. They were married on a gorgeous autumn day at Buddy and Cecile's country estate home in North Georgia. Benjamin and Kendra are now the happy parents of two beautiful children.

Letters from People Changed by the Holy Spirit

1. "Dear Pastor Carrin, The first time I came to your meeting, I weighed 86 pounds, suffered from bulimia and anorexia and vomited as much as 30 times a day. I want to tell you what happened to me the three nights I came. The first night I shook so violently as you preached that I could hardly sit there. The next night I left early and went home with fierce thoughts of suicide. Thank God, I returned to the service again. The third night when I met you at the door, I tried to speak, but my body froze like a pretzel. I could not talk. You took me to a private room with several other women, put your arms around my head and prayed. When you did that, I felt something like hot oil pour down my head and body. One of the women gave me a 'word of knowledge' about my suicidal anger the night before. That final, wonderful night I was delivered. After you left, I went to the restroom and looked at myself in the mirror. For the first time, I did not see myself as big and ugly. I not only looked normal—I was normal. I want you to know that I have been free ever since!"

2. "Dear Charles, As a result of brain surgery 20 years ago I had a condition called ataxia. My left arm would shake uncontrollably when I extended it. When I raised my hands to praise the Lord I was embarrassed

that people would think my tremor was weird. One evening at a service where you were preaching, you touched my hand, and I fell to the floor. I was going to stand up when someone said: "Just stay there and receive." So I did. Soon I felt a funny feeling go up through my left leg to my arm. When I stood, I found I could stretch out my hand, and the tremor was gone! Now I can raise my hands in worship with no tremor!"

3. "Dear Charles, On March 10, 1995, I was using a table saw and almost amputated my four fingers. The doctor performed surgery to reattach the nerves and tendons. I had been in pain with my fingers and wrist ever since. When you laid hands on me, I fell under the power of the Holy Spirit, and He touched me in a way I never knew before. The next evening, while doing my therapy, the bones in my wrist began to pop, and the pain immediately went away. God heals and answers prayer!"

4. "Dear Pastor Carrin, My children and I visited my mom during the holidays three years ago and one Sunday while attending Grace Fellowship you had an altar call for healing. At that time my son Matthew who was nine years old was having terrible migraine headaches. They were so severe he would have to go to bed. Matt went forward that day, you anointed him with oil and prayed over him. Pastor Carrin, the other day it dawned on me, he has not had a headache for three years! The Lord used you that day, and I wanted to bless you and let you know! I thank you again for being such a willing vessel. The Lord bless you ..."

4. "Dear Charles, I am a medical doctor and was healed of pain and weakness in both hands that have bothered me for seven to eight years— sometimes hurting all day and night. During your group deliverance, I felt tremendous pressure rise through my chest that just disappeared with a big sigh ..."

6. "Dear Brother Carrin, I want to thank you for what you have meant to my life. I brought my daughter to you (she was 17 at the time), and you prayed for her. It was the beginning of a restored life for her. As a child, she was labeled as 'learning disabled' and was afflicted with epilepsy, migraines, and numerous other things. She has not had one seizure, nor one migraine since you prayed for her. It is truly a miracle. I believe we are close to complete restoration! The Lord is good ... I love you. The day you prayed for her I saw Jesus with His arms around my daughter. I will never ever forget. Thank you!"

7.   "Dear Pastor, I first came across you in 1992 when I was living in Nashville, Tennessee. A friend of mine recorded one of your sermons entitled 'An Eleven Days Journey That Took 40 Years,' Deuteronomy 1:2. That was probably one of the best sermons I ever heard. Later, you laid hands on me and my 20 years of substance abuse came to a close. In truth, it was the power of the Holy Spirit that did the healing. You were the instrument of His work. I thank God, and I thank you."

8.   "Dear Charles, I had a fibroid tumor the size of a grapefruit that drained the life out of me. Actually, all you did was speak to the spirit of infirmity. A month later I went back to the doctor, and the fibroid had shrunk to nothing."

9.   "Dear Brother Charles, My family doctor sent me to a specialist who told me I had damaged the tendons in my shoulder. The pain never ceased. On June 6, 1999, I went back to the doctor for more anti-inflammatory and pain medication. That night I attended a revival meeting at our church, where you were preaching. I told you about my situation. When you put your hands on my hips and prayed for me the pain left for the first time in 4 and ½ months, Praise THE LORD!"

10. "Dear Brother Charles, May 31, 1996, while skating I took a spill onto a concrete floor and shattered my left pelvis ... From there I made a slow recovery. I could not climb ladders and could not walk without noticeable limping. April 1998, I went to a Men's Retreat in Hinton, Oklahoma, where you were preaching. You laid hands on me, and to my amazement, I could run and jump without pain. In April of 1999 the Dr. took more X-rays, and to everyone's amazement, the X-rays showed no break of any kind on my pelvis. The Dr. said, 'You have had Divine healing from the Lord because with any kind of break there is always evidence that the break was there. Your pelvis shows you've never had a break.' — But I have over 40 X-rays that say I did. So let me tell you, that the Lord not only touched me but healed me completely—which I will always remember every time I run or jump or climb a ladder."

11. "Dear Charles, A few years ago I attended a church where you preached. A friend of mine had invited me, and during the altar call, he urged me to go up. I requested that you pray for my healing from Type II diabetes and high blood pressure. Both were in severe form, especially

for a 16-year-old. When you placed your hand on me, and God moved, I was healed! Today, I'm 22 years old, still healed, baptized in the Holy Spirit, blessed beyond my wildest dreams, healed of mental illness, placed in a wonderful truth-preaching church, and moving to greater and greater heights!!! Just look what God can do for a former outcast with no hope to survive, expecting only to fail. I went from hopelessness and homelessness to joy and hopefulness."

Yours in Christ, R.S.

12. Power in the "Laying on of Hands:" The day the prisoner in the Atlanta Penitentiary laid hands on me, and I was filled with the Holy Spirit, I did not realize that same power and anointing would remain in me and that I would minister to others with the same results. Forty years later it was still happening. More importantly, Jesus said, "Freely you have received, freely give ..." (Mathew 10:8). He also said of anointed disciples, "They shall lay hands on the sick, and they shall recover" (Mark 16:17, 18). Immediate with my baptism in the Spirit I began ministering to others and seeing God make phenomenal changes in their lives. Many times, I did not know the person's actual need, but I didn't have to. All I needed was to be faithful, and God did the rest. The following letter is one of the most beautiful I have ever received. Every word of it is true, and at the time of my 70th Anniversary, the writer was very alive and active. She wrote:

"Dear Brother Charles, Please, allow me to tell you about the awesome and powerful way God touched me in a service you held at Christ Chapel in the summer of 1993. I had only known Jesus for a few months and had never been in a meeting where the Holy Spirit moved with "signs and wonders." I had never been knocked to the floor by the power of God and, furthermore, did not believe in such things. When you came to town, I excitedly attended your services and heard some excellent teachings. I was not, however, expecting the rest of what I got! Let me explain the physical condition I was in.

The year before, I ruptured three discs in my neck, had no insurance, no money, and could not afford a doctor. Many nights I did not sleep because I had an aching in my right arm that was far worse than any toothache I had ever experienced. As the weeks went by, my arm became numb. This scared me enough to see the doctor. X-rays and an M.R.I. not only confirmed the ruptured discs but revealed that the nerve that went to my right arm had been deprived of blood long enough that it was dead. The doctor explained that because of my delay in coming to him, it was too late to restore the nerve. Even surgery would not help. In time, the arm would atrophy. I was in traction for six weeks, the pain in my back was reduced to a constant, miserable ache, and there was very little feeling left in my fingertips. I could not even pick up my Bible with my right hand, or open doors, and was learning to write left-handed.

That was my condition when I went to your meetings. I loved your teaching, so I kept coming to the services even though I believed that all those people 'falling under the power of the Spirit' was not real—but I had to admit there was a 'Presence' there I could neither explain nor deny. This particular night, we had just begun singing when you came down the aisle toward the pulpit, stopped suddenly at the row where I was standing, spun around and pointed at me. You told the ushers to bring me out. I was scared to death! The only thing I knew for sure was that I absolutely was not going to fall. You reached toward me, and as your hands barely touched my shoulders, I felt a power—a force—an energy, like I had never come in contact with before. In less than a second, I was flat on the floor! You just said, 'She's Yours Holy Spirit,' and went on your way.

As I lay there, I couldn't believe this was happening to me. I wondered, could this possibly be God? What am I doing here on the floor?! Charles Carrin did not knock me down. So, how did I get here?' I thought, 'This is embarrassing. People are singing and praising God, and here I am on the floor. I'll bet everyone is looking at me. I'm getting up!' Then, I sensed a small, quiet 'feeling' deep within me urging me not to move. But, I thought, 'There is no way I am going to lie here and humiliate myself.' So I got up and went back to my seat. Within a minute you were back. You pointed to me again and said for the ushers to bring me to you. When I stepped out, you said almost with an urgency: 'Now, please! Receive everything God has for you!' And I was on the floor again. This time I knew it was God, it was true, and His power was on me. As I lay there, I humbled myself and asked Him to forgive me for getting up before. I told Him I would lie there as long as He wanted me to and that I wanted all He had for me.

It was then it started. I felt a power moving in my body. I could actually, physically, feel something like high-voltage electricity in me. But it didn't hurt. It was like velvet-covered electrical currents. It moved down my spine to the very end then came back up again. Next, it went down my right arm and back up. It did this over and over again. My right arm and spine felt it more than anywhere else, and my legs were shaking and trembling. I don't know how long I lay there with the Hand of God touching deep inside my body. But I was so filled with joy because I then knew that God is not only alive, but He still touches and talks to us today. All the arguments in the world would never stand up to my personal experience with God.

My daughter had witnessed all the agony and suffering I had endured. She and I have a beautiful and unique relationship; she is my best friend, I am hers, and when we got home she was about to explode with anticipation at what God had done. As I explained about the power, she jumped up in the middle of my story, ran to the kitchen, and returned with a full, unopened gallon of milk. I thought she had lost her mind. 'Take this!' She said. I reached for it with my left hand, but she jerked it back. 'No! Mama, take it with your right hand!' Before I realized what was happening, I took that gallon of milk with my injured hand, swung it over my head again and again as we laughed and cried together. *I was healed.* That was the summer of 1993, and this is now 1997. That horrible, agonizing pain has never returned to my neck or back. I have written this entire letter with my right hand! My right arm continues to work perfectly. I give all praise and glory to Jesus! He has made me whole! He has set my feet upon the solid Rock. Glory, Honor, and Power to His holy Name!

I thank God that He has faithful, obedient servants who refuse to listen to the popular majority but insist on hearing only our Creator, our God, our loving Father. Thank you, Brother Charles, for bringing to my home town the Truth of God's Word!"

In His love, Rose Smith, Florence, Alabama.

A Final Example of the Holy Spirit's miraculous guidance

In the Greek New Testament, the Holy Spirit is identified as the "one who calls alongside of us." He instructs us what to say and to bring into our dimension the power of His dimension. Hearing Him is not always easy. We live in a noisy, demanding world and sometimes it takes effort to discern His voice. Let me illustrate: Once, in Rome, I was escorting a group of Americans through the Forum area, was below ground in the old Mamertine Prison, when an elderly lady in our party fell and fractured her hip. For the moment, I panicked, not knowing how to get help or whom to call. Rome is a city of millions; I did not speak Italian and was unfamiliar with their telephone system. We were scheduled to fly home the next day, and the lady insisted that she not be taken to the hospital. Without knowing why, I suddenly left her, raced up the steps, and began running down a crowded sidewalk to a huge, circular intersection a block away.

The sidewalk was mobbed, traffic was snarled, there were no traffic lights, and the area where I headed was jammed with cars. Many were blowing their horns. As I ran, my actions seem illogical. In my mind, I said, "Charles! This is foolish! You don't know where you are going! Go back to the woman and help! Go back!" Even so, I kept running. The moment I reached the intersection, out of breath and confused as to why I was there, I looked up, and a short distance away saw an American Missionary driving toward me. We had met that morning for the first time. He recognized me and waved, I signaled him to come, told him of the crisis, and in a few minutes, the injured lady was on her way to the hotel. I made no phone call, contacted no help. Yet, here I was, a stranger in a city of millions, and the Holy Spirit directed me with absolute precision to the exact spot I needed to be. There was no way my meeting the missionary was accidental. God, Himself, guided me and the missionary to be in that special place.

I close by telling this story for a special reason. It was the Holy Spirit's guidance like this example that became the hallmark of my final years of ministry. That historic day in Miami in 1948, when I looked up and saw the vision of myself preaching, the Holy spirit indicated that the final half of my ministry would be dramatically different from the first. He has fulfilled that word!

ABOUT THE AUTHOR

CHARLES CARRIN'S ministry spans the final half of the twentieth century. He was ordained in 1949 and in his youth traveled with men who preached in the 1800's. For the first twenty-seven years of his ministry, Charles was a hyper-Calvinist Baptist pastor and Presbyterian seminarian who denied the miraculous works of the Holy Spirit. Mid-way in his ministry that abruptly changed. Personal crisis forced him to acknowledge Scriptures he had previously ignored. It was a time of intense pain and testing. The truths he saw were frightening; they had power to destroy his denominational ministry and at that point he had no hope that another, more wonderful ministry awaited him.

As a result of his submitting to God in that crisis, Charles emerged with an amazing anointing of the Holy Spirit. Today, his ministry centers upon the visible demonstration of the Spirit and imparting of His gifts. This new ministry has taken him to London's Westminster Chapel, the Toronto Airport Christian Fellowship, Europe, Asia, Africa, and Central and South America. He, R.T. Kendall, the former, 25 year pastor at Westminster Chapel, and Jack Taylor, former Vice President of the Southern Baptist Convention, travel together holding "Word, Spirit, Power, Conferences."

As an evangelist/writer, Charles' articles have appeared in major Christian magazines in the United States and abroad. He travels extensively, teaching believers how to operate in the power of the Holy Spirit. Charles and his wife, Laurie (now deceased), have one daughter and son-in-law, Neal and Cecile Carrin McGuire, a married grandson, Benjamin, and his wife Kendra, and two great-grandchildren.

Read other books by Charles Carrin:
On Whose Authority
Word Spirit Power
The Edge of Glory
Sunrise of David Sunset of Saul
Spirit-Empowered Theology
Island in the Sun

www.charlescarrin.com

Made in the USA
Middletown, DE
21 May 2023